Mexico Mystique

PRINCIPAL CULTURE AREAS AND SITES OF MESOAMERICA

HUASTECA

TOTONAC

EL TAJIN •

• TULA • TLAXCALA •

• ZEMPOALA

TEOTIHUACÁN •

TENOCHTITLÁN •

VERACRUZ

TOLTEC AND **AZTEC**

• PUEBLA

TR
ZAP

MIXTECA
ALTA

MONTE
ALBÁN •   • MITL

ZAPOTEC A
MIXTEC

N

SAGE BOOKS

THE SWALLOW PRESS INC.
CHICAGO

Mexico Mystique

The Coming Sixth World of Consciousness

Frank Waters

DZIBILCHALTÚN

COZUMEL ISLAND

CHICHÉN ITZÁ

UXMAL

LABNÁ

MAYA

TIKAL

OLMEC

NZO

LA VENTA

PALENQUE

YAXCHILÁN

BONAMPAK

LACADONES

IZAPA

COPAN

KAMINALJUYÚ

ASAY

First Edition
First Printing

Sage Books are published by
The Swallow Press Incorporated
1139 South Wabash Avenue
Chicago, Illinois 60605

This book is printed on recycled paper

ISBN 0-8040-0663-6
LIBRARY OF CONGRESS CATALOG CARD NUMBER: 74-18579

map by Chuck Asay

Contents

Introduction

FOR MORE THAN FOUR AND A HALF CENTURIES Mexico has held for the world a peculiar fascination. It confronts us, scholars and tourists alike, with a confounding mass of contradictions which no one has been able to reconcile.

With its palls of smog over large cities, its tall rise buildings, its network of freeways, its agrarian, economic, and political advances, its lush pleasure resorts, Mexico today seems strictly modern and dedicated to the technological future. Yet there are vast expanses of almost impenetrable tropic jungle, steaming savannah, mountain wilderness, and empty plains. In them rise pyramids of cut stone as large as those of Egypt, ruins of ancient cities magnificent as those in Greece, new stone idols on mountain tops, and fresh flowers and sacrificed turkey cocks deposited at hidden shrines. This Mexico is oriented equally to the ancient past.

The people themselves are a contradictory racial and psychological mixture of American-and-European-educated people of Spanish descent and native Indians; there are still fifty tribes speaking only Indian languages, some of whom are still Stone Age recluses living in mountain caves and jungle compounds. These two ethnic groups for centuries have been gradually fusing into a new race unique in the world—the *mestizo*. This fusing, however, is not a smooth blending. Even in the individual it is a violent and unconscious conflict between opposite polarities which wrings from the heart that ironic laugh known as the *vacilada*, derived from the verb "to vacillate." But it is also a triumphant cry; for, as William Blake wrote, "Without contraries there is no progression." And of all peoples in the world the Mexican *mestizo* is slowly and surely reconciling on all levels the two poles of his nature.

Traditionally we *Imperialismo Yanqui* neighbors to the north, with our ingrown Anglo-Saxon prejudice against Indians, have had no *simpatía* for Mexico's spiritual strivings. There is indeed a great psychological difference between Uncle Sam, who is polarized to the masculine, rational pole of our dual nature, and Mother Mexico, who is attuned to the feminine and instinctive. It is perhaps natural that we interpret in light of our dominant materialistic philosophy the ancient records of her long, proud past—innumerable codices, histories, legends, narratives, artifacts, and archaeological ruins. We generally lack the intuitive imagination to cope with the baffling origin of her first prehistoric peoples; the strange similarity of their cultures to those of the East; the meaning of their religious symbols and hermetic myths. All this we are too readily inclined to discount as romantic nonsense in order to proselyte our theory that history shows but the development of economic and political states.

Yet another view is emerging from the deeper level of esoteric theology, analytical psychology, and mythology. Since Jung's discovery of the collective unconscious, we are no longer obliged to regard ancient Nahuatl and Mayan gods as idolatrous pagan images concocted by a primitive people merely to bring rain and ward off evil spirits. They are primordial images of soul significance rising from the unconscious into consciousness where they are given form and meaning. A universal meaning as pertinent now as it was two thousand years ago. So today, despite the flood of archaeological and anthropological reports, documented histories, and popular writings of all kinds, there is still a Mexican mystique.

All these current contradictions between national cultures and ethnic races, and between our own minds and hearts, mirror a duality that has plagued mankind since the most ancient of days. The antinomy is expressed in many ways: light and darkness, male and female, good and evil, spirit and matter, instinct and reason. God and Satan, the conscious and unconscious. The conflict between these bipolar opposites and the necessity for superseding it is the great theme running through the mythology, symbology, and religious philosophy of pre-Columbian America—the Mexico mystique.

The present text does not presume to answer the many questions this mystique poses, for it is assuredly enshrouded in the mystery of mankind's journey from a common origin to a common destiny. But hopefully the text may outline the subjective area in which the key to its mystery must finally be sought.

Part One, *The History,* gives a brief summary of the primary cultures of ancient Mesoamerica as they are pragmatically known today. The major section, Part Two, *The Myths,* extends the limit of this history into the immeasurable depths of mythology expressed in hermetic myths, religious symbols, astronomical cycles, and mathematical computations of time far beyond our comprehension. Two main exploratory approaches have been made into this inexhaustible realm: one into the hermetic myth of Quetzalcoatl as recorded by the Nahuas, so concerned with the meaning of space; and the other into the Mayan concept of time. Here in the last section is offered an interpretation of the Mayan Great Cycle whose beginning was projected to 3113 B.C. and whose end was predicted for A.D. 2011. While the interpretation is purely speculative, it is based on sound research. The astronomical configurations of the planets on these two dates have been mathematically calculated in a study included as an appendix; and two astrological interpretations of their possible effects—one physical and one psychological—have been given by reliable authorities in their respective fields.

The conclusions reached in this inquiry tend to show that the ancient civilization of Mesoamerica was basically religious; that its spiritual beliefs still constitute a living religion perpetuated by the contemporary Pueblos of the Southwest; and that this common religious system of all Indian America embodies the tenets of a global belief expressed in terms of Christianity, Buddhism (and other religious philosophies of the East), and in modern Western analytical psychology. These confirm a widespread conviction that mankind throughout all its stages of existence has apperceived and reflected in some measure the spiritual laws governing its evolutionary progress, and reveal that the pre-Columbian peoples of Mesoamerica achieved a profound religious system which can be validated by the deepest perceptions of inner truth we can now bring to it. These conclusions are in direct opposition to the currently popular anthropological theory that man is but a social animal, evolving his culture from savagery through barbarism to civilization only through sociological pressures.

Since this book is an imperfect reflection of the work of so many others, its indebtedness extends to more individuals than can be named. Yet I must mention a few who particularly aided my research in many different ways: Dr. Alfonso Caso, director of the Instituto Nacional Indigenista, Mexico City; Mr. Howard Leigh, associated with the Frissell Museo de Arte Zapoteca, Mitla, Oaxaca; Mr. Ross Parmenter, Oaxaca; Mrs. Gertrude Trudy Blom, director of Na Bolom, Centro de Estudios Cientificos, Las Casas, Chiapas; Dr. Thelma Sullivan and Mrs. Doris Heyden, Mexico City; Dr. Ralph McWilliams, head of the Foreign Language Department of Highlands University, Las Vegas, New Mexico; Mrs. Roberta S. Sklower and Mr. Dan Lairmore of Albuquerque, New Mexico; Mrs. Giovanna D'Onofrio; Mr. Robert Kostka, Brookfield, Illinois; Mr. John Manchester, Mr. Charles Asay, who prepared illustrations, and Mr. Elva J. Scroggins, who typed the manuscript, all of Taos, New Mexico.

Thanks are due to the many universities and museums in Mexico, Guatemala, and the United States which gave me free access to their libraries and collections. The Instituto Nacional de Antropologia e Historia kindly issued me a *permiso* to all archaeological zones throughout Mexico. Finally, I must acknoweldge with great appreciation the grant awarded me for research in Mexico and Guatemala by The Rockefeller Foundation, and for its administration by Colorado State University.

Part One
The History

I

The Bearded White Conqueror

1 MOCTEZUMA AND THE AZTECS

HERNANDO CORTÉS AND HIS SPANISH *conquistadores* landed on the gulf coast of Mexico near present Veracruz on Good Friday, April 21, 1519. The time—between the spring equinox and Easter—was deeply significant. It marked a great turn in world history, the beginning of the conquest of America by Europe, and the replacement of one race's faith by another which posited in a new form the same hidden meaning of the old.

Perhaps there is no short sequence of events in all history as preposterous and exciting, as repulsive and sad, as the destruction of the mighty Aztec nation by Cortés and his little band of freebooters. Behind this bloody pageant lies another record of events foretold by portents to the people of Mexico.

Ten years before the Spaniards arrived there began to appear omens of disaster.[1] The first was a fire shaped like a flaming ear of corn that appeared in the eastern sky at midnight and burned until the break of day. Then in swift succession the temple of Huitzilopochtli, on the site known as Tlacateccan (House of Authority), was burned to the ground, followed by the destruction of the temple of Xiuhtecuhtli, which was struck by a lightning bolt. The fourth wonder was a fiery comet divided into three parts which flashed through the sky while the sun was still shining. The fifth portent came when the Lake of Texcoco foamed and boiled

3

with rage, destroying half the houses in Tenochtitlan. Soon this was followed by the voice of a weeping woman night after night, crying out in a loud voice, "O my sons, we are lost! Where can I take you?" The seventh omen was a strange bird resembling a crane that was trapped by a fisherman in the lake. The bird wore in the crown of its head a strange mirror in which could be seen reflected the *mamalhuaztli,* the three stars in the constellation Taurus, to which the people offered incense three times a night. The eighth omen appeared on the streets of Tenochtitlan in the form of monstrous beings with two heads. They were taken to the emperor Moctezuma, but the moment he saw them they all vanished.

Foreboding signs were also reported in Tlaxcala, where more omens appeared shortly before the arrival of the Spaniards.

Moctezuma questioned his magicians about the mystery. None could tell him when or from where disaster would come, although they managed to escape from the prison in which he cast them. Whereupon Moctezuma ordered that their wives and children be killed, their houses torn down, and even the foundations uprooted.

Then came a "common" man from the shores of the great sea to report "a small mountain floating in the midst of the water, and moving here and there without touching the shore." His ears and toes were cut off, and he was thrown into prison. Messengers were sent to the seacoast. They confirmed the report of two great towers or small mountains floating in the sea which carried strange people. "They have very light skin, long beards, and their hair comes only to their ears."[2] Moctezuma lowered his head and did not speak a word.

His anger, fear, and anguish is not easily understood without a quick glimpse at his background. Several centuries before, nomadic tribes of primitive Nahuas began to migrate into Mexico from the north. They were known as Chichimecas, or "barbarians", because they were hunters of wild game, dressing in the skins of the animals they killed. The last and most insignificant band to straggle into Anahuac, the great central Valley of Mexico, were the Aztecas, their name deriving from their mythical homeland of Aztlán. Miserable and homeless, they finally established themselves in 1325 on a marshy island in Lake Texcoco and founded the settlement of Tenochtitlan, the capital of their future empire, now Mexico City.

The land around them was far from being an empty wilderness. Earlier Chichimecan tribes had founded new towns and established *señorios,* or capitals, in ancient towns occupied by descendents of a former, civilized people known as Toltecs, the Nahautl term for "master craftsmen."

From the start the Aztecs showed a love for war, lust for power, and political organizing ability. Making military alliances with one city-state after another, they became independent enough in 1376 to elect their first king. Their choice revealed how impressed they were by the rich heritage of their civilized predecessors, as well as a vaulting ambition. They elected Acamapichtli, a descendant of the rulers of the Toltecs, and began to proclaim themselves the inheritors of Toltec culture.

During the reign of their fourth king Itzcoatl, from 1427 to 1440, their assumption of superiority was established more firmly. Itzcoatl destroyed all the historical Toltec records and instituted a new Aztec version of history with its accompanying religion.

The ancient Toltec religious beliefs, which had survived in some measure for a thousand years or more, was based on a myth about Quetzalcoatl: a god who had manifested himself as a white, bearded man, taught the people all the arts and sciences of civilization, and then disappeared with the promise to return someday in the year of his birth, Ce Acatl. The religion that stemmed from the older hermetic myth of his own "Passion" embraced the concept of penitence, purification, and redemption, and did not sanction human sacrifice.

This concept the Aztecs could not accept. They were a warring, pragmatic, practical people dedicated to building up their state. Hence they instituted in its place the worship of Huitzilopochtli, their own early tribal god, who, personifying the sun, had to be nourished with human blood to insure his life and energy. So now began a program of continual, wholesale human sacrifice that demanded ever more and more victims.

Throughout the reigns of the next four rulers, war and religion were synonymous. The boundaries of the state were extended to include most of Mexico. One of the prime purposes of the military

campaigns was to take captives. Ripping their hearts out of their
bodies with an obsidian knife and raising them still pulsating to
the sun, was the supreme sacrifice that insured the life of the
"People of the Sun."

The Aztec system of government is difficult to define. It was
neither a close-knit empire nor a loose federation of independent
tribes. An imposing civilization had been developed with an omnipotent central government, tribute states, a society divided into
castes, and professional guilds of merchants, teachers, architects,
painters, feather workers, jewelers, dancers, musicians, scribes.
"Look for some craft or occupy yourself with agriculture," the
father said to his child. "The land is our mother and must be cared
for, and always requites our love. Or carry the merchant's staff,
or the warrior's shield and mask, or do penitence in the temple, to
become a priest. For where has it been known that man live not
by craft, but by nobility alone?"

Tribute was exacted yearly from city-states and far provinces.
Pochtecas, or traveling merchants supported by the state, brought
back gold and silver, feathers, cocoa, foodstuffs, slaves, turquoise
from the north, and even emeralds from Colombia. From all this
trade and tribute the island-capital of the empire, Tenochtitlan,
grew into a resplendent metropolis later called the "Venice of the
New World." Three causeways connected the city with the mainland. From its great central plaza rose pyramid-temples, *calmecac*
schools for priests and nobles, *telepuachcalli* for training youths in
war, the palaces of the rulers, living quarters for nobles, priests,
and merchants. Here were held the public rituals and human sacrifices, and to it came the processions of merchants and ambassadors from distant lands, the flotillas of canoes loaded with produce
and merchandise.

Such was the immense Aztec empire in 1502 when Moctezuma
II ascended the throne as its ninth hereditary ruler. Upon meeting
him later, Bernal Diaz in his history of the Spanish conquest reported:

"He was about forty years old, of good height, well proportioned
and slender; he was not dark, but of the color natural for an Indian. He did not wear his hair long, and had few whiskers. His
face was a little long but pleasant, while his eyes were attractive,

and he showed in his person and in his glance both affection and, when necessary, seriousness. He was most clean, bathing every day, in the afternoon. He had many women, daughters of lords, and two high chieftains' daughters for wives. He was completely free from unnatural offenses, and the clothing he put on one day he didn't use again. . . .

"His cooks prepared over thirty kinds of dishes for every meal, and they placed small pottery braziers under them so they wouldn't get cold. They cooked chicken, turkey, pheasant, partridge, quail, tame and wild ducks, venison, wild pig, hares, rabbits. . . . He sat at a low stool, soft and rich. The table was also low and made in the same design as the seat . . . spread with white cloths and napkins. Four beautiful and clean women brought water for his hands in deep basins called *xicales*.

"From time to time they served him in cups of pure gold a certain drink made from cacao. . . . There would be ugly humpbacks who were jesters. Still others sang and danced. . . . Placed on the table also were three painted and decorated tubes filled with *liquidambar* mixed with an herb they call *tabaco*. After he finished eating, after the dancing and singing and removal of the table, he would take a little smoke from one of these tubes, and with it fall asleep."[3]

This portrait of a cultured and sensitive ruler was confirmed by his personal background. He had been well-trained in war, politics, and religion to serve as head of state, commander of the army, and high priest. For the last function, he had attended the *calmecac,* the school for religious neophytes being trained for the priesthood. Here he learned the history of the Toltecs and the transcendental religion of Quetzalcoatl whose image was painted on the wall. This religion appealed to Moctezuma, for, although it was distorted for the general populace, there was still a temple to Quetzalcoatl in the great central plaza, and the head priests of all temples traditionally still bore the name of Quetzalcoatl.

As a result of his priestly training Moctezuma became too religiously inclined to crave temporal power. When he was notified of his election as head of state, the electors found him sweeping down the steps of the great temple "to show that he desired not the Emprey." But upon taking office, Moctezuma dutifully fulfilled his responsibilities. Proving his bravery in battle, he extended his realm to finally include 371 towns from which he exacted tribute. He ruled well. Justice he administered impartially and rigorously, often disguising himself to investigate how his ministers executed their offices.

Yet for all his attainments, he could not reconcile his personal belief in the teachings of Quetzalcoatl with the constant war-and-sacrifice demanded by the state religion of Huitzilopochtli, which he was sworn to uphold.

A similar conflict of beliefs had been solved forthrightly by the king of Texcoco some years before. Netzahualcoyotl was a naturalist, a great engineer, a poet, and he had made his capital a center of learning as Tenochtitlan was a center of military strength. Undoubtedly he was an adept in the religion of Quetzalcoatl, and acknowledged no other god than the one supreme "Creator of Heaven," to whom he erected a nine-story tower and composed sixty hymns in verse. He then prohibited all human sacrifice. Shortly thereafter, that he might not be blamed for contradicting the doctrines of his ancestors, he again permitted it with the provision that the victims be only prisoners of war. Far ahead of his time, divinely inspired, Netzahualcoyotl still reflected the deeply buried feeling of all Mexico.

But he had died years ago and Moctezuma was torn by a personal conflict he was too weak to resolve.

His psychological split kept widening and deepening. He gradually gave up military direction of his government toward the constant aim of war-and-sacrifice, surrounding himself with magicians, augurs, astrologers, and men learned in the interpretation of signs, symbols, and portents. What concerned him increasingly was the old, old prophecy of Quetzalcoatl that someday, during the year of his birth, 1 Reed Ce Acatl, he would return to reestablish his ancient rule.

That year had now come. It was the year 1519 when messengers brought him news that strange men, bearded and white of skin, had landed on the east coast of Mexico. There was no doubt that they were Quetzalcoatl and his gods who had arrived. The Aztec cycle was finished; the end of his domain had begun.

"Moctezuma could enjoy no sleep, no good," reports Sahagún.

"Never could one speak to him. That which he did was only as if it were in vain. Ofttimes he sighed; he was spent, downcast. He felt no delight in savory morsel, joy, or pleasure. Wherefore he said: 'What will now become of us? Who, forsooth, standeth in command? Alas, until now, I. In great torment is my heart, as if run through with chili water, so that it burneth and smarteth. Where, in truth, may we turn, O our lords?' "[4]

More messengers arrived with paintings on hennequen depicting the white strangers clothed in iron, mounted on deer high as rooftops, and with dogs tall and fierce, their tongues hanging out. "And Moctezuma was filled with a great dread, as if he were swooning. His soul was sickened, his heart was anguished. . . .

"He would flee; he wished to escape . . . He would hide himself; he would vanish; he would take refuge and conceal himself from the gods. And he had in his heart and thought to himself, and conceived the idea, consulted within himself, spoke and asked himself: Would he enter some cave? And much did he consult with those to whom he confided his heart. . . . They said: 'There are some who know the road to Mictlan, and Tonatiuhichan, and to Tlalocan, and to Cincalco, that one may rest. Thou must determine what place is thy need.'

"And now he wished to go to Cincalco. Well was it made known; it was so noised abroad.

"But this he could not do. He could not hide nor conceal himself. He was weak; was no longer fired; he was incapable. Unverified and unfulfilled were the words of the soothsayers, through which they had changed his mind, provoked him, turned his heart, and taken vengeance upon him by seeming to be wise in knowing the way to the places named.

"Moctezuma could only await the gods; only steel his heart and tax himself. He quieted and stilled his heart, and resigned himself to whatsoever he might behold and marvel at."[5]

In this agony of guilt, this paralysis of indecision, he awaited the irrevocable destiny of his people, of all America.

2 CORTÉZ AND THE SPANIARDS

Cortés was thirty-four years old when his armada of eleven ships made landfall at Veracruz. He had been born in Medellin, a small town in the Extremadura region of Spain. His parents were of good family and sent him at the age of fourteen to the University of Salamanca. Two years later he returned home.[1]

Overly fond of women, he was injured by a fall from a roof while attempting to visit one of them, and always carried the scar of the escapade. Not until he was nineteen did he sail to Santo Domingo, capital of Espanola and the West Indies. The governor offered him land but Cortés rejected it, saying he had come to make a fortune and not to settle down as a farmer. Soon he obtained an *encomienda* of Indians, a grant of land with accompanying unpaid, forced Indian labor for life. Under the *encomienda* system, Indians were sold for four pesos apiece; those who resisted were burned or hanged, and those who escaped were hunted down by dogs. As a result the population of Espanola had declined from more than 200,000 in 1492 to less than 14,000 in 1514.[2] Successfully rich as an *ecomendero*, Cortés began to look for a new world to conquer.

Making friends with Diego Velasquez, the governor of Cuba, he was commissioned to outfit a trading expedition to New Spain at his own expense. Cortés promptly enlisted a force of five hundred adventurous freebooters. The governor, becoming alarmed, ordered Cortés to abandon the project. Cortés immediately set sail.

On the coast of Yucatan he defeated the Mayas in minor battles and picked up two interpreters. One of them was a young woman whom the Spaniards baptised as Doña Marina. First giving her to one of his men, Cortés later took her as his own mistress, and she bore him a son whom he named Don Martin. More important, she served as a loyal and invaluable informant and advisor of the Spaniards throughout the Conquest. As the Malintzin, or Malinche, she is still known by the people she betrayed; and it is her voice they hear mourning by the rivers and in the mountains.

Landing at Veracruz, Cortés declared himself independent of Velasquez and responsible only to King Charles V of Spain. To attest this he dispatched one of his ships to the Crown with all the loot he already had obtained, "keeping nothing for ourselves."

It is thus quite evident that Cortés' venture was not an expedition sent from Spain, authorized and initiated by the Crown. It was a private undertaking capitalized by Cortés and a band of freebooters who betrayed the governor of Havana who had initially commissioned them for trading purposes and then revoked his permission. Cortés' own character was already clear. He was a typical man of the feudal age of decadent Spain: uneducated, irreligious, lusting for fame, power, and gold. As he later replied to Moctezuma's question as to why he had come, "We are troubled with a disease of the heart for which gold is the only remedy." He was unbelievably brutal and cruel. He had an inborn genius for treachery and betrayal. But, above all, he had determination to surmount all fears and obstacles. If he had not come, another like him would have soon arrived as the pawn of a cosmic destiny that had to be fulfilled.

At Cempoala, a Totonac city not far north of his landfall, Cortés, upon learning that the Totonacs, like many other city-states, resented the tribute forced from them by Moctezuma, enlisted the help of the Totonac chief. Meanwhile messengers and ministers from Moctezuma arrived bearing gifts rich beyond the imagination of the Spaniards.

"A disk of the finest gold representing the sun and large as a cartwheel," reported Bernal Diaz who had accompanied Cortés. "It was a wonderful thing to see . . . and worth over ten thousand pesos. By this gold we knew they had good mines, knowledge that was worth more to us than twenty thousand pesos.... Twenty ducks made of gold and other beautifully cast pieces representing dogs, tigers, lions, and monkeys.... Ten necklaces of the finest workmanship, a dozen arrows with bow and string, and two staffs, all of the finest gold.... Crests and fans of gold and silver with rich green feathers.... And so many other things I can no longer remember."[3]   Fray Bernardino de Sahagún describes still more: "The array of Quetzalcoatl, comprising a serpent mask made of turquoise, a quetzal feather head fan, a neckband of precious green stone bands with golden shells, a spear thrower of turquoise with the head of a serpent, and obsidian sandals. There followed the array of the god Tezcatlipoca, and of the lord of Tlalocan, also beautifully fashioned."[4]

These fabulous art treasures Cortés sent to Spain to curry favor with the king. The great artist Albrecht Dürer viewed them in 1520 and wrote in his diary: "Also I saw things which were brought to the King from the New Golden Land: a sun entirely of gold, a whole fathom broad; likewise a moon entirely of silver, just as big; likewise sundry curiosities ... fairer to see than marvels.

"These things are all so precious that they were valued at a hundred thousand gulden worth. But I have never seen in all my days what so rejoiced my heart, as these things. For I saw among them amazing artistic objects, and I marvelled over the subtle ingenuity of the men in these distant lands. Indeed, I cannot say enough about the things which were there before me."[5]

In return for these fabulous gifts, Cortés sent Moctezuma a rusty helmet to be filled with gold nuggets and an armchair to sit on when they met. To the Aztec ambassadors he gave glass beads and three Holland shirts.

Then in August he began his march of conquest with four hundred Spaniards, sixteen of whom were mounted, and two thousand Totonac warriors.

After two battles with the Tlaxcalans, the Spaniards were welcomed into the city of Tlaxcala with food and women. Traditional enemies of the Aztecs, the Tlaxcalans were persuaded to ally themselves with Cortés despite the exhortations of Moctezuma's

envoys. Again the march resumed, with the addition of five thous-
and Tlaxcalan warriors.

Their route led to Cholua, the sacred city whose Toltec pyramid
—the largest in Mexico and greater in volume than the pyramid
of Cheops in Egypt—was dedicated to Quetzalcoatl. Camping on
the outskirts of the city, Cortés was invited into the city on the
condition his Tlaxcalan allies be kept out. Again Cortés resorted
to strategy. He agreed, he and his men being graciously received
by "priests and choruses of boys and girls, singing, dancing, and
playing on instruments . . . The people brought bread and fowls,
and took the guests to great salons, and that day and the next they
feasted."

On the third day all the priests, nobles, chieftains, and common
folk, "unarmed, with eager and happy faces, crowded in the great
courtyard of the Temple of Quetzalcoatl to hear what the white
men would say." The Spaniards closed the entrances, and at a
signal fell upon them. "Those of Cholua were caught unaware.
With neither arrows nor shields did they meet the Spaniards. Just
so, they were slain without warning. They were killed by pure
treachery; they died unaware."[6]

The Tlaxcalan warriors then rushed in to complete the massacre
of between three and six thousand people, to loot and destroy the
city.

The later official excuse of the Spaniards was that they had
learned the Cholulans were in league with Aztec warriors to am-
bush them. And yet Cortés' letters to King Charles V record
other atrocities during his long march: "I burned more than ten
towns, of more than three thousand houses. . . . Before dawn I fell
on two towns, in which I killed many people. . . . I fell upon a large
town. . . . As I surprised them they were unarmed. The women
and children ran naked in the streets. And I fell upon them and
caused them some loss and harm."

Permitting the Totonacs to return to Cempoala, Cortés and a
force of Tlaxcalans crossed the high pass between Popocatepetl
and Ixtaccihuatl, the Spaniards dressing their wounds with the
fat of the Indians killed on the way. They then descended to the
great Plain of Anahuac and on November 8 approached the southern causeway across the lake to the Aztec capitol of Tenochtitlan.

Here, in the midst of flotillas of canoes and vast crowds of gaily bedecked people on the causeway "kissing the ground with their hands as a sign of peace," Moctezuma, attended by his lords and nobles, descended from his litter to greet Cortés.

"Is this not thou?" asked Cortés warily. "Art thou Moctezuma?"

"It is so; I am he," replied Moctezuma, hanging around Cortés' neck a necklace of "eight golden shrimps executed with great perfection and a span long."

"O our lord, thou hast arrived on earth; thou hast come to thy noble city of Mexico . . . Lo, I have been troubled for a long time. I have gazed into the unknown whence thou have come—the place of mystery. For the rulers of old have gone, saying that thou would return . . . And now it is fulfilled; thou has returned. Arrive now in thy land; visit thy palace that thou mayest rest thy body."[7]

Moctezuma then conducted the Spaniards to Axayaca's palace where they were quartered with royal comfort and courtesy.

Cortés, accompanied by Bernal Diaz and a few other men, was taken to visit Moctezuma in his own sumptuous palace nearby. They saw the armory filled with richly decorated arms of all kinds, the huge aviary containing every species of birds, a zoo for wild animals, vipers and snakes, the tribunal rooms where trials were held, the repository where tributes were stored, workshops filled with craftsmen in gold and silver, feathers, precious stones, and cotton cloth, the gardens of flowers and fragrant trees, medicinal and cooking herbs, with pools of fresh flowing water . . . "It was something to remember," wrote Bernal Diaz later as an old man of eighty-four, "and now that I am writing about it, it all comes before my eyes as though it happened yesterday."

The Spaniards were then taken by Moctezuma to the great central pyramid surrounded by a stone wall carved with writhing serpents. Meticulously observant, Diaz counted the 114 steps up which they climbed. On the truncated top stood two temples: one dedicated to Huitzilopochtli, painted white and blue, and one to Tlaloc, its walls white and red. From here they could look down upon Tenochtitlan, the metropolis of Mexico, the Venice of the New World, larger in extent and more populous than London and Paris. Shining white in the sun, with colored houses and temples, it looked like a city floating in a great blue lake.

"We could see all three of the causeways that led into Mexico: the road from Itzapalapa, by which we had entered, the Tacuba road, and the road from Tepeaquilla. We could see the fresh water that came from Chapultepec, the bridges on the three causeways, built at certain intervals so the water could go from one part of the lake to another, and a multitude of canoes arriving with provisions and leaving with merchandise. . . . Temples built like towers and fortresses, all whitewashed. We could look down on the flat-roofed houses and other little towers and temples. . . . There were soldiers among us who had been in many parts of the world, in Constantinople and Rome and all over Italy, who said that they had never seen before a market place so large and so well laid out, and so filled with people. . . . It was like the enchantments they tell of in the legend of Amadis."[8]

Inside the temples stood images of the gods covered with gold, pearls, and precious stones. Before them were braziers in which were burning the hearts of three Indians sacrificed that day. The long hair of the priests, the altars, the walls, and floor were so crusted with blood "that in the slaughterhouses of Castile there was no such stink."

Hurrying out, Cortés suggested to Moctezuma that these horrible idols, evil devils, be replaced by a cross and an image of Our Lady. Moctezuma was greatly shocked. "Sir, if I had thought you would so insult my gods, I would not have shown them to you. Please do not say another word to their dishonor."

It is a great loss to us that the many subsequent dialogues between Cortés and Moctezuma on religion were not fully recorded; they would have revealed the essential difference between the Old World and the New, and the future of America for the next five hundred years. Yet, Sahagún and Diaz reveal enough to show Cortés' slow psychological torture and murder of Moctezuma's faith and personality.

As they talked they played *totoloque*, a game with gold pellets. Pedro de Alvarado kept score for Cortés, always cheating by scoring an extra throw. Moctezuma smiled at this; and when he won, he divided his wager of gold and jewels between the Spanish soldiers on guard.

Cortés was not too interested in religion nor *totoloque*. He demanded the royal treasure walled in the palace. Moctezuma opened up the *Teocalco* to reveal an incalculable wealth: three heaps of gold weighing more than six hundred thousand pesos, grains of gold fresh from the mines, plates of silver, *chalchihuitl* jewels, each stone of which was worth two *cargas* of gold (the weight a man could carry on his back during a day's journey), pearls, wonderfully fashioned jewelry, cotton cloths embroidered with quetzal feathers, engraved arms, and table services of gold and silver.

The greedy Spaniards melted down all the metal, setting aside the Royal Fifth for King Charles, another fifth for Cortés, and dividing the rest among them according to their rank, the common soldiers getting only one hundred pesos as their share. Not content with this wealth of a continent, Cortés insisted that his men be shown the mines from which it came.

Back at Veracruz, where Cortés had left a garrison, the Totonacs had killed two Spaniards. Their governor, or *cacique*, was imperiously summoned to Tenochtitlan with his son and fourteen nobles. Quauhpopoca did not evade or apologize, but gave his reasons for killing the Spaniards. Cortés promptly burned all the sixteen men in front of the palace, and then shackled Moctezuma in irons.

Now at last Moctezuma recognized that the Spaniards were not gods, but men like himself. Even so, he maintained his quiet dignity and showed every courtesy to his captors. His imprisonment turned his people not only against the Spaniards, but against himself.

In the mounting unrest, Cortés hastened to Veracruz with seventy men and a load of gold. Governor Velasquez of Cuba had sent an armada of nineteen ships carrying about one thousand men under the command of Pánfilo de Narváez to arrest or kill Cortés and his "thieves." In a minor skirmish, Cortés and his force of Tlaxcalan warriors defeated Narváez. Bribing Narváez' men with the gold he had brought, Cortés induced them to join him. He then returned to Tenochtitlan with thirteen hundred soldiers and two thousand Tlaxcalan warriors.

While he had been gone, the dreadful had happened again. The annual feast of Toxcatl celebrated in honor of Huitzilopochtli was

held in the great courtyard of the temple. All the celebrants were
dressed in ceremonial attire—"the great captains, the bravest warriors, the youths and the recruits, those who had fasted for twenty
days and those who had fasted for a year—were sworn to dance
and sing with all their hearts, so that the Spaniards would marvel
at the beauty of the rituals."⁹

When the Dance of the Serpent began, "when the dance was
loveliest and song was linked to song," the Spaniards under the
command of Alvarado attacked.

"They cut off the arms of the drummer; they cut off his head,"
report surviving Aztec codices. "They attacked all the celebrants,
stabbing, spearing, striking them with their swords. . . . These fell
instantly to the ground with their entrails hanging out. Others
they beheaded. . . . They struck others in their shoulders, and their
arms were torn from their bodies. . . . Some in the thigh and some
in the calf. . . . Others in the abdomen, and their entrails all spilled
to the ground. Some attempted to run away, and their entrails
dragged as they ran. . . . Some attempted to force their way out,
but the Spaniards murdered them at the gates. Others climbed
the walls, but they could not save themselves. . . . The blood of the
warriors flowed like water and gathered into pools. . . . The stench
of entrails filled the air. The Spaniards ran into the communal
houses to kill those who were hiding. They ran everywhere and
searched everywhere; they invaded every room, hunting and
killing."¹⁰

Cortés and his new force arrived, only to be besieged in the
palace. He besought Moctezuma to plead with his people to stop
fighting, as he wished to leave the city.

Moctezuma, who already had suffered psychological and spiritual martyrdom, replied gently, "What more does Malinche want
of me? I do not want to live, or to listen to him, because of the
fate he has forced on me."

Nevertheless, he was persuaded to speak from the rooftop to
the milling crowd below in affectionate terms, urging them to stop
the war as the Spaniards would leave Mexico. The answer was a
shower of stones: whether these killed him or he was murdered
by the Spaniards is not known. It is said that his body was cast
forth with that of his lord Itzaquauhtzin. The body of Moctezuma

was burned on a pyre, and "it seemed to lie sizzling and smelled foul as it burned" writes Sahagún. Itzquauhtzin's body was taken by boat to the temple courtyard of Quauhxicalco where with great honors it was burned.

For four days there was fighting, and for seven days more the Spaniards were confined in their quarters. Then at midnight, in a drizzling rain, they left Tenochtitlan. *La Noche Triste!*—"the sorrowful night" of June 30. A woman fetching water espied them and gave the alarm. Warriors swarmed to the attack. Half of the Spaniards lost their lives, encumbered by their burdens of gold, and thousands of Tlaxcalans. Cortés himself received a serious head wound and lost two fingers.

Now, if ever, was the time for the mighty empire of the Aztecs to rid itself of a handful of intruders. But leaderless and betrayed, its will and heart broken, it could not. The surviving Spaniards reached Petalco, a canal on the Calzada de Tacuba, where the Otomis gave them succor. The climax had been reached.

The tawdry anti-climax soon followed. After a year of careful preparation Cortés returned with Spanish forces augmented by 200,000 Indian allies and twelve brigantines built, transported, and reassembled at Lake Texcoco. With them came the greatest conqueror of all—smallpox.

The siege of Tenochtitlan lasted eighty days. The Aztecs fought desperately against the blockade. "The people were tormented by hunger, and many starved to death. There was no fresh water to drink, only stagnant water and the brine of the lake.... The only food was lizards, corncobs, and the salt grasses.... The people ate water lilies and seeds of colorin, deerhides, and even pieces of leather.... They ate even dirt."

More than 30,000 warriors from Texcoco among those fighting with the Spaniards, and more than 240,000 Aztecs were killed or died of smallpox. "Almost all of the nobility perished; there remained alive only a few lords and the little children." It was all over.

3 DEFEAT OF THE MAYAS

The conquest spread rapidly in all directions. Sandoval, with a large force of Indian allies, was sent south of Veracruz to conquer the land and to search for more gold. Orozco subdued the Mixtecs and Zapotecs of Oaxaca centering around the ancient cities of Monte Alban and Mitla. Olin, in turn, invaded the land of the Tarascans to the west, around lakes Patzcuaro and Chapala. Then Cortés, inflamed by reports of great riches in the Maya kingdoms to the south, sent his favorite captain, Alvarado, to conquer the Mam, Cakchiquel, and Quiché Mayas in Guatemala.

Alvarado, leading a large command of Spanish horsemen and foot soldiers and Indian allies, advanced rapidly into the highlands of the Quichés, the most powerful nation. Near Quetzaltenango, often called "Under the Ten" for its surrounding ten mountain peaks, he defeated the Quichés, killing their leader, Tecum Uman. As a gesture of peace, the Quichés then invited Alvarado into their capital of Utatlán. The ancient metropolis had been established five hundred years before and had been governed by kings of nine generations. According to records, it contained the temples of their gods, twenty-four palaces of the nobility, and was beautified by countless works of art.

Instead, Alvarado seized the kings outside the city and burned them to death before their terrified subjects. He then ordered the city to be destroyed, writing his reasons to Cortés in a letter dated

19

April 11, 1524: "And as I knew them to have such a bad will towards service to His Majesty, and for the good and peace of this land, I burned them and ordered the city burned and leveled to the ground, because it is so dangerous and so strong that it seems more like a house of thieves than the abode of people."

Zaculeu, a fortified citadel and ceremonial center of the Mam Mayas near the village of Huehuetenango; and Izimchi, fortress capital of the Cakchiquel Mayas, fell also to Alvarado, becoming Guatemala's first Spanish capital.

Meanwhile word reached Cortés that Spanish troops under Olid sent to take possession of Honduras had turned traitorous. So in the fall of 1524 Cortés himself, leading a hundred and forty Spaniards and three thousand Indians, undertook his celebrated march from Veracruz through the soggy savannahs of Tabasco and across the base of the Yucatan peninsula with its vast rain forests, morasses, and tropical rivers to Honduras. With him he took Cuauhtemoc and the *cacique* of Tacuba.

The last Aztec ruler, the young lord Cuauhtemoc, had tried in vain to organize resistance to the Spaniards after Moctezuma's death, but his effort was too late. He gave himself up to Cortés upon the promise of honor and protection. At the village of Yaxzum, in the swampy Chontal Maya country of Acalan, Cortés tortured him and the *cacique* in an effort to wring from them the location of more hidden gold. The *cacique*, it is said, groaned with pain under the torture. Cuauhtemoc, who is today Mexico's most popular hero, rebuked him by quietly asking, "Am I then lying on a bed of roses?" Cortés then hanged them both on the trumped-up charges they were conspiring against him.

All winter Cortés' army fought its way through the dense tropical *selva*. "The forest," reported Cortés, "was such that we could see nothing but the ground where we stood. . . . I consulted my compass by which I had often guided myself, though we had never been in such a plight as this."[1] Struggling through swollen rivers and treacherous swamps, they reached a river five hundred paces wide and four fathoms deep, which could be crossed only by a bridge. The exhausted Spanish soldiers rebelled. Whereupon Cortés ordered his men "to take no part in building the bridge, for I would do it with the Indians." Within four days the Indians built a bridge with more than a thousand beams up to ten fathoms long, hewed from trees which they felled.

In April 1525 the army finally reached the seacoast of Honduras to find that Olid had been executed. Cortés then sent his army on the long march back through Guatemala to Mexico while he returned by ship.

Two years later Francisco de Montejo, who had served under Cortés, was granted the title of *adelantado* with permission .to exploit northern Yucatan at his own expense. Montejo lost his fortune trying to subjugate the Mayas, and turned the venture over to his son who in 1542 managed to establish the present capital of Merida on the site of the ancient Maya town of Ichansiho.

In their subjugation of Yucatan, Guatemala, and Honduras, the Spanish never realized they had conquered an aspect of Middle American civilization as great as that of the Aztecs in Mexico. During his celebrated march to Honduras, Cortés had passed through an area marked by some of the greatest cities of ancient America. Cortés did not see them. They were already abandoned ruins obscured by towering rain forests, twisting vines, creepers, and luxuriant jungle growth. Like Teotihuacan near Tenochtitlan, the Aztec capital which he had razed, these Mayan ruins expressed the mystery of a time extending back into antiquity. Nor were the Montejos impressed by the stupendous ruins of Chichén Itza, Uxmal, and Mayapan, which had marked a later renaissance of Maya culture in northern Yucatan.

It had been the custom of the Mayas to erect *katun* stones every twenty years. The fateful Katun 8 Ahau period of twenty years took place every 256¼ calendar years. Every preceding period for a thousand years—those beginning in 672, 928, 1185, and 1441— had marked great changes or catastrophes. In the Katun 8 Ahau period corresponding to 1441-1461 the tri-city League of Mayapan broke up and Mayapan was utterly destroyed. The Itza Mayas, fleeing from the ruin, migrated back to the jungles of Guatemala, establishing their new capital of Tayasal on an island in Lake Peten Itza, a location similar to the Aztec capital of Tenochtitlan on an island in Lake Tezcoco.

This destruction was followed by the Spanish conquest and settlement during the sixteenth century. A century later, in 1697, a

force of only 108 Spaniards under Martin de Ursua dispelled the
5,000 Itzas at Lake Peten Itza, finally completing the conquest of
the Mayas. The Itzas fled without giving battle because the date
was only 136 days before the last Katun 8 Ahau period prophesied
as the end of their rule. This again was similar to the time 1 Reed
Ce Acatl prophesied as the end of Aztec rule. Thus there came to
a close the civilization of what Morley, the Maya scholar, calls
"the most brilliant aboriginal people on this planet."

4   A NEW PERSPECTIVE

The conquest was utterly complete. Bands of Spaniards roamed through the country laying waste to the land. Monuments and palaces were destroyed; temples were torn down and their very foundations uprooted for the gold and jewels they embodied; whole cities were levelled to the ground. Reported Bernal Diaz, "There were burned all the royal archives; all the chronicles of their ancient things; and also the other things which were like literature or stories were destroyed." Of a civilization once as great as any in the world there remained scarcely more than ruins.

We stand appalled at the ruthless destruction and at the greed, ignorance, and murderous hate which achieved it. A civilization that had evolved "one of the few really great and coherent expressions of beauty so far given to the world . . . and historically as important as was that of the Greeks in Europe," says Spinden; and Morley, "a more accurate knowledge of astronomy than the Egyptians down to the Ptolemy period in 300 B.C. and whose calendar was more accurate than the Gregorian calendar of Europe introduced in 1582; a system of hieroglyphic writing; an architecture that achieved with mathematical precision a pyramid which was the largest structure in the world for cubic content;—what more could it have evolved if it had been granted a few more centuries?"

And yet our emotional revulsion at this great waste is tempered by a larger perspective. The conquest of Mexico by a handful of

Spanish invaders was made possible only by tens of thousands of Indian allies. Cortés was not the power, but the trigger for their revolt. The Aztec empire of countless tribute city-states and provinces was ready to come apart at the seams. Only the enforced demand for sacrificial victims held the government in power, and this need was based on the Aztec's lust for temporal power. They had distorted the spiritual values in the early Toltec religion of Quetzalcoatl in which the mass of people still believed deep in their hearts. And so in them, as in weak and sensitive Moctezuma, there existed a growing guilt, a widening schism that gave vent to their ferocious fighting as Cortés' allies. So too among the Mayas could be discerned the gradual weakening of the primal spiritual force that had initiated their early classic empire, followed by its complete rupture, and then a gradual dissolution of all cultural values.

This impasse in the New World was matched by that of the Old World of Europe, itself decadent and diseased. In Spain, civil war with the Moors had desolated Granada. Barbary pirates were scourging the coasts. Heretic England was looming as a menace to and to whip it up again the Holy Inquisition had distorted it into a and to whip it up again the Holy Inquisition had distorted it into a tool for gaining temporal power with a cruelty excessive as that of the Aztec state. At the slightest suspicion of heresy men were tortured to death. Property, homes, and personal effects of Moors and Jews were confiscated, forcing tens of thousands of them to flee for their lives to all seaports in hope of finding passage anywhere. Columbus could hardly obtain ships and find an obscure port to sail from, so crowded they were.

But he discovered the new thought, the new hope, which might have breathed life into diseased and dying Europe. A whole New World untouched, vast and rich beyond all imagination. Espanola confirmed it. Cortés' conquest of Mexico proved it. And Pizarro's later conquest of Peru amply refuted all doubts.

It is idle to conjecture what may have happened had the art, science, and religion of the New World sparked into flame the dying embers of civilization in Europe. For Spain's royal treasury was empty, and the State depended upon the help of the Church to fill it with the untapped treasure of America. To be sure, there were a few great humanitarian friars like Bartolome de las Casas, an early slave owner who in middle age received a spiritual enlightenment and for the rest of his life labored for the Indian cause. But Diego Rivera's mural caricatures of brutal and fanatic Spanish priests bespeak the greater truth. The purpose of the Holy Inquisition which took over the rule of the New World was not to spread Christianity. It was to build up Spain's temporal power.

Thus the dual tragedy of America and Europe.

How old it is, and repeated so often, the saying that history repeats itself in a succession of civilizations conquering by the sword and dying by the sword. We cannot deplore the Spanish burning of Aztec and Maya codices without deploring the Aztec burning of ancient Toltec records.

The contemporary sociologist Gerald Sykes draws an interesting parallel between the Aztecs and Toltecs in Mexico, and those of today in modern America. "If we add a modernizing 'h' to Toltec, we get 'Toltech', embodied by such men of thought as the poet, the physicist, the philosopher. If we add a modernizing 'h' to Aztec, we get 'Aztech', or such men as storekeepers, statesmen, chiefs of staff. The Aztechs have achieved unprecedented control over nature through the application of scientific methods they did not create. . . . Like the old Toltecs, the new Toltechs—the scientists and artists of our own day—must submit to the authority of a more primitive kind of man who happened to be on hand when thought to which he had contributed nothing produced a bonanza. . . . A division of men into Aztechs and Toltechs is not a play on words, but an attempt to deal accurately and flexibly with complex everyday realities that have existed since the beginning of civilization."[1]

If Sykes is right, we here in America and throughout the world are now facing the same old schism between opposite dualities. It is as if time has never moved; as if all the great events of history, the rise and fall of civilizations, are but passing shadows cast on an immovable screen.

In Mexico today there is no monument to Cortés who impressed upon the country the mark of his Crown and Church, his tongue and culture. But in Mexico City, the national Ministry of Education is housed in a vast sixteenth century convent built with stones from an Aztec temple. In its central court are placed four statues, facing the four quarters of the world. They are Quetzalcoatl, Plato, the Buddha, and Las Casas.

Why Quetzalcoatl and the Buddha instead of Christ? What links Plato and Las Casas? The relationship of these four disparate figures prompts us to inquire in later pages if beneath the temporal history of the Conquest there lies an unfolding cosmic pattern which these figures commonly apperceived.

II
The Pool of Life

Even before the conquest of Middle America was completed, many Spanish friars and historians were mystified by the great civilization they were destroying. What was the origin and nature, the religion and culture of these native people who had erected such magnificent cities with their pyramids, temples, and monuments? Sahagún, Duran, Acosta, Clavigero, Torquemada, and Landa, with Ixtlilxóchitl, Tezozómoc, and many others probed the mystery with their early volumes. Today, centuries later, we are still probing.

Unraveling pre-Columbian history is like peeling an onion. The layers are so infinitesimal that one never gets to the heart. The custom nowadays is to separate each, view it microscopically, and label it by whatever potsherd, site, culture, or period differentiates it in detail from the others. The disadvantage of this excessive classification is that it promotes too many specialists in too many fields. Archaeologists, anthropologists and ethnologists, linguists and historians, each with his own axe to grind, disagree with each other as new discoveries are being made too fast for correlation with finds in other fields.

"Particularly in these fields (archaeology and ethnology)," writes art historian Alexander von Wuthenau, "it is important to overcome the 'disease of our time', exaggerated specialization, with its menace of atrophying the integral man."

What actually is the complete onion, the Mexican mystique?

The civilization of pre-Columbian Middle America, or Mesoamerica, covered at the outset a span of some 2,700 years—roughly

27

from 1200 B.C. to A.D. 1500. Archaeologists now divide this span into three "horizons": the Preclassic, ending about A.D. 300; the Classic, ending about A.D. 900; and the Postclassic, terminating with the Spanish conquest in 1521. The time-scale and its nomenclature is arbitrary and variable. Now coming into vogue are the terms "Theocratic" and "Militaristic," "Early" and "Late Urbanism," and "Late Epiclassic" instead of "Postclassic". Meanwhile the present "horizons" are being broken down into periods variously called "Upper, Middle, Lower" or "Full and Middle"; and these are further divided into many sub-periods. Another time-scale is based on the stratification of potsherds, resulting in more names: Ticomán, Zacatenco, El Arbolillo, etc. Adding to the confusion is the growing multiplication of names for peoples, phases, and sites, (Tenocelme, Tetlamixteca, Nuine, etc.) newly coined by ambitious specialists anxious to make names for themselves. More hair-splitting is developing as anthropologists disagree on the difference between a culture and a civilization or whether a great population center was a city or a ceremonial center.

In *Maya History and Religion,* the noted Maya archaeologist J. Eric S. Thompson observes: "Archaeology is in mortal danger of losing itself on the bypaths of abracadabra. . . . A fantastic amount of time and effort is spent in labeling pottery with what are for the most part uncouth, unpronounceable names (some taken from Spanish not even correctly spelled). The report on one smallish site contains no fewer than 177 named varieties. . . ." He also refers to the 2,800 footnotes to the first two volumes of a bulky report.

As there are reported to be twelve thousand archaeological sites in Mexico alone, the prognosis for such bookkeeping is not promising.

What we are doing in this monstrous job of peeling, analyzing, and cataloguing the infinitesimal layers of the onion is compounding miniscule differences instead of seeking the unifying concept that welded all Mesoamerica into one integrated civilization.

Covarrubias, an outstanding authority on Indian art, asserts with many others that there were two prehistoric centers of civilization in the Americas: one in Middle America and one in the high Andes of South America. Middle America or Mesoamerica comprises the area from the northern part of Mexico south to Guatemala, Honduras, and El Salvador. Archaeologist Alfred V. Kidder defines it as that area "occupied in prehistoric times by peoples of allied advanced cultures heavily weighted on the ceremonial side." If one accepts this definition, the area should be extended to include the Pueblos of the Southwest in the United States on its northern perimeter.

The ancient Nahuas themselves conceived their world as a flat disc surrounded by a ring of water that merged with the heavens on the horizon, forming a complete circle, a great pool of life. The analogy is apt. Mesoamerica was indeed a vast, fecund pool fed by subterranean streams from many directions; subterranean to us who have not yet charted their invisible currents. Periodically, in different places, bubbles broke its surface. These bubbles constitute what we may call cultures, but they were all embodied in the same great pool of civilization and each contained all its constituent elements.

Let us now take a brief look at some of the most important from the limited viewpoint of what we factually know about them so far.

1 THE OLMECS

It is generally agreed that the mysterious Olmec culture was the first big bubble to break surface. Its known lifetime endured from 1200 B.C. to about 400 B.C., the only preclassic culture that did not continue on site into the classic period. But because its influence spread so far and endured so long in other cultures, it is considered the mother culture of all Mesoamerica.

Olmec invariably carries the adjective "mysterious." Who the Olmecs were, where they came from, and what happened to them is not known. The most mysterious thing about them is that their culture appeared fully formed and well-organized from the very start, as if it had been transplanted from somewhere else.

The name Olmec, derived from olli, the Nahuatl word for rubber, was tacked on to them centuries later. Their heartland lay in the rubber country on the Gulf coast of Mexico, watered by the Papaloapan and Tonalá rivers. The archaeologists Bernal and Caso assert that this area was the "Mesopotamia of the Americas," pointing out that the birthplaces of most great civilizations lay in well-watered river basins: that of the Sumerians between the Tigris and Euphrates, that of the Egyptians along the Nile, and the Chinese in the basin of the Hwang Ho, the Olmec region containing the largest volume of water in Mesoamerica. Recent discoveries, however, suggest that this area may not have been their original homeland.

Here in Veracruz, however, they developed their first known center at San Lorenzo which shows the earliest Olmec radiocarbon date of 1200 B.C. Another major site in Veracruz was Tres Zapotes. The principal site was La Venta in Tabasco, established sometime before 800 B.C. La Venta occupied a small island of only two square miles in a swamp along the Tonalá River. Here the Olmecs constructed a round clay pyramid 420 feet in diameter and 103 feet high with 11 vertical ridges, resembling a petalled flower. They also excavated three huge pits floored with a thousand tons or more of slabs of green serpentine inlaid with mosaic jaguar masks. There were tombs of basalt columns, a sarcophagus with a lid in the shape of a stylized jaguar, and large stone altars. All the structures were laid out along a central axis.

If the architectural remains are surprising, the sculpture leaves no doubt that the Olmecs were the first and finest sculptors in Mesoamerica. Tomb ornaments included objects of amethyst, turquoise, obsidian, quartz, magnetite, amber, and pyrite. Carving jade with stone tools, they produced exquisite pieces rivalling those of the Shang dynasty in China (1500-1027 B.C.) with which they have been compared: small figurines and statuettes, ceremonial axes, funerary offerings of jewels, ornaments, and anthropomorphic jaguars. Their stelae, monuments of basalt decorated with sculpture, are magnificent. The largest at La Venta, Stela C, stands fourteen feet high and weighs some fifty tons. Yet their monolithic sculptures of giant human heads and altar statues hacked out of coarse basalt are most expressive of their enigmatic genius.

As there was no stone on the swampy island, it was apparently quarried from the extinct volcano Cerro Cintepec in the Tuxtla mountains some eighty miles to the west. It was then dragged to the Coatzacoalcos River, transported along the Gulf and up the Tonalá River by rafts and canoes.

There is no use making a pilgrimage to La Venta, now utilized as an oil field. But the site has been recreated in an imaginative outdoor museum on the shore of the lagoon, "Lake of Illusion," on the outskirts of Villahermosa. On a winding path cut through the mosquito-infested jungle growth, one may encounter these monolithic sculptures in their natural setting. There are still more re-

mains in the old but superb Museo de Tabasco on the river bank
in Villahermosa.

Not a single Olmec skeleton has been found, but the twelve
colossal sculptured portraits discovered at San Lorenzo, La Venta,
and Tres Zapotes show evidence of influence from foreign sources.
Those famous, gigantic stone heads! No bodies. Just heads, standing up to ten feet high and weighing up to eighteen tons. They
have round faces with flat Negroid noses and thick lips, and puffy
slanted eyes with the Mongoloid epicanthus fold, portraying a combination of the features of both races.

They recall the anthropological belief in an early mixture of Negroid and predominantly Mongoloid types in India and Indonesia,
resulting in a stock which later mixed with Oceanic Negroids. This
ultimately produced the Polynesian race which passed through
the Malay Archipelago and Melanesia to populate all the islands
of Polynesia, including Easter Island. This prompts the inquiry
whether the Olmecs came from Polynesia, as Covarrubias believed.

All their colossal heads wear what can be described only as
football helmets whose purpose is unknown. They remind us of
the gigantic stone heads on Easter Island surmounted by great
cylindrical stone blocks, sometimes topped by a small white cap.
These *pukae* have never been scientifically explained. Esoteric
sources suggest they represent an evolutionary stage of archaic
mankind when the etheric body was not yet tightly connected to
the hardening physical body, and projected beyond it in the head
region. It also has been suggested that the small white cap on top
marked the opening on the head above the sagittal suture, the
fontanelle, through which man received cosmic knowledge, according to many world-wide beliefs. It is equivalent to the Hopi
kopavi, or "open door," to the Creator, and the spot on the head
marked by the scalp-lock of many Plains tribes. The historically
few inhabitants of Easter Island were far from being such an archaic race, and the great stone heads perpetuate the myth that the
first men to live on the island were survivors of the world's first
race.

The Olmecs themselves were not an archaic people. Their gigantic stone heads may not prove to be an anthropological record of

their racial derivation, whatever it may be. But they are a psychological record of an early stage of mankind when consciousness was beginning to emerge from the unconscious. No necks, no bodies. Just huge heads emphasizing the new significance of the head-center.

But full consciousness had not yet broken free of the unconscious, the substratum of man's essential being, which can be equated with the maternal earth itself. This hold of the earth still upon the Olmecs is reflected by their obsessive concern with the jaguar which was a symbol of the forces of earth and night. It is shown in the typical "Baby Face" of the great heads, the open "Olmec Mouth" being curved downward and usually likened to the feline mouth of a jaguar. The figure and symbol of the jaguar, rather than that of a humanized deity, appears in all forms, in jade and stone, in axes and mosaics.

The Olmec jaguar cult was diffused throughout all Mesoamerica. In one mural after another the jaguar motif appeared later on the walls of Toltec, Maya, Zapotec, and Aztec temples, along with sculpture and jaguar "thrones." If the jaguar was not deified by the Olmecs, it served as a cult animal, or *nagual*, a spiritual counterpart or guardian. Still today this intimate relationship is perpetuated by the Indian belief that each man from birth is associated with such a *nagual*, and that whatever happens to one happens to the other.

Similarly, the jaguar's Mesopotamian counterpart, the lion, was a much-portrayed cult animal in Babylonia. In the mysteries of Mithras, the grade of religious initiation known as the "Lion" was the fourth of seven degrees, the mid-point on the neophyte's path from the lower to the higher stages of consciousness.[1]

What we can read in these colossal heads, then, is an emerging consciousness still earthbound in the maternal unconscious, and striving upward toward freedom. A wonderful sculpture in the Museo de Tabasco portrays it best. It is in the form of a semi-humanized jaguar seated in a posture of worship, arms stretched downward to its legs, head raised imploringly toward the sky.

That help did come is suggested on monuments and altars by sculptures of figures far different from the round "baby faced" Olmecs—by figures with thin faces, aquiline noses, and beards, wearing ornate headdresses—"visitors" as Covarrubias calls them. Some of the altars are great rectangular stone blocks on whose sides are carved life-size figures. Altar 5 in the La Venta out-door museum shows in high relief a priest seated with crossed legs, with a thin face, and wearing an ornate headdress, who is holding in his arms a baby with Olmec features. The theme is re-peated on the north and south sides of the altar, and is a frequent motif on all altars. The sizes of the figures are not representational, but merely indicate their relative importance. For Olmec sculp-ture is far from being primitive; the famous work of art known as the "Wrestler" shows competence in the realistic portrayal of hu-man anatomy. Hence these altar figures can be regarded only as highly symbolic. The man and child do not represent a paternal relationship, but that of priest and acolyte, possibly that of a more advanced culture from outside nurturing an emerging primitive people.

Who these later and culturally advanced "visitors" were, and where they came from, is suggested by the art historian Alex-ander von Wuthenau.[2] During fifteen years of investigation of thousands of pre-Columbian terracotta pottery heads and figures, he found portraits of five different racial types: Mongoloid, Chinese, Japanese, Negroid, and all types of white people, espe-cially Semitic types with and without beards. Engraved on Stela 3 at La Venta, the central figure, with its thin face, long aquiline nose, and drooping beard, could be Semitic or Chinese. Just as significant are statuettes found at Tlatcilco in the central valley of Mexico. They are of an old man bearing on his head a charcoal brazier. He has been identified as Huehueteotl, the "Old God" or God of Fire, said to be the first humanized god to emerge in Meso-america. Von Wuthenau, however, points out that most depictions of him show Semitic features and non-Indian beards. Like Covar-rubias and anthropologist Charles R. Wicke, he believes that the cradle of Olmec culture was either on the Pacific slopes of Guer-rero or in Oaxaca.[3] Recent archaeological finds in Guerrero seem to suggest this.

Carlo T.E. Gray, a retired steel company executive, and Gillett Griffin, curator of primitive art at Princeton University, were led in 1963 to the discovery of some of the earliest paintings yet found in the New World. They lay deep underground in Juxtlahuaca Cave near Colotlipa, Guerrero. There were three paintings and three drawings on the walls. One of the polychrome paintings depicted a figure five feet tall, wearing an Olmec style helmet, quetzal-plumed, and dressed in a jaguar skin. He is holding a rope which is attached to a small figure sitting with crossed legs, whose features show an aquiline nose and pointed beard. His face is painted black, as those of priests. Its resemblance to the figure engraved on Stela 3 at La Venta is undeniable.[4]

Quick, literal interpretations are usually found to be out of order, and I am not plugging this one. But on the assumption that the Olmecs founded their culture in Guerrero and then moved to the Gulf coast, it is suggested that they made nominal captives of newly-arrived members of an advanced culture in Guerrero, and then elevated these visitors to importance as priests and teachers when they moved eastward to the Gulf coast.

Gray and Griffin a few years later discovered near Xochipala, Guerrero several burial sites containing innumerable ceramic figures. All were naturalistic, exquisitely modelled even to anatomical details, and showed a free flow of form and expression not equalled in Mesoamerican art until much later.

However significant these and other discoveries in Guerrero may be, one thing is certain: the beginning of Olmec culture must be pushed back considerably. And when it is, the present belief that the central valley of Mexico was the cultural birthplace of Mesoamerica will be out-dated. Several centers appeared here on the present outskirts of Mexico City early in the preclassic period. At Cuicuilco was built a conical pyramid faced with uncut stones about eighty feet high. When the small volcano of Xitle erupted shortly before the beginning of the Christian era, it was partially covered with the lava now forming the *pedregal* south of the University. Tlatcilco, another major site, produced a great variety of interesting earthenware: jars, bowls, braziers, masks, and small feminine figures with overdeveloped thighs and two heads. How crude and primitive they are, compared to the exquisite figures from Guerrero!

How could this village with its primitive culture have been the motivating center of the great civilization that spread over all

Mesoamerica, as is now commonly asserted?

All its remains, according to Bernal, reflect the presence of fertility rites and a cult of the dead. But they were still based on primitive magic. Tlatcilco had no organized religion nor professional priesthood. Moreover, all the objects bore the unmistakable Olmec style. Tlatcilco, he concludes, was no more than a crude highland village, an outpost of the spreading Olmec culture.[5]

Just how far it spread is not certain. Every major ruin from central Mexico south into Guatemala shows evidences of its style. Bernal postulates that the Olmec sphere constituted the first Mesoamerican "empire"—a sphere of influence expanded primarily for diffusion of its religious ideology, and utilizing outpost colonies for trade, as for the importation of jade from Costa Rica. There are indications that its influence spread as far south as Peru where the Chavin art style and the religious jaguar motif seem too strikingly similar to those of the Olmecs to be coincidental.

It is possible that Olmec culture also spread north to the Mound Builders of the Ohio Valley in the United States. By 1000 B.C. or earlier these broad-headed Adena people were constructing huge burial and effigy mounds, their great Serpent Mound being the largest effigy mound in the world. They were the first mound builders in the region and could not have derived this custom from any earlier occupants; the long-headed Hopewell and the Mississippian mound builders to the south followed much later, between A.D. 500 and 700. The Adenas were also the first brachycephal, or broad-headed, people in the Ohio Valley, introducing the same style of head-shaping or deformation found among the earliest skulls discovered in Mexico. From these facts it has been concluded that the origin of the Adena culture was in Mesoamerica.[6]

One might venture to guess that it was indeed a derivative of the widespread Olmec influence, for the apex of both was reached about the same time, 800 B.C. This is contradicted by the fact that the Adena people can be traced back to 2450 B.C.—centuries earlier than the earliest known date for the Olmecs. Could this indicate a case of the tail wagging the dog; that the Olmecs stemmed from the Adenas instead? Or is it possible both stemmed from one source and reflected a common prototypal culture?

Enough of these tantalizing conjectures. They only confirm the mystery of the beginning of Olmec culture. A mystery that also surrounds its end.

Apparently San Lorenzo was the first Olmec site on the Gulf coast to be occupied. It was abandoned and its monuments buried about 850 B.C. About the same time, La Venta rose as the preeminent site. It and its monuments were abandoned about 400 B.C. This marked the virtual end of the Olmec "empire." Tres Zapotes continued to be occupied until it too was abandoned, its monuments being destroyed. It was then reoccupied by a later people digging holes to seek jade offerings. Here, inscribed on Stela C, was found the earliest recorded Olmec date—31 B.C. It was recorded in the dot-and-bar system, indicating that writing and a calendar had been developed long before. For this reason, the end of the Olmec culture is often placed at the beginning of the Christian era. Why all these sites were abandoned, and where the Olmecs went, is unknown.

So in the enigmatic Olmec culture we confront, first off, the Mexico mystique. The mystery of its origin and of its end. And above all, the mystery of the people themselves—of the round-faced Olmecs and the thin-faced visitors—who left here a superlative art without any antecedent steps.

2   THE MAYAS

No other pre-Columbian culture has evoked so much admiration and speculation as that of the Mayas. It has been studied assiduously for decades by archaeologists, anthropologists, ethnologists, historians, linguists, astronomers, and artists. The mystery of its origin and development still remains unsolved.

There is one reason. Bishop Diego de Landa in 1552 publicly burned at Mani almost all hieroglyphic records of Maya history and religion, as well as destroying hundreds of "idols," inscribed stelae, and altar stones. Then, by some strange quirk, he collected details of Maya life, published a century later in his *Relación de las Cosas de Yucatán*, the primary source of Maya information.

There remain only three hieroglyphic records, named after the cities in which they are preserved: the Codex Dresdensis in Dresden, the Codex Peresianus in Paris, and the Codex Tro-Cortesianus in Madrid. As only a third of the Maya hieroglyphs have been deciphered, the codices have not been fully interpreted. None of them seem to be historical; they contain divinatory almanacs, eclipse tables, tables of movements of the planet Venus, and matters dealing with religious aspects.

There are few textual records. The *Popul Vuh,* the sacred book of the Quiché Mayas written in historical times, was composed in Quiché using letters of the Spanish script, and deals primarily with the creation myth. The *Books of Chilam Balam* are mytho-

logical histories. And *The Annals of the Cakchiquels* relates events
of the Spanish conquest and gives a genealogical history of the
Cakchiquels. In all these records, religion and myth blur the confused outline of factual history.

As far as they have been deciphered, the inscriptions on stelae,
lintels, and temple panels offer little help. With few exceptions, all
are utterly impersonal, giving no names of places or persons, obit-
uaries of rulers, records of wars or conquests. They are restricted
to religious, astronomical, and astrological matters. What we have
left, then, are architectural ruins whose magnificence has excited
the wonder and imagination of the world.

The Maya area includes all the Yucatan Peninsula, southern
Mexico, and most of Central America. It is divided into three
parts: the northern area which juts out into the Gulf of Mexico;
the central area which includes the Petén department of Guatemala; and the southern area extending to the Pacific. It was long
supposed that Mayan culture originated in the Petén, probably
because the region was richest in archaeological remains. Another
theory holds that it originated in the Olmec area. It is believed
that the Olmecs originated the dot-and-bar calendar system, just
when we do not know. But sometime between the third and first
century B.C. the Mayas originated for the first time in history the
mathematical concept of zero and developed the Olmec chronological system into a calendar more accurate than the Gregorian
calendar introduced in A.D. 1582. Obviously there was a cultural
connection with the Olmecs, when and where we don't know.

Between 800 and 900 B.C. the Mayas built at Kaminaljuyú, on
the outskirts of what is now Guatemala City, some 200 earthen
temple mounds, one a truncated pyramid whose base measured
230 by 300 feet. Another eighty temple mounds were built at Izapa
in Chiapas, Mexico. All these and others recall the round clay
pyramid of the Olmecs at La Venta and the hundreds of mounds
built in the Ohio Valley by the Adenas.

But far earlier than this there appeared on the northwestern tip
of the Yucatan Peninsula what may have been the first large city
in Mesoamerica—Dzibilchaltún. Its ruins, only a taxi drive from
Merida, were not excavated until 1959-1960, and its significance
has not yet been widely appreciated. Yet it is the fox in the hen-

coop theory of straight-line evolution from savagery to civilization. Dzibilchaltún covered an estimated area of fifty square kilometers, possibly containing from fifty to seventy-five thousand inhabitants. Surrounding its great plaza were five platforms whose ceremonial structures were connected by causeways, revealing an acropolis pattern subsequently followed by classical Mayan centers. Fronting the plaza was a pyramidal base supporting a temple—"Structure 450"—which was formed by four superimposed structures showing six periods of occupation. Two other structures have been dated at 310 B.C. The lower base of Structure 450 has not yet been dated, but it is believed that Dzibilchaltún was settled between 2000 and 1000 B.C.[1]

The dispersion of tribes all over Yucatan, the Petén and central Guatemala, southern Mexico, even to British Honduras, is an unsolved puzzle. One group moved up the Gulf Coast to Veracruz, becoming known as the present Huastecas. The Chontal Mayas established themselves in the swampy delta of the Usamacinta and Grijalva rivers in Tabasco, Mexico. Others settled in the mountain highlands of Chiapas, Mexico where their numerous descendants still live today. The migratory routes of the Quiché, the Cakchiquel, Itza, and Mam tribes are shrouded in myth and contradictory historical interpretations, as we shall see. What a maze of cowpaths through this vast wilderness of Maya-America they made! A rootless people aimlessly migrating from somewhere to somewhere else, seeking the light of a guiding star that would indicate the place where they could convert their inward longings into outward reality.

Then suddenly, in the third century of the Christian era, the Mayas received a mysterious, invigorating impulse, religious in nature. It must have awakened in them the mystery of time, a sense of the transitoriness of life, and the obligation to record the passage of worldly periods; and it resulted, says Spinden, in "one of the few really great and coherent expressions of beauty so far given to the world, and their influence in America was historically as important as was that of the Greeks in Europe."

They began erecting stelae, great stone monuments recording the passage of the twenty-year *katun* periods marking the founding of their cities and the general course of their history. There began the great classic period of architectural splendor during which rose nineteen major cities and dozens of lesser size and importance. With the inscribed stone monuments appeared another unique characteristic, corbeled roof vaults, "the false arch." Clay mounds gave way to stupendous pyramids of cut stone, majestic temples and palaces adorned with fantastically carven facades and lintels, exquisite sculpture, solar observatories, water reservoirs and irrigation systems, and all the practical applications of an advanced civilization.

Why did this phenomenal birth of classic Mayan civilization take place only in the central area? One might suppose it would have occurred in the northern area, at the tip of the Yucatan Peninsula where Dzibilchaltún, founded a thousand years before, was still occupied. Or that the new great cities would have been built in the Guatemala-Chiapas highlands which offered better living conditions. It is also curious, considering the amount of sea trade around the peninsula, why they were not built along the coasts instead of in the tropical lowlands a hundred miles inland. The great ceremonial sites largely centered in the almost impassible heart of the Petén in Guatemala, and in the rain-forest of the Usamacinta valley in Chiapas, Mexico. Their overgrown ruins are hidden so well that Bonampak was not discovered until 1946. If they are difficult of access today, how much so were their sites to the founding Mayas. And what tremendous effort was required to cope with this hostile tropical wilderness! Knowing the compelling religious motivation of the Mayas and their deep knowledge of mathematics and astronomy, one may well wonder if the sites were picked astronomically, perhaps as centers of astrological influence from various celestial bodies. It might be interesting to see if their geometric ground pattern reflected in any way those of the constellations.

How indescribably beautiful they all are! Embalmed in meditative silence, they lie in a time-dimension unfamiliar to us, their mystery appealing to something in our deeper selves. Sublime Palenque bespeaks it best. It lies on the slope of a rain-forested hill in the valley of the Usamacinta. Over its ruins fly macaws and parrots, always in pairs, and there sounds at night the roar of howler monkeys. Maya tradition affirms this was the birthplace

of the gods. Also of mankind. According to the *Popul Vuh's* creation myth, the yellow and white ears of corn from which the flesh
of the first men were formed came from Paxil and Cayala. These
mythical places lay in the region of Palenque. Paxil has been interpreted as "the separation of the waters," evidently meaning
the land which first emerged from the watery abyss.

Pythagorean tradition affirms Palenque is the geographical center of the area embraced by the continental land mass of America.
Its architecture is said to exemplify the highest Pythagorean art
developed in America, combining the abstract precision of mathematics with the emotional power of poetry and music. Palenque's
great Palace reputedly corresponds to the Parthenon at Athens.
To the east, flanking a small plaza, are three exquisite temples: the
Temples of the Sun, the Cross, and the Foliated Cross. Each
houses a magnificently carved tablet. The Temple of the Sun may
be the most perfect of all Mayan buildings. At the center of its
tablet is a carving identified by Pythagoreans as the aegis of Zeus,
showing the Gorgon's head and tassels as described by Homer,
which Athene carried as her shield. It is supported by two full-
figure numerals marking the number of Neith, 77.[2] Modern archaeologists interpret it as the mask of the Jaguar Sun, before two
crossed spears.

Indo-Chinese motifs as well as Grecian appear. The controversial tablet in the Temple of the Foliated Cross is said to be the
sculptured counterpart of one at Angor Vat in Cambodia. Both
show a godlike being, a tree of life with plantlike arms extended
to each side, giving the figure its name. This Foliated Cross is
interpreted realistically as a maize plant; but Robert von Heine-
Geldern, an authority on the archaeology of Southeast Asia, points
out its Buddhistic origin as representing the celestial tree on top
of Mt. Meru.

Another bone of contention is the water lily or lotus motif as
prevalent in Maya art as it was in the Buddhist art of Cambodia,
Burma, and India. The unusual parallel, observes Heine-Geldern,
lies in the fact that the part of the lotus depicted is the rhizome,
or root, usually invisible because it is submerged in water or
buried in mud at the bottom.

Whatever extraneous influences it may show—Egyptian, Greek,

Chinese, or Indo-Chinese Buddhism—Palenque exerts universal appeal as the loveliest Mayan center. It reflects the mystery of its origin, its superlative architecture, and art in its living ruins.

Tikál, in the heart of the Petén, was the largest and most spectacular. Within an area of six square miles were built 3,000 structures, the ceremonial center containing six lofty pyramids, one reaching a height of 212 feet. Its Stela 29 is the oldest dated stela, bearing the date A.D. 292. Stela 9 at Uaxactun eleven miles away bears the date of 328. There followed the rise of the second largest metropolis, Copan in British Honduras, the Mayan astronomical center; Piedras Negras and its twelve-foot stelae; spectacular Yaxchilan with its marvelous lintels; Bonampak, so renowned for its brilliantly colored mural paintings. . . .

One cannot deny the driving religious impetus that brought them all into being. It was felt about the same time in Teotihuacan, the "City of the Gods," the religious center and capital of the original far-flung Toltec empire in Mexico. It too supplied a powerful contributing influence to the development of the Mayan cities. Shortly after A.D. 400 Kaminaljuyú in central Guatemala came under the domination of the Teotihuacan Toltecs who rebuilt it in a miniature likeness of their capital, with stepped-pyramid temples. Teotihuacan religious influence spread rapidly throughout the lowland centers, into Tikál itself. Representations of Teotihuacan gods on stelae and pottery vessels suggest they were beginning to replace Maya gods.

Then abruptly the great Teotihuacan empire collapsed. There is no record of just when, how, or why its great metropolis was partially destroyed and later abandoned sometime between 750 and 800 A.D. Whatever happened, the fall of Teotihuacan signalled the end of the classic Maya civilization which Morley called the "Old Empire." The last dated stelae were inscribed at only three sites in 889, ending the unbroken sequence of dated inscriptions that had begun in 292. Copan ceased to erect hieroglyphic monuments in 800. There is no evidence of war, disease, a change of climate. The magnificent cities were simply abandoned to be engulfed by tropical growth, as had those of the Olmecs; and there are indications that the inhabitants of Tikál themselves also mutilated stelae and portions of temples before leaving.

Not until a century later did there begin here a renaissance of Maya culture known as the postclassic, or "New Empire." Wholly militaristic, it seems to have been impelled by the later Toltecs from Tula, Mexico. The new empire bore little resemblance to the old. Chichén Itza, its most important center, is today the most popular of all Maya sites. It embraces hundreds of buildings within an area of some three square miles. Twenty or thirty of the largest have been beautifully restored and lie scattered without plan on well-kept grounds that resemble a college campus trod by thousands of student-visitors. The most imposing structure is the so-called Castillo or Temple of Kukulcan, a nine-step pyramid seventy-five feet high with a stairway on each of its four sides leading to the temple on top. Impressive as are all other structures —the Temples of the Warriors and of the Jaguars, the Platforms of Venus and of the Tigers and Eagles, the largest ball court in Mesoamerica, and the Tzompantli, or "Wall of Skulls"—Chichén Itza lacks the homogeneity of Tikál, the fragile beauty of Palenque, the poignant sense of communication still possessed by the jungle-covered ruins of Yaxchilan. Some of its older structures in what is called "Old Chichén" reflect classic simplicity, but the galleries of colonnades, columns of warriors, the *tzompantli*, merlons, tigers, and eagles devouring human hearts, undulating serpents and columns of serpents head-down, tail-up, suggest that Tula and Chichén Itza were constructed by the same builders.

Uxmal is the most appealing of northern Yucatan ruins. Built between 600 and 1000 A.D., the structures show little Mexican influence. Dominating them is the curious oval-shaped Pyramid of the Magician, nearly one hundred feet high. "Thrice-built," it consists of five structures superimposed one upon the other during successive epochs. The temple on top, reached by a dangerously steep staircase, has a carved facade representing a huge mask of the rain god Chac whose open mouth serves as the doorway. The massive Palace of the Governors, with its perfect proportions, Morley called the finest single building in America, although to me it cannot begin to compare with the exquisite Temple of the Sun in Palenque. The Nunnery, a vast court flanked on all four sides by stone buildings whose upper facades are completely carved, is equally impressive. All the buildings at Uxmal are set on natural terraces over a wide area, and with their comparative simplicity and harmonious proportions give a sense of compactness and relationship of masses.

A number of outlying ruins in the *monte,* or dense tree-high brush, await fuller excavation. At Kabah only three of eighty building sites have been uncovered. One is the popular Codz-Pop with its completely carved facade of Chac masks. Another is the famous Triunfal Arco, the only Maya free-standing arch, under which passes a stone-paved road to Uxmal nine miles away. There are X-Lapac, Sayil with only two structures visible of its seventy-five known sites, and many others in the distinctive *puuc* style with a pinkish tinge to their limestone walls.

Labna, remotely isolated in an amphitheatre of the *puuc,* or hill country, is the loveliest of all Yucatan ruins. Its arch is famous for its size and intricate decoration. From it leads a paved cause-way across a great level plaza to the palace, adorned with friezes, mosaics, columns, and Chac masks. From one corner protrudes a human head within a serpent's open jaws. The building is longer than the Palace of the Governors at Uxmal, and it was unfinished when it was mysteriously abandoned. Over the door is the deciphered date of 869. Nearby is a pyramid whose temple on top wears a roof-comb adorned by life-size human figures on the corners, and which was built about 600 A.D.

The renaissance, then, was a period of declining Maya culture under Mexican influence. The religious compulsion was gone and the sense of a divine destiny. Government was secular and militaristic, duplicating that of Toltec Tula. It ended about 1200 A.D., resulting in disastrous wars among city rulers. The destruction of Mayapan between 1441 and 1461 marked the collapse of the New Empire just 56 years before the first Spaniards dropped anchor off the coast of Yucatan.

A number of symbols appear repeatedly in art and architecture throughout the course of Maya history. The earth-dragon, or crocodile, the screech owl, snail, butterfly, the bloodthirsty bat, and other forms of animal life served the commonfolk as *naguales,* or guardian spirits, and took their places in the sacred calendar as names and gods of the days. Of importance to the priesthood was the jaguar, the key symbol of the Olmecs. The most notable representation is the gorgeous throne for the high priest discovered in the sanctuary of a sealed chamber within the pyramid-temple of Kukulcan in Chichén Itza. It is carved in the shape of a jaguar, painted bright red, with eyes of jade and fangs of flint, and spots on its coat made of inlaid jade discs. There is another jaguar seat on a low platform in front of the Palace of the Governors at Uxmal.

The most outstanding symbol is the serpent. Almost every structure at Chichén Itza is adorned with serpent heads, rattles, or motifs in some form. This of course reflects the late cult of the Plumed Serpent believed to have been brought to Yucatan by the Tula Toltecs. Jose Diaz-Bolio, in a small guidebook derided by scholars, opposes this belief with the theory that the Plumed Serpent cult originated among the Mayas, traveled north to Mexico, and was later brought back to Yucatan in a more sophisticated form. On this premise he asserts that Maya art, architecture, geometry, and religion all derive from the Maya rattlesnake, *Crotalus Durissus Tzabcan*. Its skin pattern, the four-vertex *Canamayte* which in Mayan means "Four Corner Square," shows a basic symmetrical design. Coinciding with its rhomboid pattern are the outlines of the Maya thatched roof house, the pyramid, the temple roof-vault, or "false arch," the design on a Maya blouse, and even the flattened forehead of the Maya himself.[3] Of whatever value, these are pertinent observations. They reflect the fact that the symbol of the serpent, like that of the jaguar, stems back to an apperception of the forces of nature in archaic times.

Certainly the symbol of the serpent was not restricted to the late renaissance period in Yucatan. In earlier classic centers the serpent appears in its natural form. The monolithic sculpture of a man with a snake wrapped around his shoulders and hanging down over his breast stands at the entrance to Kabah. In Old Chichén one of the four square columns standing in front of the Templo de los Falos shows the figure of a priest holding a snake in his mouth. At the base of the Hieroglyphic Stairway temple complex in the classic center of Copan, Honduras sits the sculptured figure of a priest holding a snake in his mouth. He is clenching it a few inches back of the head which rests against his left cheek, so it cannot strike, its body dangling on his right as if he could stroke it with prayer-feathers to prevent it from coiling. This sculpture could well be that of a contemporary Hopi snake-priest during the annual Hopi Snake Dance in Arizona.

At Palenque's famous Temple of the Inscriptions, dated 692, a frescoed panel on one of the pillars on the facade of the temple on top of the lofty pyramid depicts the body of a snake. It is connected with a simulated small tube, like a prolongation of its body, that leads down through the interior of the pyramid to the burial crypt eighty feet below. Here on the tomb-covering is engraved a triangular-shaped serpent's head connected by the tubing to the tail on the facade above. This replicates similar tubes protruding from the burial places at the Olmec ruin of Tres Zapotes and from the Zapotec tombs in Monte Alban.

All this serpent symbolism posits a cult of the serpent which existed throughout all Mesoamerica from ancient times; which took form in the Teotihuacan religion of Quetzalcoatl, the Plumed Serpent; which extended far north to the Adena Mound Builders of Ohio as shown by their great Serpent Mound; and which is still perpetuated today in the rituals of the Zuñis in New Mexico and Hopis in Arizona.

Writes Spinden: "When we can bring ourselves to feel the serpent symbolism of the Mayan artists as we feel, for instance, the conventional halo that covers the ideal head of Christ, then we shall be able to recognize the truly emotional qualities of Mayan architecture."[4]

3   THE ZAPOTECS AND MIXTECS

The Zapotec bubble broke surface in the great central valley of
Oaxaca south of the Mexican plateau. Probably as early as 1500
B.C. the rugged hills and valleys were inhabited by small groups.
Then about 600 B.C. or slightly earlier, the Zapotecs began to
occupy the top of Monte Alban, a high rise of hills fifteen hun-
dred feet above the floor of the valley.

The area borders that of the Olmecs who strongly influenced
the Zapotecan culture being born at Monte Alban. The stone slabs
with incised bas-reliefs of *danzantes,* or dancers, are undoubtedly
Olmec in style. But how different are these large human figures,
hunchbacked, distorted, showing genitals, with coarse features,
and in many strange postures, from the free-flowing Olmec figures
found in Guerrero and the artistic representation of the "Wrestler" found in Veracruz.

Associated with them in the same period, between 600 and 300
B.C., were large stelae numbered 12 and 13. They contain eleven
glyphs associated with numerals in the Olmec dot-and-bar system
of chronology. The Mayas adopted the dot as representing the numeral "one," and the bar as representing "five," and then invented
the "zero," which they represented by a symbol resembling a
shell. The Zapotecs, however, did not use the zero as did the
Mayas; they used a name-glyph in combination with the number;
and the decipherment of these has posed great difficulties.

Apparently the earliest recorded radiocarbon date for Monte

48

Alban is 275 B.C. But Howard Leigh, a private collector in Mitla who has traced the evolution of Glyph C, the oldest and most distinctive of Zapotec hieroglyphics, maintains that the glyphs on stelae 12 and 13 represent a date of 644 B.C.[1] If accepted, this will be the earliest known American date transcribed in writing. It will long precede the Mayan date of 36 B.C. on Stela 2 at Chiapa de Corzo in Chiapas, considered to be the oldest date recorded in hieroglyphic writing. It is still generally believed, however, that the Olmecs originated the calendar and a system of writing later developed by the Mayas and adopted by all Mesoamerica.

Every culture in Mesoamerica has scholarly adherents who maintain that it was the most important. The current Zapotec champions are as vociferous as any. They declare that the ancient Monte Albans were the first city dwellers in Mesoamerica, that they invented writing and the calendar, and, in short, founded the mother culture of all Mexico. Certainly the Zapotecs developed one of the outstanding cultures. Lying between the Olmec area to the northeast, the Mayan area to the south, and Toltec Teotihuacan area to the north, the Zapotecan culture received influences from all of them.

About 300 B.C. Mayas arrived from the lowlands to the south. By A.D. 300 still another influence had come from the great Toltec center to the north, Teotihuacan. Under these combined cultural importations there began the classical period during which Monte Alban was finally constructed in the form whose ruins we see now. It occupied not only the top of the mountain, but the summits and sides of adjoining hills, comprising fifteen square miles of urban construction. Its ceremonial plaza is one of the most majestic. Measuring 300 by 200 meters, it was flanked by great stepped platforms on the north and south, pyramidal platforms on the east and west, with ball court and tombs outside. In the center was a strange building, thought to have been an astronomical observatory. It has a curiously pointed end, off-center to the main axis, being the only irregularly-shaped structure of pre-Columbian times. One is awed by the labor Monte Alban represented. Every stone for construction, every drop of water, had to be carried up the rocky hillside. These are the majestic ruins we see today.

Despite the impressiveness of this great plaza, one notices that

it gives no view of the surrounding hills and valleys. Unrelated
to its topography, completely enclosed, it gives the feeling of an
immense tomb. This feeling is borne out by lack of evidence that
the Zapotecs originated any religious concept which was diffused
outside their own area. The major deity was Cociji or Cocijo, god
of water, equivalent to the Mayan god Chac, and the Nahuatl god
Tlaloc. The four divisions of the sacred calendar, the *tonalámatl,*
were named *cocijo* after him. If in Teotihuacan all high priests
were called Quetzalcoatl, so in Monte Alban were they considered
his living images. Seler, the great German scholar, interprets the
god Coqui as "Lord of the Growing Bright" or "Lord of Dawn," a
parallel to the Nahuatl Quetzalcoatl as the Morning Star. Pije-Tao
or Pije-Xoo ("mightly wind"), if translated into Nahuatl, he believes would be synonymous with Quetzalcoatl in his aspect of the
god of wind. Another Nahuatl importation was the god Xipe-Totec.

Ceramic remains show an abundance of animal, bird, fish, and
anthropomorphic effigies. The majority are of the jaguar, deity of
earth and death, reflecting the importance given to this Olmec
symbol and the ancient belief that the Zapotecs were descended
from the jaguar. Of secondary importance is the bat, the Maya
symbol of death and darkness. There are bat gods galore, bat
heads, bat claws, bat masks, figures half-human and half jaguar-
bat. Seler interprets the name *zotziha* not as "bat" but "bat's
house"—a dark region in the interior of the earth, a kingdom of
darkness and death.[2]

These gods and anthropomorphic effigies, largely imported from
Olmec, Mayan, and Nahuatl sources, were not incorporated in a
distinct Zapotec religious context, and did not give rise to a transcendental myth of spiritual significance.

On the contrary, the Zapotec preoccupation with death clearly
points to a highly developed cult of the dead. Individuals were
buried in tombs or directly in the ground, according to rank. The
great tombs are the distinguishing feature of Monte Alban. Some
two hundred have been discovered. Built of rock, many of them
comprised an antechamber with the burial crypt in back, the walls
covered with polychrome paintings, glyphs, and symbols, and
containing ceramic effigy figures and pots.

Despite the few murals and solid figures, Zapotec art seems to have been compressed into these pots. They were fashioned in all shapes and sizes. Human heads wearing elaborate headdresses, figures seated with hands held across breasts, masks of the bat, the jaguar, the man-bat-jaguar, Cocijo and other gods. All decoration was at the front, the backs left plain, indicating they were meant to stand on a shelf in the tombs. Moreover, they were made to hold offerings for the dead. In short they were funerary urns, giving still more testimony to the Zapotec obsession with death.

Sometime in the tenth century A.D. Monte Alban was abandoned by its inhabitants and the valley was invaded by groups of Mixtecs from the mountainous Mixteca-Alta region to the north.

Early establishing their principality of Tilantongo, the Mixtecs had participated about A.D. 800 in the conquest of Cholua with the later, or historic, Olmecs, the Nahuas, and the Popolocas. This sacred city, like Teotihuacan, was dedicated to Quetzalcoatl. It is probable that the Mixtecs helped to build the last step of its mammoth pyramid. The Mixtec invasion seems to have been slow and peaceful. The ruins of Monte Alban show no signs of destruction by war, and the great valley below remained populated at numerous sites. The arriving Mixtecs began utilizing Monte Alban's massive tombs for burials of their own important personages.

The only surviving Nahuatl codices are believed to have come from the Mixteca-Puebla region, and seem to reflect a Teotihuacan influence. The Borgia group of six hieroglyphic manuscripts are solely of a religious, ritualistic, or esoteric nature, accentuating the religion of Quetzalcoatl, the Plumed Serpent. The second group, including the *Codices Vienna, Nuttall, Selden,* and *Bodley,* are known as the history manuscripts. The *Bodley Codex* covers Mixtec history from A.D. 692 to 1466. The *Selden Codex* is a Mixtec genealogical history from A.D. 794 to 1556 of only one place, "Belching Mountain," whose location is unknown. It relates, according to Caso, how two deities descended to the mountain. On the right was 1 Death (the Sun) bearing the symbol of a solar disc. On the left was 1 Movement bearing the symbol of the quincunx with its five points, showing him to be the incarnation of the planet Venus (Quetzalcoatl); also the mask of a fleshless jaw, also symbolizing Venus as Xolotl, the dog who accompanies the Sun when it goes down in the west to illumine the Land of the Dead. The two deities, Sun and Venus, then threw darts opening a crevice in the mountain, the "Hill of Gold and Jade," from which was born 127 days later the Lord 11 Water, beginning the genealogical history.[3] All these symbols—the Belching Mountain, the Sun, Venus-Quetzalcoatl, Xolotl, the quincunx, and Movement—embody, as we will explain later, the basic tenets of Nahuatl religious belief. History cannot be divorced from religious ideology.

It is little wonder that many scholars conjecture there may have existed in Teotihuacan pictorial codices, none of which have been found, that formed the basis of these Mixtec codices.

The Mixtecs, then, were a later and more advanced people encroaching upon and superseding the Zapotecs. They are known not only for their codices, but for their great artistry. Accomplished metallurgists working with gold, silver, and copper, and using the "lost wax" process of casting, they fashioned beautiful pectorals, bracelets, necklaces, rings, and earplugs. From alabaster and onyx they carved elegant vases, from jade, exquisite figurines, from rock crystal, necklace beads; their masks of wood were inlaid with turquoise and shell mosaics; and jaguar bones they carved as delicately as Chinese miniatures. Monte Alban's celebrated Tomb 7 was originally built by the Zapotecs long before they abandoned the center. Centuries later the Mixtecs utilized it for the burial of a prominent priest or chief. Caso, when he excavated it in 1932, discovered what has been called the greatest pre-Columbian treasure yet found. It comprised some five hundred exquisite objects now displayed in the regional museum of Oaxaca. They were all of Mixtec make. The beautiful jewelry which Dürer admired at the court of Charles V, and the pieces the King gave to the Pope, so admired by Benvenuto Cellini, were undoubtedly Mixtec.

Mixtecan architecture, contrasted with the Zapotecan, is no less distinctive. Mitla, the Mixtec "City of the Dead," twenty miles east of Monte Alban, is believed to have been a sacred burial place for kings and high priests. It is the most famous of all Mixtec ruins, comprising four main buildings enclosing a central court. They are characterized by walls of stone and adobe inlaid with mosaics of small stones cut so perfectly that no mortar was necessary to hold them in place. It has been calculated that in one building alone more than one hundred thousand cut stones were fitted together with miraculous precision. Their fret and meander designs, remindful of the Greek, show a geometrical abstractness and a preciousness of artistry, but also a certain coldness. Here too are found impressive tombs decorated with stepped spiral designs in stone mosaics, and remnants of mural paintings with calendar names and glyphs. Seler years ago recognized the figure of Quetzalcoatl in painted fragments on the palace "no fewer than nine times."

A few miles away Yagul occupied a magnificent location on top of a hill overlooking the Oaxaca valley. Excavations reveal a large courtyard with an adoratory in the center and four temples surrounding it, a great palace of six patios and twenty-three rooms showing remnants of mosaic work like that of Mitla. The thirty tombs attest the same obsession with death.

Both of these major ruins indicate the fusing of earlier, basic Zapotec construction with the later intricate Mixtec decoration. Neither of them equal the monolithic complex on Monte Alban which dominated the valley. But one is forced to agree with Bernal, against other claims, that the Zapotec culture was not the parent culture of Mexico because its products, style, and knowledge were not diffused to other cultures. Much of it was imported from outside, Monte Alban being only "an extraordinarily distinguished heir."[4]

Lovely Oaxaca is my own favorite city in Mexico. To its beauty and leisurely pace I owe much throughout many years. The contemporary Zapotecans are a sturdy people with a love of life and independence which has carried them through the stormy history of Mexico. Yet whenever I jolt up the steep winding road to the summit of Monte Alban and confront its ancient ruins, all connections between the Zapotec present and past seem curiously broken. The great ruins seem like empty and abandoned shells of a life that has left no lingering aura of its eternal essence. They are massive and stupendous; they compel my admiration. But they do not evoke any response to a living spirit as communicated by the Mayan pyramid-temples with their fragile roof-combs and exquisite panel frescos and lintel carvings. Nor do they awaken the awe and wonder of life, the exaltation of soul, as does Teotihuacan with its great impersonality, its imposing austerity. The stepped platforms of Monte Alban never aspire toward a peak. Massive, grim, and earthbound, they give no feeling of the spiritual urge that may have impelled their building, or that they were ever sparked by the divine flame. Nor do the famous tombs and the funerary urns, too elaborate to be cleanly beautiful and to convey a direct meaning; and these seem to be the characteristic symbol of the Zapotecs as were the jaguar of the Olmecs and the serpent of the Mayas. All carry a downward thrust. All seem dedicated to the Zapotec obsession with death—a death without transfiguration.

4 THE TOLTECS OF TEOTIHUACAN

So cultures kept breaking surface to vanish or endure ... But shortly before the beginning of the Christian era there burst forth in the great central valley of Mexico not a cultural bubble but the fountain of a civilization that splayed all Mesoamerica with its unprecedented magnificence.

> *Cuando aun era de noche,*
> *Cuando aun no habia dia,*
> *Cuando aun no habia luz,*
> *Se reunieron,*
> *Se convocaron los dioses,*
> *Alla en Teotihuacan.*[1]

This indeed was Teotihuacan, the "City of the Gods" who assembled here "while it was still night, before the light of day had dawned," and gave birth to the Fifth Sun and to the foremost civilization in Mesoamerica.

Today, two thousand years later, Teotihuacan's grandeur of conception still reflects what has been called "a well-integrated cosmic vision." The immense ruins, 30 miles from Mexico City, are dominated by the lofty four-step Pyramid of the Sun, standing 217 feet high on a base 750 feet square. Past it runs the Street of the Dead, Micaotli, nearly three miles long. At one end rises the Pyramid of the Moon, 149 feet high, from a square courtyard surrounded by 13 temples. Toward the other end lies the square Ciudela, or Citadel, enclosed by walls thirteen hundred feet long.

55

On each of three sides are four pyramidal bases for temples; on the east side are three more. In the center, embodied within a later temple, lies the Temple of Quetzalcoatl, its facade decorated with great sculptured stone heads of Quetzalcoatl, the Plumed Serpent, alternating with those of Tlaloc, the god of rain. Along Micaotli, the Street of the Dead, lie other temples and palaces that housed priests and acolytes. Farther out from this ceremonial precinct lie the great residential Palaces of Atelelco, Tetitla, and many others. And surrounding these zones was the general population area with grid pattern streets, market places, hostels for traveling merchants, canals and sewers—the whole comprising the first metropolis in the New World.

Austere and bare today, uncovered from the brush and dust of centuries, the mammoth structures give no indication of the smooth facing that covered their rough stone exteriors. But the excavated temples and palaces, some of them underground, reveal the gorgeously colored walls, murals, and friezes that made all Teotihuacan a city of color glowing in the sun. They show a variety of subjects: deities, priests, animals, men, naturalistic scenes, and inexhaustible symbolism. Some of the finest are of jaguars, jaguars devouring birds and human hearts, and jaguar priests. There are friezes of serpents. Along with these motifs encountered in the Olmec and Maya areas is that of the bird; the quetzal associated with the serpent, and the eagle perhaps for the first time symbolizing the sun. The butterfly and the butterfly god appear. All are intertwined, related in composition and meaning, as the union of bird and serpent, water and fire. The most striking representational fresco covers a wall in the palace of Tepantitla. With Tlaloc, god of rain, surrounded by entwined serpents, is depicted Tlalocan, Tlaloc's Paradise, where dozens of human beings are dancing among fruits and flowers made bountiful by the *tlaloques,* the clouds, who cast raindrops precious as jade—all comprising a symbolism to be interpreted later.

Myth amply attests that the builders of Teotihuacan were master craftsmen of all arts. As Sahagún reports: "Nothing that they did was difficult for them. They cut green stone, and cast gold, and they made other works of the craftsman and the feather worker. . . . Also they were very rich. Of no value were food and all sustenance. It is said that all the squashes were very large, and the ears of maize could hardly be embraced in one's arms.... And the small ears of maize they only burned to heat the sweat baths."[2] He goes on to say the amaranth plants grew so tall they could be climbed. And the colored cotton prospered without dyeing: bright red, yellow, rose, violet, green, azure, verdigris, and coyote-colored. It is said these Toltecs were physicians skilled in the virtues of herbs, that they were skilled in astronomy and the art of interpreting dreams.

There is no history of this ancient metropolis save that it was called Tollan. In Nahuatl, Tollan simply means "Great City." Its inhabitants were known as Toltecs, the Nahuatl name for "Master Craftsmen." There seems little reasonable doubt that this first great Tollan was indeed Teotihuacan. Sahagún is quoted as reporting in the sixteenth century: "As to the antiquity of this people, it is proven that for more than two thousand years they have lived in this land now called New Spain, because through their ancient pictures there is evidence that the famous city called Tollan was destroyed a thousand years ago or very nearly ... and as to the time it took to build it and the time it prospered before it was destroyed, it is consonant with truth that over a thousand years passed, from which it follows that this land was populated at least five hundred years before the Incarnation of our Redeemer. This famous and great city of Tollan, very rich and well-ordered, very wise and powerful, suffered the adverse fortune of Troy."[3]

Archaeological dating confirms this time-span. The great pyramids of the Sun and the Moon were built sometime between 200 B.C. and A.D. 150, followed by the erection of the Temple of Quetzalcoatl, the huge Ciudela with its numerous temples, and the great palaces and plazas; and the metropolis was first partially destroyed and then abandoned between A.D. 650 and 750.

Who the people were who built it is not known. There are no inscriptions to reveal what languages they spoke. Nothing is known of their physical appearance, as they cremated their dead. It is enough to know that this City of the Gods was the birthplace of the myth and religion of Quetzalcoatl, the birthplace of the Nahuatl culture; and to call its people by their time-honored and indisputable name of Toltecs.

The ruins of Teotihuacan, laid out with geometrical precision, still exist in a space-time continuum beyond our worldly comprehension. Its insistent impersonality, its utilization of great space equated with measureless time, its imposing austerity, still perpetuate in us today its single purpose of exalting the human soul.

The expansion of Teotihuacan's civilization has no parallel in Mesoamerica. Its influences spread east to the Gulf Coast and north to El Tajin and Panuco; west into Guerrero and Michoacan in the Tarascan country; south through the Zapotecs in Oaxaca to the Tehuantepec isthmus. By A.D. 400 the highlands of Guatemala were under Teotihuacan's domination, the Mayan site of Kaminaljuyu on the present outskirts of Guatemala being converted into a miniature replica of Teotihuacan. From there Teotihuacan influence spread through the lowland Mayas to Tikál in the Peten rainforest, to Copan in Honduras, to El Salvador and the Pacific coast.

This phenomenal expansion was not accomplished by war, but primarily at first by *pochtecas,* or traveling merchants, who established trade routes, market, and trading centers where they could obtain the prized green feathers of the quetzal, jaguar hides, cacao beans, textiles, and other goods. Through these channels were diffused Toltec art and architecture: the combination of vertical and inclined planes by use of the *talud* (slope) and *tablero* (panel), pottery styles like tripod vessels and "thin orange" ware, representations in mural and fresco art of Teotihuacan gods, symbols, and motifs.

Of all Teotihuacan exports, its religious ideology and world view were paramount. The Toltec civilization or empire was almost completely religious. It has been compared to Tibet where the Dalai Lama, the incarnation of the Buddha, headed a religious theocratic state; to a Holy Empire whose center was equivalent to Rome or Mecca; to the great Hellenistic commonwealth of ancient Greece whose intellectual and religious capital of Alexandria in Egypt fulfilled the same functions as Teotihuacan in Mesoamerica.

The multiplicity of deities and the complexity of its religious ideology cover a scope too great to condense here; it will be viewed in proper perspective in a later section of this book. But of all the gods there stands out the most appealing and most controversial figure in Mesoamerican myth and religion—Quetzal-coatl, the Plumed Serpent. However vehemently it may be asserted or denied that he was an historical fact, he looms up in the New World as a psychical symbol with the universal stature of the Buddha and the Christ.

He emerged here among the Toltecs to assume for the first time his complete mythical role of man and god. As a culture hero, the king of Tollan, he taught men all their arts and sciences, laid the foundations of Nahuatl culture. Then in penance for violating his own religious tenets, he self-immolated himself, suffered torments in the Land of the Dead, and rose triumphant as Venus, the Morning Star. The myth about him was dramatic and profound. It interjected into primitive religious belief the transcendent quality that raised it to a level of universal meaning. The doctrine formed from it grew into a national belief that spread into the nooks and crannies of all the religious ideologies throughout Mesoamerica.

Teotihuacan was not the only bastion of the Quetzalcoatl doctrine. Cholua to the east of the high central valley was built before the Christian era, about the same time as Teotihuacan which largely influenced its development. Its great pyramid, dedicated to Quetzalcoatl, was not as high as Teotihuacan's Pyramid of the Sun but was larger in volume, and remains the largest pyramid in the world. Today, overgrown with brush, it resembles a great hill on whose summit stands a Spanish-Colonial church. Recent excavations show that it is composed of four superimposed structures oriented to the east-west axis with a deviation of seventeen degrees to the north, as was the Pyramid of the Sun. On the northern Gulf coast, El Tajin later became another focus of the Quetzalcoatl doctrine; as did Xochicalco to the south, near present Cuernavaca, which also shows Mayan influence in its great carvings of the plumed serpent.

The fall of Teotihuacan is as mysterious as its rise to greatness. It is believed that the sacred city was partially destroyed about A.D. 650 by barbarian Otomis from the north. Traces of fire have been found in its carbonized beams. Other theories assert that outside attackers did not destroy the city until a century or more later, but that the collapse of its power was due to an internal crisis—perhaps a revolt of the people against its theocratic rulers.

This initiated a period of decline, a prelude to the invasions of barbarians, and Teotihuacan was finally abandoned between 750 and 800 A.D.

The fall of Teotihuacan did not end its religious influence. The Florentine Codex records the exodus of its *tlamatinime,* or learned men, toward Guatemala. It is possible, as many believe, that the immigrations into Guatemala and Yucatan recorded in the *Popul Vuh* and the books of Chilam Balam refer to the Teotihuacan dispersal. A large number of refugees settled in Cholula, perpetuating their culture until the city's conquest about A.D. 800 by the Mixtecs and "historical Olmecs." A mass migration then began to the south: to Guatemala, El Salvador, Honduras, perhaps as far as Colombia and Peru. The name of *Pipiles* has been given to these exiles. This word, according to the Nahuatl linguist Dr. Thelma D. Sullivan, means both "appendages" and "nobles," so they may well be considered priestly and noble appendages of Teotihuacan.

These conjectures have not been proved, but they do bear out the fact that a serious crisis, a subterranean tremor, shook all Mesoamerica between A.D. 650 and 800. A mysterious collapse whose cause lies in the field of religion rather than in economics and politics. Not only did Teotihuacan and Cholula fall, but the Mayan centers stopped erecting stelae and monuments were mutilated, ending the great period of classic Mayan culture. Yet the seeds of the old had been planted to grow new shoots with new forms.

5 THE TOLTECS OF TULA

Sometime before the fall of Teotihuacan, barbarian nomads from the north began entering the Valley of Mexico. With them entered one of the most confusing and controversial aspects of Mesoamerican history. Who were these barbarians, where did they come from, when?

Fray J. de Acosta who was in Mexico early enough to reach original sources of information and whose history was published in Spain in 1589,[1] gives the name of Chichimecas to the first immigrants. They were followed by a second wave of immigrants, the Navatalcas, or Nahuatlacas, which comprised seven tribes which had come forth from seven caves. Acosta names the seven tribes— the Suchimilcos, Chalcas, Tepanecans, Culhuas, Tlatluicans, Tlascaltecans, and Aztecas—dating the migration of the first at A.D. 720 and the arrival of the seventh in 1022.

Abbe D. Francisco Severio Clavigero in his history published in 1787 agrees with Acosta in naming seven tribes that came from a place called Aztlán to the north: the Sochimilcas, Chalcas, Tepanecas, Colhuas, Tlahuicas, Tlascalans, and Mexicas.[2] All these tribes bore the common name of Nahuatlacas. He asserts, however, that these seven tribes came after the Chichimecas who were preceded by the Toltecas, the first immigrants, about which Acosta knew nothing. These Toltecas left their old kingdom of Tollan in Asia under seven leaders in 596 A.D. and founded their new capital of Tollan in Mexico in 607. He then lists the names of eight kings

and the dates when each began his reign, beginning in 667 and
ending in 1031. He reports that in 660 the astronomer Huemetzin
painted the *Tecamoxtli,* the "Divine Book," now lost, recording
the Toltecas' journey to America, and their calendar and mythological transformations of their deities "concealed from common
knowledge." According to Clavigero, the Toltecas built the great
pyramids at Teotihuacan and Cholua.

Fernando de Alva Ixtlilxochitl at the end of the sixteenth century listed nine Toltec kings reigning from 510 to 885.[3] The *Codice
Chimalpopoca,* spanning the period 635 to 1519, lists six more
kings reigning from 923 to 980.[4] Ixtlilxochitl affirms that the Toltecan race was 5,768 years old.

Confusing and contradictory as are these early histories, they
cannot be discounted. They help to illumine the period of Teotihuacan's rise and fall, and the period now following. Based on
myth recorded when it was still fresh, they contain allusions and
implications to be probed later.

Since these early works, scores of documented histories have
been written. Most of them agree that the Chichimecas—a generic
term for barbarian nomads—came from the north. From the Gran
Chichimeca, asserts contemporary archaeologist Charles di Peso,
reviving the old name for all the land lying north of the Tropic
of Cancer to the 38th parallel, westward to San Francisco, California and eastward into the Great Plains as far as Wichita, Kan-
sas.[5] On that assumption the Chichimecas were members of the
Uto-Aztecan linguistic family whose ancestors had crossed the
Bering Strait to America some fifteen thousand years before and
they had slowly migrated southward through this great region of
Mexico.

Cutting through all these historical conjectures is the commonly
accepted myth of the great Chichimeca chief, Mixcoatl. Easily
routing bands of the dispersed population of Teotihuacan, he
established his capital at Culhuacan, at the foot of the hill of La
Estrella. During his campaigns near Cuernavaca he encountered
in battle a resolute young woman named Chimalman. Unable to
vanquish her, he married her. While she was pregnant, Mixcoatl
was assassinated by one of his leaders who then usurped his
throne.

Chimalman died upon giving birth to a son who was educated by his maternal grandparents who lived near Tepoztlán. This ancient town was not far from the fortress-temple-city of Xochicalco, the third important center of the Quetzalcoatl religion. Here the boy, named Ce Acatl Topiltzin, adopted the beliefs of the Quetzalcoatl teachings.

Grown to manhood, he killed his father's assassin and assumed leadership of his people. Mixcoatl's remains he found and buried in the Hill of the Star, erecting a temple on top where he could be worshipped as a god. He then moved his capital from Culhuacan to Tula, Hidalgo, about sixty miles north of present Mexico City. Here in 968, as the king of Tula and the high priest of the mythical Quetzalcoatl, he became known as Quetzalcoatl.

The ancient Quetzalcoatl religion which he upheld was opposed to human sacrifice, but a great number of barbarians under his rule were militaristic and worshipped a war god, Tezcatlipoca. Rebelling against Topiltzin's attempts to make them embrace his own religion, they forced him to abdicate his throne in 987 and to leave Tula.

Huemac, the last ruler of Tula, reigned for seventy years. A revolution in 1168 then forced him to flee to Chapultepec where he reportedly committed suicide in 1174. Under the onslaught of fresh barbarians from the north, Tula was destroyed in 1224.

Even on this established chronology the ascribed dates are contradictory. For the beginning of Topiltzin's reign in Tula, his departure, and the destruction of the city, the National Institute of Anthropology and History of Mexico gives the dates quoted above, 968, 987, and 1168. The Institute's museum at Tula, 965, 987, and 1156. Bernal gives 980, 999, and 1224. This of course is splitting hairs, but other records are still more contradictory. According to the *Codice Chimalpopoca* and *Anales de Cuauhtitlan,* which date from 1570, Topiltzin Quetzalcoatl became king of Tula in 873 and reigned till 895. But according to Ixtlilxochitl he reigned from 1031 till 1063. Now Topiltzin could not have reigned from 873 to 895, according to the *Codice Chimalpopoca,* if Tula were founded in 968, according to the National Institute. Nor could he have reigned from 1031 to 1063, according to Ixtlilxochitl and Clavigero, if he fled Tula in 987. There is a difference here of three calendar rounds of 52 years each, whose significance will be explained later.

What actually became of Topiltzin is a mystery. The most common version is that he sailed for Yucatan. Another is a report from Texcoco that he died in Culhuacan in the year 2 Acatl, 883. A third is the transcendental myth that he went to the coast and was transformed into the planet Venus, a myth that undoubtedly refers to the original Quetzalcoatl.

Demythologizing all accounts about him, Spinden asserts that Topiltzin-Quetzalcoatl died or committed suicide in Yucatan when Venus made its last appearance as the Evening Star on April 4, 1208 and was transformed into the Morning Star on April 13, 1208; and that he may have been buried in the Temple of the Magicians at Uxmal.[6]

All these contradictory conjectures are given here not to further confuse matters, but to show that history doesn't know what really happened. The only record of the travails of the human spirit is myth. In it these perplexing questions may find answers far different than we expect. But for the moment the contradictions also introduce a heated controversy in which we innocent bystanders are caught in the middle.

The ruins of Tula, or Tollan Xicocotitlan, lie near the "crooked hill," Xicuco, from which it takes its name. The buildings are grouped about a large plaza with a monolithic altar in the center. To the north rises the thirty-foot Pyramid of Quetzalcoatl, below which stand fifty-one huge square pillars forming a colonnade or vestibule. There are still some remains of the facing of the five steps of the pyramid. The panels show bas-reliefs of human faces emerging from the mouths of plumed serpents, eagles devouring bleeding hearts, a procession of jaguars. On the flat top stand the enormous stone pillars that supported the roof of the temple: cylindrical serpents head down and tails upward, and square columns depicting warriors. Behind them stand the celebrated four Atlantean statues: enormous fifteen-foot-high caryatids of warriors armed with darts, and wearing breastplates of stylized butterflies, their squat faces brutal and expressionless.

To the north of the pyramid-platform is the *coatepantli*, or "serpent wall," garnished with a frieze of Greek frets and people being devoured by serpents. And beyond, a ball court. West of the pyramid stand round pillars and large carved stone benches that mark the site of what is known as the "Burnt Palace." On the eastern side of the main plaza rises another pyramid in ruinous state, facing another unexcavated structure across the plaza.

As a whole, Tula lacks homogeneity. It stood at a crossroad of space and time: between two peoples and at a decisive moment when the fulcrum was tipped to the militaristic future. The plumed serpent symbol of Quetzalcoatl and the armed warrior symbol of Tezcatlipoca—these are the two conflicting motifs of its unprepossessing style. Without warmth, it has nothing of the humanness and beauty of the old Maya centers, the majesty of Teotihuacan with its grandeur of conception, its transcendental appeal. Séjourné calls it "a second-rate civic center which, except for a few remarkable sculptures, contains only crude copies of imported motifs and thus cannot possibly have been the cradle of a glorious culture."[7]

The confusing situation in the ninth or tenth century, or whenever Tula was founded, presents too thin ice for anyone to skate over with impunity. Yet in 1941 a congress of the Sociedad Mexicana de Antropologia affirmed that "the mistaken views identifying the Toltecs with the Teotihuacans have been proved wrong," and passed a resolution to the effect that Tula had been the ancient Tollan—not Teotihuacan which a thousand years before had been the birthplace of the Fifth Sun, the myth of Quetzalcoatl, and the first great civilization of Mesoamerica.

No layman has any business entering the continuing squabble, but much of its bitterness is losing edge. Uneasy doubts have set in. Many authorities are voicing the opinion that a one-to-one Tula-Tollan correlation is untenable. The clash between the peaceful adherents of Topiltzin-Quetzalcoatl and the militaristic adherents of the Tezcatlipoca cult in Tula assumes wider and deeper significance. The historian Chadwick in a scholarly dissertation postulates that the history of Toltec-Tula in the *Codice Chimalpopoca* is copied from Mixtec codices, being the history of the first and second dynasties of Tilantonongo as related in *Codices Bodley, Selden, Vindobonesis, Nuttall,* and others. Mixcoatl's capital of Culhuacan, he believes, was Zaachila in Oaxaca. Moreover, he suggests that the first battle between the Quetzalcoatl and Tezcatlipoca dynasties took place in Teotihuacan where the Quetzalcoatl forces routed those of Tezcatlipoca. The struggle continued in Cholua where Tezcatlipoca defeated Quetzalcoatl. The latter then conquered the Mixteca, becoming overlord of Tilantongo. Finally after three successors, the Tezcatlipoca dynasty defeated that of Quetzalcoatl.[8]

This argument, if it proves true, may clear up the differences between the dates of Topiltzin's rule by proving that there were two Quetzalcoatls, or ruling priests of Quetzalcoatl: one, Meconetzin, or 9 Wind "Stone Skull," reigning from 875 to 959, and the other Topiltzin, or 8 Deer, reigning from 1031 to 1063. It will also accentuate the importance of the Mixteca-Puebla region. There is a growing feeling that the Mixtec codices were inspired by earlier Teotihuacan codices, although none of these have been found.

Yet what we are confronting in these worldly allegories is not a struggle for temporal power between two opposing secular dynasties. For Quetzalcoatl and Tezcatlipoca are opposing deities, one beneficent and the other ubiquitous, whose battles began in Heaven at the creation of the First World. So it is on this celestial plane we must finally search for the cause of the schism in Tula which reflects the primary concept of duality common to all of Mesoamerica.

The Toltec-Tula culture, in short, was that of a semi-barbaric, militaristic society built upon the ruins of the high religious culture of Teotihuacan whose elements it adopted but failed to assimilate. Its importance lies in the influence it exported to Chichén Itza in Yucatan, and that as a transitional military culture it opened the way for the domination of Mexico by the aggressive Aztecs.

6 THE AZTECS

On the crest of a new wave of Chichimecas from the north in 1224 A.D. rode the great chief Xolotl. He established several *señorios*, or capitals, one of which was Tenayuca, now a town on the northwest outskirts of Mexico City. Here still stands what may be the prototypal pyramid that centuries later served as the model for the great Aztec pyramid in Tenochtitlan. Four-stepped, it has two stairways leading to two temples on top instead of the one stairway common to Toltec and Maya pyramids. Encircling it at the bottom is a *coatepantli,* or "wall of serpents," similar to that at Tula. To the north is a monumental sculpture of a coiled serpent, head pointing to the position of the setting sun a month before the summer solstice, and, to the south, another pointing to the setting sun's position a month after the solstice. The obsessive concern of these barbarians with the symbolism of serpents, eight hundred of which are found at Tenayuca, and with the setting sun, undoubtedly was engendered by surviving groups of Toltecs.

Xolotl finally established his capital at Texcoco on the eastern shore of Lake Texcoco. A powerful ruler, he reigned for half a century. According to the *Codice Xolotl,* he was followed by three more nomadic rulers and five sedentary rulers before the breakup of his dominion. Under the rule of Nezahualcoyotl, the poet-king in the fifteenth century, Texcoco became the seat of learning and the arts, the "Athens of Mexico."

On the heels of this late invasion of Chichimecas there straggled into Anahuac, the Valley of Mexico, a miserable band of savages dressed only in the skins of animals they killed with darts. These Aztecas were the last and most insignificant of the seven tribes to come forth from Chicomoztoc, located in their legendary homeland of Aztlan, an island in the middle of a lake, the "Place of Herons." Clavigero gives a time-table for their wanderings, stating that they left Aztlan in 1160 and arrived in Tula in 1196 where they stayed nine years before moving on. Finally, in 1325, on a marshy island near the western shore of Lake Tezcoco, this miserable straggling band founded what was to become the great capital of the Aztec nation, Tenochtitlan.[1]

Their rise to power was largely due to their fanatic dedication to war. But also they were politically acute enough to form alliances with one neighboring tribe after another to defeat the others. They first allied themselves with the Tepanecs of Azcapotzalco who still preserved remnants of Toltec culture. In 1367 their combined forces destroyed Culhuacan, the ancient capital of Mixcoatl whose rulers still claimed direct descent from Toltec kings. A few years later, allied with Tlatelolcos, they took Xolotl's *señorio* of Tenayuca.

This program of successive military alliances not only built up their confidence, but their material resources with the booties of war. It accomplished something else equally important. It impressed upon them the rich heritage of their civilized predecessors, the Toltecs. So in 1376 they chose as their first king Acamapichtli, a descendant of the Toltec rulers of Culhuacan which they had destroyed. Thereafter, they claimed by right of succession the Toltec heritage.

By the time of their fourth king, this idea was firmly established. Itzcoatl, the son of Acamapichtli, when elected in 1427, immediately proclaimed himself "Lord of the Culhuas," referring to the people of Culhuacan, the capital of the remnant Toltecs. Defeating Azcapotzalco with the help of Texcoco, Itzcoatl appointed as advisers Tlacaelel and Moctezuma I, his nephew and the son of Huitzilihuitl, the second king. He then proceeded to establish a cultural and religious basis for Aztec military domination by first destroying the records of the Toltecs. As related in the *Codice Matritense*:

> They preserved an account of their history,
> but later it was burned,
> during the reign of Itzcoatl.
> The lords of Mexico decreed it,
> the lords of Mexico declared:
> 'It is not fitting that our people
> should know these pictures.
> Our people, our subjects, will be lost
> and our land destroyed,
> for these pictures are full of lies . . .'[2]

The identity of Tlacaelel and his role in this book-burning orgy has long been disputed. Clavigero, for example, writes: "Acosta makes Tlacaelel the grandson of Itzcoatl, and at the same time uncle of Moctezuma, which is evidently absurd; Moctezuma was the son of Huitzilihuitl, brother of Itzcoatl; of course he could not be the grandson of the grandson of Itzcoatl." Moreover, Clavigero insists that Tlacaelel was but one of the names of Moctezuma, another being Ilhuicamina, "Archer of Heaven," as represented in the Mendoza collection of paintings with the heavens pierced with an arrow. Torquemada, another early historian, doubts that Tlacaelel ever existed, saying that his name might have been applied to Itzcoatl.

The contemporary historian Leon-Portilla establishes Tlacaelel's importance.[3] He and Moctezuma the elder, Ilhuicamina, were born in the year 10 Rabbit (1398) on the same day, having different mothers but the same father, Huitzilihuitl. It was he, rising swiftly to prestige and power, who persuaded Itzcoatl to destroy the Toltec records and substitute in their place a new Aztec version of history. The priests rewrote the ancient prayers and hymns to Quetzalcoatl, praising Huitzilopochtli as the supreme god; and Tlacaele began persuading the people that their divine mission was to dominate all the nations of the earth in order to nourish Huitzilopochtli, the Sun, with sacrificial blood.

Itzcoatl then initiated new campaigns which extended his rule beyond the central valley. Upon his death Moctezuma I ascended the throne, retaining Tlacaelel as his most influential adviser. In his reign from 1440 to 1469 the Aztec empire was consolidated

throughout all of central Mexico. Its crude island capital of Tenochtitlan was rebuilt into a magnificent metropolis connected
with the mainland by three broad causeways.

The great central plaza was the hub around which revolved the
life of the empire. Enclosed by a *coatepantli*, or serpent wall, it
contained seventy-two stone buildings: pyramid-temples, the
tzompantli, a rack of human skulls imbedded in mortar, a ball
court, *calmecac* schools for training of priests and nobles, *telepuachcalli* for training youths in citizenship and war, the palaces
of the rulers, and living quarters for priests and nobles. Dominating all stood the Great Pyramid, rising about one hundred feet
high. Its two stairways of 114 steps were garnished at the bottom
with great stone heads of serpents and led to two temples on top:
one, blue and white, dedicated to Tlaloc; and the other, red with
white dots representing skulls, dedicated to Huitzilopochtli. Bernal Diaz in his history of the Spanish conquest gives the classic
description. The best visual picture now is given thousands of
people daily underneath this ancient central plaza, the zocalo of
today. There in the main arcade of the enormous central station
of Mexico City's magnificent new Metro subway system is displayed a miniature replica.

In elevating the comparatively insignificant tribal god of the
early Aztecs to the position of the creative deity of the Aztec
empire, Itzcoatl and Tlacaelel were not able to obliterate all vestiges of belief in the hermetic Quetzalcoatl teachings. Hence, in
the middle of the great plaza was erected a circular temple of
Quetzalcoatl in his aspect of the god of wind, its doorway representing the mouth of a serpent.

The religion of Quetzalcoatl had prohibited human sacrifice.
This was in opposition to the newly established religion of Huitzilopochtli which maintained that he, personifying the sun, had to
be nourished with the precious fluid, the nectar of the gods, to give
him life and strength for his daily struggles against the moon and
stars. In order to firmly inculcate this concept, an appropriate
number of sacrificial victims would be needed to properly dedi-
cate the great pyramid in Tenochtitlan. Where could they be obtained?, queried Moctezuma.

Tlacaelel's answer, quoted by Leon-Portilla, was pat enough.

There was no need to go to war to obtain victims to inaugurate the temple. "Rather, let a convenient market be sought where our god may go with his army to buy victims . . . as if he were to go to a nearby place to buy tortillas." The market, he continued, should be situated in Tlaxcala, Cholua, and other nearby places. If it were farther away, the flesh of those barbaric peoples would become old and stale. Instead Huitzilopochtli must be able to feed himself with them "as though he were eating warm tortillas, soft and tasty, straight out of the oven."

Human sacrifice in Mexico was not new; it had been carried out since ancient times to a limited degree. But this program of perpetual and wholesale sacrifice set a precedent and presented the difficult problem of finding a close "market" to provide the human "tortillas."

Tlacaelel again offered a ready solution: a perpetual war between two states which agreed to engage in battle periodically. Neither would endeavor to destroy the other, to sack its towns, to acquire its territories. The objective was simply to capture prisoners for sacrifice, a dead enemy being of no value. So began the "Battles of Flowers," or "Flowery Wars," between Tenochtitlan and its neighboring cities. Tlaxcala soon became the most fruitful source of victims. By mutual agreement Tlaxcala was allowed to maintain its independence with the provision that during periodic "Flowery Wars" it would provide Tenochtitlan with a new supply of captives to be sacrificed to Huitzilopochtli.

So it was that a single man obscure in history was largely responsible for creating from an ancient tribal myth a religious-political structure to support the immense Aztec empire. That it was wholly militaristic at base was not new; the Toltec-Tula regime had set the precedent. But it established a pseudo-religious basis for war and human sacrifice. At the death of Moctezuma I, Tlacaelel was offered the throne. He refused, preferring to remain an adviser to the succeeding king Axayacatl.

Axayacatl, the sixth king and a descendant of the first king, Acamapichtli, finally conquered Tenochtitlan's only rival, the city-state of Tlatelolco whose pyramid may still be seen in La Plaza de las Tres Culturas de Tlateloloco in the heart of Mexico City.

Tizoc's short reign followed that of Axayacatl, and upon his

death he was succeeded by his brother, Ahuizotl. During the first
year of Ahuizotl's reign, 1487, the great temple was finally completed and dedicated with the sacrifice of hordes of victims. The
reported number varies from twenty to eighty thousand, undoubtedly a gross exaggeration. Yet whatever the number, the
cruelty and rapaciousness of this despot spread southward to the
border of Guatemala.

In 1502 Moctezuma II was elected as the ninth hereditary ruler
of the vast empire now at its peak. The head of an immensely
complicated social, political, and economic system, he was an
emperor embodying all the temporal power of an autocratic despot. As the nominal head of a state religion, he was in addition a
high priest to whom was ascribed the attribute of divinity. Moctezuma's sensitive character was unable to support such a burden.
And in the seventeenth year of his reign, when he was but forty
years old, destiny intervened to end his rule and the course of the
Aztec empire. The year was 1519 and Cortés had landed on the
east coast of Mexico.

On the basis of the Aztecs' continuous bloody human sacrifices,
it is customary to discount them as uninspired barbarians, wholly
materialistic. This is but one side of the coin. The other is emerging ever more clearly through their grandiose architecture, monolithic sculpture, lyric poetry, and the philosophical discourses by
their priests and learned men. If the Aztecs were bloodthirsty barbarians with an itch for power, they were also a sensitive people
with high moral ethics. They were, in short, a people like most
peoples, expressing both sides of their dual nature. Only on their
own terms can we understand them—the metaphysical terms expressed in their mythology.

7 IN-FLOWING STREAMS

Into the vast pool of Mesoamerican cultures there must have been in-flowing streams from farther shores.

The hard-line theory of orthodox anthropology affirms that there was a major migration of Stone Age peoples from Asia to America over the Bering Strait land bridge some twelve to fifteen thousand years ago; and that within seven thousand years they had spread south to Tierra del Fuego on the southern tip of South America. Eventually they established two main centers, one in the fetid jungles of Mesoamerica and the other on the forbidding *altiplano* of Bolivia and Peru. Here, completely isolated from all contacts with other continents, they developed high civilizations. Moreover, affirms the doctrine, these Asiatic immigrants who came to be known as American Indians were homogeneous.

The earliest known specialized projectile points in the New World are said to be 13,200 years old. Human skeletal remains have been discovered, notably that of a woman at Midland, Texas and that of a man near Tepexpan, Mexico, both estimated to be ten thousand years old. These bear out the academic fraternity's conclusion that Mesoamerica was initially occupied by nomadic hunters and gatherers about 10,000 B.C. But here looms a great gap. There are no evidences of their slow evolution into settled, civilized people. All their first cultures, as we have seen, appear fully formed, with corn agriculture, sophisticated art, social organization, and religious ceremonialism.

Mounting evidence contradicts the present Bering Strait theory. Sophisticated stone tools, dated as about 250,000 years old by several techniques, have recently been found in a stream bed at Hueyatlaco, near Puebla, Mexico.[1] Such a shocking great age for man in the New World seems so unreasonable that no conclusions have been drawn, although Louis Leakey and Ruth Dee Simpson previously had proposed pushing the history of man in America back 50,000 to 100,000 years. More finds point to that direction. Artifacts with a radiocarbon dating between 25,000 to 32,000 years have been found on the Old Crow River in the Yukon. Human tools near Cobleskill, New York believed to be at least 70,000 years old. Carbon associated with a stone scraper at Tule Springs, Nevada with a date of 28,000 years. And evidence of human presence near San Diego, California dating from 20,000 and 35,000 years.[2] None of these (and other similar finds) are accepted as valid by the academic fraternity.

Of the many maverick scholars who dispute the theory of the single Bering Strait crossing, the anthropologist Harold Sterling Gladwin offers the most specific theory of different migrations from Asia across the Strait.[3] The first migration was of Asiatic Austroloids between 25,000 and 15,000 B.C. who left their imprints on skull types found in Ecuador and Brazil. The Asiatic Negroids comprising the second migration between 15,000 and 2,500 B.C. are identified with Folsom Man and the Basketmakers. The third migration, 2,500 to 500 B.C., was of peoples from northern China and Siberia who became the ancestors of the Algonguin tribes which stretched across northern United States. The fourth migration of Eskimos from Siberia about 500 B.C. remained along the Arctic fringe of North America. Following the breakup of the Chou dynasty about 300 B.C., the fifth migration was of Mongoloids who spread down into the Southwest and Mexico from northern China.

In addition to these five Bering Strait migrations, there followed a sixth migration between 300 B.C. and A.D. 500 which came directly by boat across the Pacific. It consisted of Melanesians who became the American Caribs, and Polynesians who became the Arawaks, as attested by the innumerable Oceanic traits on the Pacific Coast from Mexico to Peru.

From these stocks derived the physical characteristics of the principal groups in America. As a summation, Gladwin asserts that the prototypes of all cultural traits north of Mexico were confined to China and northeast Asia, whereas those of Mexico southward into Peru were derived from Polynesia, Melanesia, India, and the Near and Middle East.

Such an anthropological breakdown of racial types and physical characteristics can be continued as indefinitely as the archaeological classification of potsherds. One thing seems certain. The American Indians were not a homogeneous race. They were composed of many different stocks migrating from many different sources at many different periods.

Even during the Conquest, European observers could not believe native Indian savages could have built up from scratch their monumental civilization. Francisco Lopez de Gómara, biographer of Cortés, was the first to suggest that the aborigines of America had come from the mythical continent of Atlantis. Other conjectures followed. Gregorio Garces in his *Origin de los Indios de el Nuevo Mundo* of 1607 reviewed eleven major postulations: that the Indians of America were Carthaginians, Jews, Tatars, Mongols, or Norsemen; or came from Ophir, Tarshish, China. Lord Kingsborough's nine-volume *Antiquities of Mexico* (1830-48) was compiled to prove that the Mexicans were descendants of the Ten Lost Tribes of Israel, and the thesis of Compte de Waldeck's *Romantic Travels* (1838) was that they had descended from the Egyptians.[4] It is quite probable that some of all these peoples crossed both the Atlantic and Pacific to Mesoamerica centuries before the Christian era.

One of the most outstanding historians of these voyages is Dr. Henriette Mertz. The earliest she recounts is recorded in the oldest Chinese classic, the *Shan Hai King,* "The Book of Mountains and Seas," compiled during the reign of Emperor Shun, 2250 B.C. Long considered a fairy tale in China, Miss Mertz' documented and mapped interpretation reveals it to be a factual travel record across the "Great Western Sea" to America, an exploratory expedition of some six thousand miles north to Canada and south to Mexico from the "Great Luminous Canyon where the Sun Was Born," the Grand Canyon of the Colorado.

Her second account is an interpretation of the Chinese classic,

Kuen 327, written in A.D. 499 during the Sung dynasty. This is the record of a Chinese Buddhist priest, Hwui Shan, who voyaged across the sea to a country called Fu-sang, identified as Mexico.[5]

In another great work of reconstruction, Miss Mertz interprets Homer's classic, *The Odyssey,* as the factual account of a voyage made about 1150 B.C. across the Atlantic to the coast of North America.[6] And at successive meetings of the International Congress of Americanists, she presented papers on two Atlantic voyages to South America. One was based on *The Argonautica,* the epic account by Appolonius Rhodius of the voyage of the ship "Argo" about 1200 B.C. to the mouth of the Rio La Plata on the east coast and upriver to the *altiplano* of Bolivia. The other confirmed Herodotus' record of a voyage made by the Egyptian king Sesostris (Senusert II) to the Bolivian region of Colchis.

More outstanding work has been done by Cyrus B. Gordon, chairman of the Department of Mediterranean Studies at Brandeis University, famous for deciphering both Minoan Linear A and Eteocretan inscriptions from Crete. He has recently deciphered the inscription on the Parahyba Stone found near Parahyba, Brazil in 1872 ,as the record of the voyage of fifteen Canaanites across the Atlantic from Ezion-geber to the "New Shore" of Brazil in 531 B.C. after a two-year voyage around Africa during which ten other ships were lost. Ezion-geber was located in Edom on the fringe of Judah where the Israelites were seafaring partners of the Phoenicians, their combined Hebrew-Phoenician nautical operations beginning when King Solomon and Hiram I of Tyre embarked on joint overseas trading expeditions in the tenth century B.C. From this inscription and others, Gordon posits many other Canaanite and Aegean voyages to the New World.[7]

All such studies of migrations, voyages, and findings are rejected by the present establishment, which seems determined to throw out the baby with the bath water. This poses the bitterly contested question of "Diffusion"—the bugaboo of Mesoamerican research. The academic Isolationists stubbornly adhere to the Bering Strait theory, maintaining that civilization in America developed independently in complete isolation from the rest of the world. The Diffusionists assert, to the contrary, that the emigrants and voyagers to America did not carry their furniture, tools, art, and handicrafts. What they brought were carried in their heads—their religious ideology, art motifs, beliefs, and customs. Miguel Covarrubias, an outstanding authority on Indian art, has produced in two magnificent books a comprehensive text with more than a hundred superb drawings of art motifs common to the Old World and the New.[8]

Scholars in many fields have called attention to the similarities between the Late Chou decorative styles of China and the friezes at El Tajin; the tripod vessels of Han China and Teotihuacan; the Hindu and Mexican calendars; Hindu Buddhist and late Classic Maya iconography.

Heine-Geldern points out that the Burmese game of *pachisi* and the Aztec game of *patolli* both involve the symbolism of the four quarters of the world and their directional colors. The central temple of Angor Thom, Cambodia, bears a relief depicting a scene similar to the Flying Pole Dance, *Los Voladores,* still performed at El Tajin in Veracruz .The half-columns flanking temple doorways and walls, so characteristic of Cambodian architecture, are also a feature of the *puuc* style of the Maya in Yucatan, especially noticeable at Labna. The Mayan murals at Bonampak depict the same thrones, litters, parasols, and fans on poles as used by high personnages in southeast Asia. He sees evidences of Chinese influences coming between 650-200 B.C., whereas contacts between southeast Asia and Middle America were frequent between A.D. 100 and 600.

At the national meeting of the Society for American Archaeology held at Santa Fe, New Mexico in 1968, a symposium was held to discuss pre-Columbian contacts between the hemispheres. Twenty-seven papers and four commentaries were given. In an appendix to his own paper, John L. Sorenson presented a table documenting nearly a thousand cultural features shared by Mesoamerica and the Near East.[9] This presents a good case for the Diffusionists.

If we cannot accept the Isolationist premise that the Western Hemisphere was devoid of human life until it was populated solely by an influx of homogeneous immigrants from across Bering Strait some 12,000 to 15,000 years ago, neither can we agree with extreme Diffusionists that America's culture was later imported lock, stock, and barrel from overseas. Both of these views are restricted by the blinders worn by their adherents. Transportation cannot account for the similarity of primordial images and myth motifs stamped on the human soul in both hemispheres. How far back in time they were stamped we do not know, save that their abstract patterns reveal a spiritual impress that must have been made upon mankind in past ages so remote we vaguely call them "antediluvian." Nor can we be assured that mankind developed in straight-line evolution from brute prehumans to *Homo sapiens* with an accompanying rise of culture from savagery to civilization. Undoubtedly civilizations whose achievements equalled or exceeded those of our own today existed in an antiquity far beyond our short history. Civilizations that must have appeared and disappeared in rhythmic intervals in tune with astronomical cycles.

This element of periodicity appears when we discard our inhibitions and blinders. The origin of Mesoamerican civilization is still out of perspective. The known history and nature of its primary cultures as sketched in this section is all we have to work with. But from them a few fundamental conclusions can be drawn.

8 LIFE SPANS AND WORLD CYCLES

The outstanding feature of all these cultures is their related-
ness; they cannot be isolated. In their long span of about twenty-
seven hundred years one culture overlapped or succeeded another
in rhythmical progression, each manifesting its own unique characteristics while remaining basically interrelated.

Of all the major cultures, only three which originated in the preclassic period B.C. endured into the classic period ending about
A.D. 900. These were the Zapotecan culture of Monte Alban, the
Toltecan culture of Teotihuacan, and the Mayan. If we would discover a common denominator in Mesoamerican civilization, it
seems reasonable to look for it in these three primary focuses, and
the only measure of its strength and validity is the influence it
exerted.

The Zapotec culture reflected imported Olmec, Maya, and Teotihuacan influences; but as mentioned earlier, nothing distinctive of
its own was diffused outside. Mayan influences spread far, the
Maya-perfected calendar system being adopted throughout all
Mesoamerica and remaining in use until historical times. The wid-
est and deepest influence was exerted by Teotihuacan. Purely
religious, it achieved a spiritual synthesis that remained unpar-
alleled in the New World until the Spanish introduction of Christianity.

These two focal points, the Nahuatl and Mayan, may be considered as representing the opposite poles of Mesoamerican civili-

79

zation. They show many differences in art and architecture. That of the Mayas is expressed in a style opulent, elaborate, and decorative. Facades of temples are covered with masks, volutes, spirals, and frets. They are surmounted with delicate, lace-like crests called "roof-combs" which have no structural function whatever. That of the Nahuas, or Toltecs, in Teotihuacan seems its direct antithesis. With the geometrical arrangements of pyramids, temples, and palaces, its architecture is dedicated to the austere and abstract. The art of the palaces, however, reveal gorgeous murals symbolic of cosmic figures and forces that suggest a pictorial counterpoint to the hieroglyphic writing of the Mayas. It is no paradox that the Mayas were obsessed with the abstract notion of time and the Nahuas were engrossed with that of cosmic space. To plot the position of a point on a curve, one needs two co-ordinates, one of space and one of time. And so it seems that we can regard these two cultures as expressing the two co-ordinates of Mesoamerican civilization.

The approximate coincidence of their life spans shows a remarkable similarity. There is no accounting for their mysterious birth and growth about the same time. Yet it is quite apparent that both reflected from the start a vast concept integrating their architectural grandeur and beauty, their mathematical and astronomical preciseness, their art and philosophy; a concept that could have come only from an unprecedented and powerful religious impulse.

Nor is there any acceptable reason for their mysterious collapse about the same time. Many theories have been offered to explain their fall. War, disease, a change of climate, have gained few supporters. The most popular hypothesis is economic failure—the "high cost of living" as Morley puts it—due to the failure of the "slash-and-burn" agricultural system to support the increasing population; an hypothesis first advanced by the United States Department of Agriculture. We can question this agricultural collapse theory by asking why the croplands from the Valley of Mexico, through the central valley of Oaxaca, to the tropical valley of the Usamacinta and the jungles of Guatemala, all became exhausted about the same time.

Now coming into vogue is a political theory: that the general populations revolted against the theocratical rules of their priests and nobles. This is based on the current belief that all primitive cultures everywhere gradually evolved into theocratic states which in turn evolved into some other social structure when their populations revolted. But just why all the populations from central Mexico to the lowlands of Guatemala chose the same time to revolt is not explained.

Perhaps it is natural that we view the collapse of these resplendent cultures or civilizations in light of our own materialistic philosophy. So fully conditioned are we by this traditional European view of history as expressed by Toynbee's theme of "challenge and response" that we fit into its pattern the rise and fall of his postulated many successive civilizations. A society, he asserts, is challenged by environment, war, economic, political, and other rationalized pressures. As long as it successfully responds to these challenges it continues to expand; when at last it fails to respond, it perishes. This is wholly a secular, linear view of history. There are never any mysterious upsurges of spiritual forces from deep in the soul of mankind, no strange cataclysmic plunges into obscurity. Religious systems are viewed by Toynbee only as by-products of the merging of these secular systems which constitute the "intelligible field" of historical study.

But all religious systems embody this depth, a dimension we are not conditioned to perceive. So we are utterly confused by the mytho-religious civilizations of classic Mesoamerica, for there is no doubt whatever that the Teotihuacan Toltecs and the lowland Mayas created "holy empires" completely religious in nature.

Writes Thompson, the great Maya scholar: "The Maya rose to heights of spiritual grandeur, unfortified by which they could never have freed their culture from the shackles of a poor soil, a deleterious climate, inadequate methods of agriculture, and a pitifully restricted range of tools. Our own culture is the opposite of that of the Maya, for materially it has infinite wealth and resources, but spiritually it is desperately impoverished. ... In such a sad plight we may well humble ourselves to inquire how and why the Maya, endowed with scant material resources, made a success of their life, whereas we, with all nature at our command, have fallen woefully short of that objective. The general answer to that inquiry, if we have the humility to make it, must lie in the greater spiritual wealth of the Maya. . . ."[1]

Toynbee in later years questioned his earlier assumption that the major religious systems were but by-products of the merging of the various secular systems; suggesting instead that religion itself may be the "intelligible field," and that the purpose of civilizations is to spread it among mankind. And with the final completion of his colossal twelve-volume *A Study of History,* he ventures to state that racial elements are "distinctive psychic or spiritual qualities, possibly innate in certain societies of human beings, which may prove to be the positive factor impelling these societies towards civilization."

Hence we must look to the field of religion for the cause of a civilization's rise, duration, and fall for a cyclical view of history different from Toynbee's linear view. Only from such a perspective can we perceive more clearly the civilization of Mesoamerica, and this involves the factor of time.

As early as the fourth century B.C., Plato maintained that everything that has a genesis is foredoomed to eventual disintegration, and that this breakdown is connected with the periodic rhythm of all life. This belief was more fully developed in the fifth century A.D. by the Greek philosopher Proclus who asserted that everything in the world has its own *aeon,* or measured period of existence. The lifetime of a plant, bird, or animal is not accidental nor can it be continued indefinitely. Each has its duration hidden within its genus, man's *aeonian* life-cycle ranging about seventy years as mentioned in the Psalms. The same measured periods of growth and decline apply to civilizations, which also manifest the stages of organic growth. This cyclic view dominated Hindu as well as Grecian philosophy, as illustrated by the great Hindu cycles of *kalpas* and of four *yugas* which correspond to the four worlds or eras of Nahuatl and Mayan mythology.

But all great civilizations like our own are composed of component parts or cultures often distinctive enough to be called civilizations themselves, having their own unique characteristics and measured lifetimes. Many attempts have been made to establish a time-scale for their rise and fall. The great sixteenth century German astronomer, Johannes Kepler, reconstructed history upon his determination that the points of the triangles formed

by the great conjunctions of Saturn and Jupiter move through
what he called the "four elements" in about 800 (794⅓) years,
and that they move through the whole zodiac in 2,400 (2,383)
years. The four elements are represented astrologically by:

Fire: Aries, Leo, Sagittarius
Earth: Taurus, Virgo, Capricorn
Air: Gemini, Libra, Aquarius
Water: Cancer, Scorpio, Pisces[2]

A period of 720 years was set in 1611 by John Napier, the inventor of logarithms, and Sir Napier Shaw's assertion of 744 years
is based on a lunar-solar cycle which embraces sunspot periods,
lunar and synodic revolutions, almost every possible cosmic influence upon earth. Having exhausted all these potentialities, the
culture or civilization then dies.[3]

Rodney Collin, in formulating his theory of celestial influence,
made a new logarithmic approach from the phases of man's life-
cycle to the corresponding phases of a culture. He proposed 800
years roughly (777 years exactly) for the lifetimes of the seven
cultures or civilizations making up the present great Western
civilization. And this corresponds to the mean length of 794 years
for the last three Chinese cycles.[4]

That each culture with its growth, maturity, and decline has
an organic lifetime as definite as that of plant or man was also
the basis of Spengler's history as opposed to Toynbee's theory of
purely mundane responses to social, economic, political, and other
challenges.

How closely do the lifetimes of the component cultures of Mesoamerican civilization conform to the seven to eight centuries as
given by all the postulations quoted above?

Table 1 shows that the Olmec culture, from the date of 1200 B.C.
for San Lorenzo to the abandonment of La Venta about 400 B.C.,
endured 800 years. The classic Maya lifetime is set at 725 years,
from A.D. 200 to 925, by the foremost Maya scholar, J. Eric S.
Thompson. The Zapotec span was 700 years, between A.D. 300 and
1,000 when the structures at Monte Alban were begun and abandoned. The Mixtec was 774 years, according to the *Bodley Codex*

which gives its history from A.D. 692 to 1466. And the lifetime of
the Toltec-Teotihuacan culture endured 800 years, from 150 B.C.
when construction of the Pyramids of the Sun and Moon was
begun, to A.D. 650 when the immense city was partially destroyed.
Indeed, this life span of from seven to eight centuries seems to be a
measure of a major culture. Those which replaced or were virtual
extensions of them—the "new empire" of the Mayas, that of the
Toltecs of Tula, and that of the Aztecs—endured only from two
to four centuries; and, significantly, they were militaristic rather
than religious.

Table 1
Lifetimes of Primary Mesoamerican Cultures

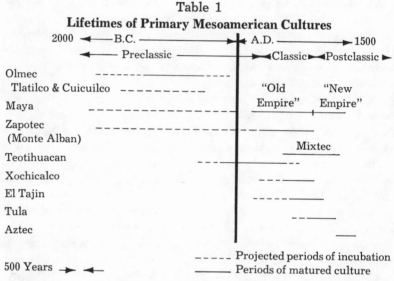

What determines the lifetime of a civilization as a whole? If we
grant that the small planet Earth is not isolated from the solar
system and the greater universe of which it is surely a living part,
we can readily accept the belief that the changing configurations
of the heavenly bodies exercise different influences upon Earth
throughout their durations. These changes are clocked by the
great Precession. The axis of the revolving earth describes a circle
every 25,920 years. This circle of 360 degrees is divided into twelve
zodiacal sections of 30 degrees, more or less. The time required
for the axis or the vernal equinox to pass through each of these

sections is 2,160 years. This zodiacal period is commonly regarded as an "age," such as the Age of Taurus, Aries, or Pisces, and believed to manifest the characteristics determined by the influences of their dominating constellations.

Kepler, as already noted, believed that the great conjunctions of Saturn and Jupiter passed through the whole zodiac in 2,383 years; whereas the progression of the ecliptic takes 2,160 years. These bases of measurement are not commensurate, but they do show a relative correspondence. So we may accept here the 2,160-year measurement of a zodiacal age and the lifetime of its corresponding civilization.

Determining the life-cycle of Mesoamerican civilization presents somewhat of a problem. Its end is definitely marked by the fall of the Aztec empire in 1521 A.D. At the risk of seeming to fit a fact to a supposition, its beginning should occur about 639 B.C. to conform to a 2,160 year lifetime. But the zodiacal Age of Pisces, in which all of the component cultures blossomed except the Olmec, began about the time of Christ; and this earlier date would push backward the beginning of Mesoamerican civilization into the preceding Age of Aries with a different planetary configuration.

Yet there is some justification for risking the supposition. The date of 639 B.C. coincides with the approximate date of 600 B.C. given for the end of the period Bernal calls Olmec II, the great period of Olmec efflorescence, the apogee of its cities, and the diffusion of its culture to peoples who developed their own distinctive cultural patterns long after its decline and death. In this respect we can still regard the Olmec as the "mother culture" which, like all generations of cultures, handed down its heritage to those succeeding. But because the birth and development of the Olmec culture took place before the advent of the Teotihuacan culture which hailed the beginning of Mesoamerican civilization, can we also consider it apart, paradoxical as this may seem? Its major lifetime existed in a different zodiacal age under different planetary influences, the Age of Aries. The period before that of Olmec maturity, the period termed Olmec I, which goes back to the earliest established date of 1200 B.C. for San Lorenzo, shows what Bernal calls an "ancient ancestral pattern" without a trait of the later civilization. Certainly the Olmec origin will be traced back centuries earlier, revealing a culture stemming from a yet unknown background.

Conjectural as the effect of zodiacal cycles and planetary influences upon Mesoamerican civilization may seem, it emphasizes how little we know about Mesoamerica before the Christian era. And how much less we know of the relationship between Earth and the other planets which also represent stages of development in the whole of the universe. This is why the effect of cosmic cycles on the temporal cycles of man on Earth is so important if we would understand ancient Mesoamerican civilization and religion. The priest-astronomers of the New World, like those of the Old World, were quite aware of these cycles, their meaning and effects, as revealed by Mayan mathematics, astronomy, and astrology.

This will be fully covered in the last section of the present book. But as it lies outside the limits of documentary history, in the subjective realm of religion, our only available approach to it is through the universal language of myth.

Part Two
The Myths

I

The Five Suns

1 THE UNIVERSE

HUMAN HISTORY IS A CHRONOLOGY of the external life of man.
Mythology is history at a far deeper level. It does not
begin with those epochs when man fashioned flint points
to kill prehistoric beasts and pecked on rocks the first record of his
existence. Its realm is not his physical life as revealed by his bones
and artifacts, but that of the groping spirit within him which too
has left its record in imperishable memory.

Esoteric theology holds that in the early stages of man's evolution, long before he developed articulate language and rational
thought, his external impressions were reflected in images. Moreover, it holds that in the course of his further evolution man will
reach the state where he can evoke these primeval images, all his
archaic past, from this indestructible picture-consciousness or
memory bank, the *akashic* record.

Modern depth psychology terms it the "collective unconscious,"
a deep, universal, and impersonal layer of the unconscious which
contains the entire psychic structure developed by all mankind
throughout the ages. Its contents, which Jung calls "archetypes,"
are these "primordial thoughts," the "unconscious images of the
instincts," the universal images that have existed from man's picture-consciousness in the remotest times.

The *akashic* records of esotoric theology and the archetypes of
analytical psychology are parallel but not quite identical. Archetypes have been likened to the impressions of seals indelibly

89

stamped on the collective unconscious. They empower myths which have a universal meaning, but the origin of the seals themselves is unknown. Nevertheless the two can be roughly equated as universal images stemming from the time when man intuitively apperceived far beyond his sensory boundaries a universe governed by laws and forces beyond those of nature.

Perhaps his earliest symbol for this was the *uroboros,* the circle formed by a snake eating its own tail. Its hieroglyph in ancient Egypt designated the universe embracing heaven and earth, the waters and stars. The "Great Round" of the *uroboros* as the symbol of primordial unity, enclosing the infinitude of all space and time; the Greek *pleroma,* the fullness of divine creation; the snake itself symbolizing timeless time. Mesoamerican mythology reflects this universal concept. The Aztecs, spokesmen for the Nahuas, believed the earth rested on the back of a saurian monster of some sort: serpent, crocodile, or lizard. This *cipactli,* according to the Mayas, was immersed in a world-pool of water filled with waterlilies. The earth itself, as conceived by the Aztecs, was a flat disc surrounded by a great ring of divine water that merged with the heavens at the horizon. From the name *Cem-Anáhuatl,* "the complete circle," for the land surrounded by water, was later derived the name of Anáhuac for the central plateau of Mexico, a limited portion of the whole.

The ring of water surrounding the "complete circle" has further significance. For water, as shown by the marvelous photographic studies made by Schwenk in Europe, always tends to take a spherical form, a totality, by the spiralling course of its rivers, the meandering loops of its streams. This archetypal form is reflected by all living creatures in their muscles and bones, in seashells, in the horns of an antelope, in man's own bloodstream. Water is a living element with a spiritual nature, reacting to the phases of the moon, sensitive to planetary influences.[1]

The universe extended horizontally and vertically from the land disc in the center. It was divided into four quadrants, each bearing a directional color: white for the east, blue for the south, red for the west, and black for the north.

Above the horizontal world were thirteen heavens and below it were nine hells. (See Plate 1.) Between the heavens were pas-

PLATE 1

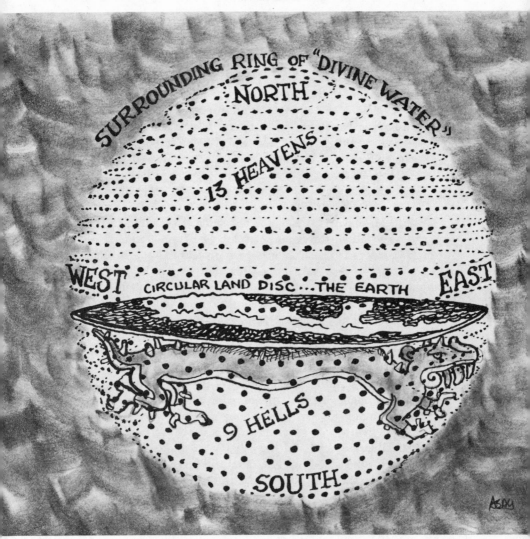

Drawing by Chuck Asay

sages allowing the celestial bodies to move from one to another in their orbits. In the lowest heaven traveled the moon. The second heaven was *Citalco,* "the place of the stars" and the constellations: the tiger *Tezcatlipoca* (the Big Bear), *Citlalxonecuilli* (Little Bear), *Colotl* (Scorpion), the *Mamalhuaztli* (the three stars that form the head of Taurus), and the very important *Tianquiztli* (the Pleiades). Our present sun, *Tonatiuh,* journeyed in his orbit in the third Heaven of the Sun. The fourth heaven was the domain of the "Big Star," *Citlálpol,* the all-important planet Venus. In the fifth heaven were the "smoking stars," the comets. The sixth and seventh were the colored heavens of night and day, and the eighth a place of storms. The last three were the dwelling places of the gods, the last two constituting *Omeyocan,* the Place of Duality, the abode of *Ometéotl,* the supreme deity and ruler of the universe. The nine hells below were the abode of the dead.[2]

The Maya variant is much the same. According to the *Chilam Balam of Mani,* the earth was flat, but "four-pointed, four-sided, four-bordered." Each side bore a directional color, but differing from that of the Aztecs: red for the east, yellow for the south, black for the west, white for the north, with a fifth color, green, for the center. Upholding the sky were four standing gods or Bacabs: the red Bacab standing at the east, the yellow Bacab standing at the south, the black Bacab at the west, and the white Bacab at the north. At each side also stood a sacred ceiba, or wild cotton tree, with its corresponding directional color, the giant green ceiba standing in the center of the world, roots in the underworld, branches in the upperworld, corresponding to the World Tree of many mythologies throughout the world.

There were also thirteen heavens above. Not superimposed vertically, one on top of the other as in the Nahuatl version, but placed in six ascending steps from the east to the seventh, and descending in six more steps to the west. In a similar fashion the nine hells or underworlds were arranged in four descending and then four ascending steps from the fifth at the bottom.

This structure of the universe is reflected in the form of the stepped pyramid whose steps mark the path of ascension toward the spirit. The triangular-shaped sides of the pyramid is one of the basic symbols of mankind. While its base, the square, represents the earth, and the circle represents heaven in its uroboric fullness, the triangle placed between them symbolizes the relationship, the means of communication, between them. The pyramids of Mesoamerica were ritually used for this purpose.

This pyramidal structure of the ancient Mesoamerican universe is still embodied in the ceremonialism of the Navajos in the aptly named Four Corners area of the American Southwest. The core of the universe was a great pyramidal rock extending from the underworlds to the upperworlds. It was oriented to the four directions, its sides glowing with their colors: white on the east, blue on the south, yellow-red on the west, black on the north, corresponding to the color symbolism of the Aztecs. When the people first emerged to this world from the underworld below, they planted four directional Holy Mountains about it and in each was placed a Talking God. Hence they called this great natal rock the Mountain Around Which Moving Was Done, the Mountain Surrounded by Mountains, or the Encircled Mountain.

The four sacred mountains bounding the ancient Navajo homeland are physical mountains readily identified. The metaphysical Encircled Mountain is too great to be visible. But this today is how it is symbolized in a Navajo sand-painting: a great axial rock as seen from above, spreading out the world like a four-petalled flower, a four-leafed clover, a lotus.

Plate 2 depicts this Navajo concept. It is a photograph of a sand-painting made on the second day of the Shooting Chant ceremony. At the center is a circle of central water surrounded by the four directional sacred mountains in the shape of a lotus. Each is protected by a Holy Person or Talking God. Four directionally colored buffalo stand between them, their paths leading to the central water. Their breath of life comes from their hearts, out of their mouths, and prayer sticks are implanted in their hearts. A rainbow tipped with feathers surrounds the whole, with two buffalo guarding the east entrance.

This pyramidal structure of the universe is paralleled in Asian cosmography by the mythical Mt. Sumeru of the Ural-Altaic peoples and by Mt. Meru of Hindu and Tibetan Buddhists. Mt. Meru is shaped like a truncated pyramid, its four sides bearing directional colors: white on the east, blue on the south, red on the

PLATE 2

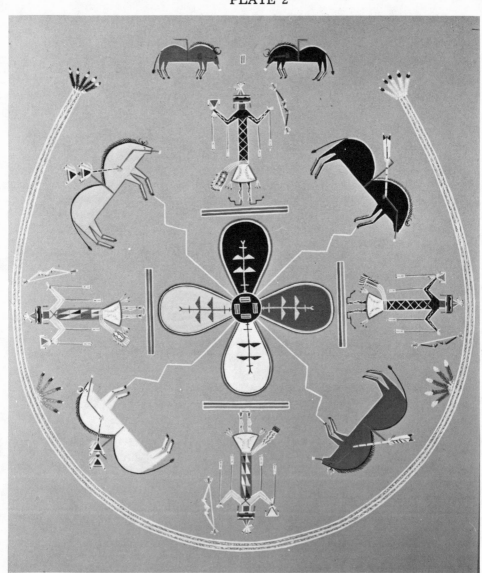

Photo by Laura Gilpin. Courtesy Museum of Navajo Ceremonial art, Santa Fe, New Mexico.

west, and yellow on the north, three of these corresponding to those of the Aztecs and Navajos. Within it are several underworlds and several heavens. Around this mighty core of the cosmos are seven concentric circles of mountains separated by seven encircling oceans. Each of these fresh-water oceans and its corresponding wall of mountains is a separate universe with its own sun, moon, and planets.

Outside these seven universes, and floating in the outer salt-water ocean of space, are four main continents spreading out in the four main directions. The southern continent is the smallest of the four, and is our planet Earth.

The Buddhist cosmos thus spreads out like a great four-petalled flower, a lotus. Each of its world-petals is protected by a Lokapala, or World Guardian, as each of the Holy Mountains of the Navajos is protected by a Talking God, and each quadrant of the Mayas by a Bacab.

To all these striking pictorial parallels must be added a common metaphysical meaning. The Buddhist cosmos, represented as a lotus, is also identical with the female aspect of the creative force, the goddess-mother called "The Lotus"; and our earthly universe is located within her "at about the level of the wrist." So too does Navajo ceremonialism explain, "When they put the extra mountains around, they took the Mountain Around Which Moving Was Done out of First Woman's belt." Zuni ceremonialism also fixes the location of its corresponding Mountain of Generation as lying just below the navel of the Earth-Mother, the goddess-mother of creation through whose successive womb-worlds the Zunis emerged to this one.[3]

Throughout all Indian America, the universe, this world, our present Earth, always has been regarded as a living entity. A mountain peak, man himself, replicates its structure. Even today the Zinancantecos of southern Mexico, descendants of the ancient Mayas, believe that the soul of man is composed of thirteen parts, corresponding to the thirteen heavens of Mayan and Nahuatl cosmology. Sacred mountain peaks figure prominently in their rituals. The summit of the peak they regard as the head, its base they term the feet, and its sides the stomach of its living body.

From all these parallels in American and Asian mythology, we can understand that the Nahuatl universe, rather than being a gigantic inanimate structure, was one vast living body informed with all the spatial forces of creation. Endurable and changeless as it might seem, it was not static. Movement, constant change, was a primary theme of Nahuatl mystico-religious belief. And so from the very origin of the universe, we see the creation of successive suns, worlds, or eras.

2 THE FIRST FOUR SUNS

The Nahuas' supreme dual Creator, Ometéotl, being omnipotent and omnipresent, existed both in Omeyocan, the "Place of Duality" in the topmost heaven, and at the navel of the universe, the center of the world. As abstract power, he created the world through the abstract forces of the four directions, represented as his sons. One after another were created four successive suns, worlds, or ages.

A number of Nahuatl sources detail their histories. The principal source is the *Codice Chimalpopoca* which comprises two other manuscripts, the *Anales de Cuauhtitlan* and the *Leyenda de los Soles* translated from the Nahuatl in the sixteenth century. Although the order of the successive worlds, eras, or suns is juxtaposed in some versions, all are essentially uniform. That given here is from the *Leyenda de los Soles.*

The first sun was *Ocelotonatiuh,* Sun of the Tiger, whose sign was 4 *Ocelotl* (Ocelot, jaguar, tiger). The world was inhabited by giants who were devoured by tigers. It was an era of dark earthbound matter.

The second sun, with the sign of 4 *Ecatl,* was the Sun of Air, *Ecatonatiuh,* represented as Quetzalcoatl in his aspect of the god of wind. In a single day most of the inhabitants were destroyed by wind, and the survivors were turned into monkeys.

The third was *Quiauitonatiuh,* Sun of the Rain of Fire, under the sign 4 *Quiauitl* (fiery rain). Its inhabitants were turned into

97

birds, turkeys.

The fourth sun was *Chalchiuhtlicue,* its sign 4 *Atl* (water). It was destroyed by a flood, and the people were turned into fish.

The destruction of these first four worlds, or suns, gave way to the creation of the present fifth sun, the Sun of Movement, *Tonatiuh,* whose sign is 4 *Ollin* (movement). How and when it was created with the men who now populate it will be related in detail later. Its significance derives from the hermetic meanings of the first four.

The cosmic forces of the four directions of the universe, represented by the four sons of Ometéotl, each in turn exert supremacy. The four successive worlds may then be equated with the four quadrants. They do not exist concurrently; one follows another as the reigning cosmic forces move in cyclic order around the circle like a great revolving wheel. For the duration of their cosmic cycle there is rest. At its end there is a cataclysm, the world is destroyed. The wheel turns and the forces of the succeeding quadrant create a new world. This informs with dynamic movement an otherwise static cosmography. It is cyclic and ordered, for the destruction of each world and the creation of another world occurs on a day carrying the numeral 4.

These four worlds created by the cosmic forces of the primary directions constitute the four primary elements of classical antiquity: earth, air, fire, and water. The sign of the first was the "tiger," synonymous with the ocelot and jaguar, which was the symbol of the earth. The second world was of the element air, the third of fire, and the fourth of water. Each of these elements dictated the form of life its inhabitants took: tiger, monkey, bird, and fish. Even the food each ate is prescribed: acorns; *acocentli,* a cornlike grain; *acecentli,* a "water corn"; and *cencocopi* or *teocentli,* one of the ancestors of modern corn. All this reflects the concept of the evolution of life-forms throughout the successive worlds or eras.

The creation myth of the Quiché Mayas recorded in the *Popul Vuh* recounts the creative evolution of man. The Creator, the Maker, and the Forefathers created the first man of mud when the world was still in darkness. Their first human creations were soft and pliable, without mind or soul, and were promptly destroyed. For the second creation man was fashioned from wood. They were stiff, inflexible, and, being without soul or mind, they did not remember their Creator. It was necessary to annihilate these men by a flood of fiery rain, their few survivors being changed into monkeys. Dawn had not yet appeared when for the third creation man was made from the dough of white and yellow corn (mixed with the blood of a snake, according to the Cakchiquel Maya myth.) Four men only were thus created, and they were beautifully formed, possessing intelligence and wisdom, able to know all: "the four corners, the four points of the arch of the sky, and the round face of the earth." But the Creator, the Maker, and the Forefathers were not pleased.

"Must they perchance be the equals of ourselves, their Makers, who can see afar, who know all and see all?" said the Creator, the Maker, and the Forefathers. "Must they also be gods? Let us check a little their desires; let their sight reach only to what is near." So they blew mist into the eyes of the four men so they could see only what was close to them.

For the fourth creation, continues the *Popul Vuh*, the gods carefully created four women to be wives of the four men. From them came the ancestors of the present race of men. In the darkness they multiplied. Neither the sun nor the light of day had dawned. So they contemplated the Great Star, the Morning Star, *Icoquih,* which comes ahead of the sun, that lights up the arch of sky and the surface of the earth, and illuminated the steps of the men who had been created and made. And when the sun came up, and the light of dawn fell upon the earth, they burned incense, and danced and sang, and wept for joy.

There are contemporary Indian parallels. Both the Navajos of Arizona and the Pueblos of New Mexico observe in their ceremonialism the same succession of previous worlds which they regard as lower worlds from which they emerged. The Hopis, who believe the present world is the fourth rather than the fifth, designate the first world with the color white and the direction north; the second world blue and south; the third world yellow and west; and the fourth world red and east. Among their religious orders is the Two Horn Society, the only order retaining the original concept of Creation. Its symbol of two horns worn on the mask of every member designates knowledge of, and ritually remembered experiences in, the three previous worlds as well as in this present fourth world. The One Horn Society, on the contrary, has knowledge only of the present world. During *Wuwuchim,* the first of the nine great ceremonials in the annual cycle, they ritually enact the Emergence to this newly created world. On toy bows given to boys too young to be initiated into a religious order, the middle section is painted white to symbolize the first world. On each side are a blue segment symbolizing the second world, a yellow segment for the third world, and a red segment extending to the tip of the bow to symbolize the fourth world.

Every ceremonial in the annual cycle refers to the same theme. Its most dramatic portrayal is given in the great *Niman Kachina* held at the time of the summer solstice. The chronology of the four worlds is observed by the four appearances of the masked kachina dancers during the day: at sunrise, midmorning, midafternoon, and at sunset. The pattern is observed by the dancers themselves. The line of dancers file into the plaza to the north side. As they dance, the end of the line slowly curves west and south but is broken before a circle is formed, just as the perfect pattern of life was broken and the first world destroyed. The dancers then move to the west side, the line curving to the south, and is broken as was the pattern in the second world. Moving to the south side and curving east, the dancers repeat the procedure in this third position representing the third world. There is no fourth position, for the Hopis believe that it remains to be seen whether life on this present fourth world will adhere to the perfect pattern or be broken again.

The same theme is also reflected in the structure of the song they sing. The first three sections recount man's successive emergences to each of the three preceding worlds, his disregard for the laws of Creation, and the world's destruction. The fourth and fifth sections of the song exhort the people to maintain this world in proper balance so as to be ready for their emergence to the perfect fifth world. This simple but profound Hopi ceremonial thus still dramatizes the ancient cosmological pattern and its teachings.[1]

The Zunis remind us that their four underworlds were embodied within the goddess mother of Creation, from which man

has been successively reborn. Rooted in the first Zuni underworld
was the Mountain of Generation, corresponding to the Navajos'
Encircled Mountain, and the Buddhists' Mt. Meru. The second
cave-world to which mankind emerged was called the "Umbilical-
Womb or Place of Gestation." Here beings separated to become
fathers of the six kinds of men: yellow, grey, red, white, black,
and mingled. The third cave-world was lighter, "like a valley in
starlight." It was named the "Vaginal-Womb or Place of Sex-Gen-
eration" for here people began to multiply in kind. In the fourth,
the "Womb of Parturition," it was "light like the dawning," and
men began to perceive according to their natures. Finally into
the present upper "World of Disseminated Light and Knowledge
or Seeing" mankind emerged, blinded by the light and glory of
the Sun Father as were the first people in the Maya creation myth
recounted in the *Popul Vuh*.

Tibetan Buddhism develops this great theme in more detail. It
traces the evolution of man through the mineral, vegetable, animal, and human kingdoms with the derivative elements of each.
From the fire element man derived his life heat. From the air
element his breath of life. From the water element his life stream,
his blood. And from the earth element the solid substance of his
body. Hence man is a derivative summation of the four states of
existence through which he has passed.[2] Like the Navajo ceremonial name for themselves, he is "Made From Everything."

But man is more than a physical organism. Hence Buddhism
asserts that from each of these four worlds or elements he derived
corresponding psychical qualities or aggregates. With fire, man
received an aggregate of feelings. With air, an aggregate of volition. With water, consciousness. And with earth, touch.

With these qualities which lift man from the level of a physical
organism to that of a sentient, conscious being, he received corresponding passions. Fire and feelings gave rise to his passion of at-
tachment and lust. Air and volition, the passion of envy. Water
and consciousness, the passion of anger. Earth and touch, the
passion of egoism.

There is another aspect to these mythical four worlds of ancient
America: the orientation to time of the four quadrants or directions. The great wheel of successive domination by the cosmic

forces of the four quadrants keeps turning, one world or era being replaced by another, involving the factor of time. The *tonalámatl*, the sacred calendar of all Mesoamerica, expresses in various ways the relationship between space and time. Its twenty day-signs are grouped in five series of four, the first sign of each group bearing the directional designation of east, the second north, the third west, and the fourth south. Looked at again, each group of five day-signs comprises five so-called "weeks" of 13 days, or 65 days. In the 260-day sacred calendar there are four of these 65-day periods, each related to one of the four cardinal directions. On a still larger scale the vastly important Nahuatl period of 52 years is divided into four periods of 13 years during which the forces of each of the four directions has a predominating influence.

A fuller discussion of the *tonalámatl* will be given later; these comments merely indicate the great significance of space, of direction, to the Nahuas. The Mayas were more engrossed in time itself. They extended these daily, weekly, yearly and 52-year cycles to great cycles of 5,200 years. We may suspect that these measured the durations of the four previous worlds and the present fifth world. We may also venture that Mesoamerican myth was based not only on the astronomical cycles of time, but on the astrological influences from the four quarters of space as the heavenly bodies changed their positions.

In summation here, man's evolution through the four previous worlds or stages is more than a mechanical process. It has taken place, as these myths tell us, on both physical and psychological levels. Now in the fifth world it must develop on a plane no longer physical but psychical, hastened or retarded by the degree of man's unfolding consciousness. There is a great difference between our present conception of evolution as a process of accumulation, and that of unfoldment of consciousness. "One cannot get out of a bag more than what has been put into it. If it is not put there in the beginning, it will not be got out in the end," writes an Eastern sage. Man's awareness of his role in the universal plan was inherent in the beginning. It has not been accumulatively evolved. It has been gradually liberated in his progression through the four worlds or eras. This concept is implicit in Nahuatl cosmology. A duration of cyclic cosmic forces had been established in each of the four quadrants, resulting in the creation of a new sun which was destroyed at the end of their cycles. But now a new fifth direction has been reached in the dead center of these four directional worlds which forms a cosmic quincunx. Here, as we shall see, the unfoldment of man's consciousness depends upon man himself.

3 THE MYTH OF ATLANTIS

The mythological creation and destruction of four previous worlds is not a unique conception of the ancient Nahuas and Mayas, or of contemporary Pueblos and Navajos. The belief was common to Hindu and Tibetan Buddhism; to Zoroasterism, the religion of ancient Persia; to the Chinese; and it is found in the myths of Iceland and the Polynesian islands. Heraclitus and Aristarchus both taught that the earth was destroyed periodically; and Hesiod, the Greek historian, recounted the destruction of four previous worlds.

Does this universal myth have an historical basis?

It seems certain that the first recorded account of such cosmic catastrophes was given to the Greek sage and law-giver Solon when he visited Egyptian priests in Sais about 590 B.C. These priests told him they preserved an accumulated knowledge of millenia, the constitution of Sais recorded in their sacred registers being eight thousand years old. One of the priests, later reported by Plutarch to have been Sonchis, told Solon: "There have been and there will be many diverse destructions of mankind, of which the greatest are by fire and water, and lesser ones by countless other means."

He then related the account of an immense island or continent larger than Libya and Asia put together, situated in front of the straits then called the Pillars of Heracles. From it a rich and powerful empire exerted rule over those parts of Libya within the columns of Heracles as far as Egypt, and of Europe as far as Tyrrhenia. There came then violent earthquakes and floods, and the continent or island now known as Atlantis sank in the depths of the sea about 9,500 B.C.

Solon gave this first account of Atlantis to his relative Dropides who passed it down to Critias' grandfather, whence it was handed down to Critias. The account finally appeared in Plato's dialogues *Timeaus* and *Critias* about 355 B.C.

How trustworthy is the account after this lapse of time, and how reliable is Plato himself?

Pythagoras of Samos followed Solon to Sais, where he studied the Egyptian mysteries. In 529 B.C. he established in the Greek colonial city of Croton in southern Italy the first school of what he termed "universal knowledge or religion," based on what he had learned in Egypt. The "universal language" required to express it was pure mathematics. With this, the Pythagoreans laid the foundations of Grecian culture, working out new laws of mathematics, harmony, architecture, and philosophy.

Plato was a Pythagorean, a "non-mathematical Mathematician," whose philosophy was based on Pythagoras' universal religion. The pupil of Socrates and teacher of Aristotle, he is now considered one of the greatest philosophers of all time. One can safely assume that his account of Atlantis was founded on authentic Egyptian tradition, and was not perpetuated as a hoax on posterity.

Discoveries in the next few centuries seemed to confirm it. The school of Pythagoreans included Pytheas of Messalia who is said to have discovered a method of measuring latitude and voyaged to Iceland and America about 323 B.C.; Hipparchus who in the second century B.C. discovered the precession of the equinoxes, the obliquity of the ecliptic, and how to measure longitude, thus founding the science of navigation; and Appolonius of Tyana who in the first century A.D. reputedly directed the first scientific survey of the world, sending an expedition to the Ecuadorian coast of

South America.

All this data, including the metrical characteristics of ancient cities as well as the boundaries of continents, was recorded in a Pythagorean cipher of measure numbers intelligible only to mathematicians and which could not be used by one nation in time of war. It is conjectured that some of this information may have been preserved in the great library of Alexandria, partially burned by the Romans under Julius Caesar, and completely destroyed by a mob by command of the Christian emperor Theodosius in 389 A.D. The few that have been preserved, and other inscriptions on monuments scattered throughout the world, are still being deciphered by modern Pythagorean mathematicians.[1]

This Pythagorean tradition is a pertinent background to Plato's account of Atlantis, for the voyages of Pytheas and Appolonius discovered a land mass beyond the Pillars of Heracles. That it still existed led Appolonius to assert that the area embraced by the Americas, in whole or in part, coincided with Atlantis. This assertion coincides with the belief of some modern scholars like Henriette Mertz. It also accounts for the Pythagorean symbols and ciphers said to be inscribed on ancient monuments in Palenque, as recounted in Part One of the present text.

However true these beliefs may be, the role of Atlantis in world mythology cannot be ignored or politely side-stepped. Unproven, derided, often considered a fairytale, the myth of Atlantis has about it something so compelling that it has endured for over twenty-five hundred years. Some three thousand books have been written about it, comprising an established Atlanteanology. If its physical reality has not been established, the myth about it is a psychological reality of prime significance. This myth is too familiar to be detailed here, but a brief outline is necessary.

All esoteric schools include Atlantis in a global pattern of human evolution. There are many variations, but all follow the same general belief in four successive continents or land masses that served as evolution centers for developing mankind.[2] The Polarian, on which the first phase of evolution occurred; the Hyperborean, scene of the second phase; the Lemurian of the third phase; and the Atlantean of the fourth phase of evolution. Lemuria roughly occupied the region between Africa and Asia now covered by the Indian Ocean and the Pacific. When it began to sink, advanced groups emigrated westward across Africa to Atlantis.

Man's evolution thus far had followed the line of descent of spirit into matter. His life in the first phase might be compared to that in the mineral kingdom, in the second to that of the plant kingdom, and in the third to that of the animal kingdom. He had fully developed a physical body from soft androgynous form, with a division of sexes. But he was not wholly corporeal, being receptive to cosmic influences and spiritual guidance. Now he was ready to begin the ascent of spirit out of matter in full self-consciousness.

This was later expressed in India in the so-called Laws of Manu dating from the seventh century B.C.

"Man will traverse the universe, gradually ascending, and passing through the rocks, the plants, the worms, insects, fish, serpents, tortoises, wild animals, cattle, and higher animals . . . Such is the inferior degree."

Hence the physical emigration of peoples from Lemuria across Africa to Atlantis kept pace with their psychical development, and marked the emergence of the ancestors of man. The discovery of the remains of the earliest "early man" in Africa, giving rise to the belief that Africa was the birthplace of mankind, is said to fit into this great pattern. For esoteric theology cautions against the belief that Lemuria and Atlantis were the only inhabited parts of the earth; they were primary centers of evolution. Only the most advanced peoples of Lemuria emigrated to Atlantis. Some stragglers remained behind in Africa; and these, with other previous inhabitants, remained in a primeval state. Theirs are the remains exhumed today, and their descendants are the unevolved primitive tribes still found in certain areas.

The four "continents"—the Polarian, Hyperborean, Lemurian, and Atlantean—served as the successive centers of evolution, and their progressive influence affected and transformed the life of mankind. As such they suggest themselves as prototypes of the previous four worlds of all later mythologies. Yet we will find later that they embody a deeper meaning.

The creation myth of the Quiché Mayas attests the belief that mankind was first possessed of perfect and complete cosmic knowledge. It relates that the Creator and the Maker, Tepeu and Gucumatz, the Forefathers, and the Heart of Heaven usually known as Huracan, in council tried three times to create human beings on earth. All were destroyed, only the fourth attempt being successful. These mythical four Mayan beings typify the four "races" or phases of evolution of esoteric theology. Hesiod also postulated four races of mankind, the first being near perfection, the others progressively more gross as they became concerned with earthly activities.

The god Poseidon, it is said, was the first ruler of Atlantis, or Poseidon's Isle. He and Cleito, his mortal wife, produced five pairs of twin boys. Each of the ten sons as a priest-king was given a kingdom to govern. Atlantis was named after the first-born son, Atlas.

The land was fertile, and contained many elephants. Critias describes in detail the central metropolis, surrounded by alternating zones of land and sea, with a canal to the harbor. Enclosing the zones were three walls: one coated with brass, another with tin, and the third with orichalcum (reportedly a golden-colored ore of copper, probably a form of brass). Inside the citadel stood the massive temple of Poseidon, its outside walls covered with silver and its pinnacles with gold; inside, its roof was of ivory, the walls, pillars, and floor covered with orichalcum. These various metals were related to the planetary forces being studied, and the symbology continued through historical times. Hesiod describes the first age as golden, the second silver, and the third bronze, as the people progressively declined. The later alchemists of Europe founded their school upon the belief that matter was activated by a spiritual principle which had descended and was imprisoned; hence they dedicated themselves to the task of releasing this spirit, the *deus absconditas,* under the guise of transmuting gross matter into gold.

Physiological differences based on psychical factors began to appear, resulting in the development of types that became the primary races of mankind. Mystery centers were established where the different groups were initiated into knowledge of the formative forces received from various planets. To the north were the Sun and Jupiter mystery centers; in the central part the Mars and Poseidon mysteries; and to the south the Saturn, Mercury, and Venus mystery centers.

For generations Atlantis prospered. A civilization developed that was said to be more advanced than ours today. Gradually the larger mass of people became corrupt and the great Atlantean empire degenerated. There then began a series of cataclysms that broke up the land mass into islands and finally sank the last vestige of Atlantis into the sea. During the breakup, selected groups emigrated east and west, amalgamating with other primitive peoples throughout the world. Those of the northern mystery centers, led by the legendary law-giver Manu, went eastward across Europe to central Asia. From here they spread southward, founding the cultures of Sumeria, Chaldea, Egypt, India, and Tibet. Post-Vedic traditions, the laws of Manu in the seventh century B.C., and the teachings of Buddha in the sixth century B.C. reflected their Atlantean background.

Groups from the southern mystery centers of Mercury, Saturn, and Venus emigrated west to Central America, while other groups landed in South America. Groups from the Mars center in central Atlantis emigrated eastward to Asia, moved on into Mongolia, and portions of them finally crossed Bering Strait to North America where they split up into various stocks and tribes.

This summary, brief as it is, outlines a fair sample of the many versions of the Atlantis myth in its full context. All reflect the parallel myths throughout the world of four previous worlds and of the flood that sank Atlantis. The Sumerian epic of *Gilgamesh*, dating back to 5,000 B.C., preserves the story of the deluge, as does the *Mahabharta* of India which recounts the tradition of Manu-Noah. The Creation Myth of the contemporary Hopis parallels these with rituals still observed. In full detail it recounts how the people became corrupt, did not "sing praises to the Creator"; how the world was destroyed by a great flood, and a few chosen people were selected to survive and make a transition to another world.

An interesting confirmation of the Atlantis myth was given by the late psychic, Edgar Cayce. Mainly known for his accurate diagnoses of physical ailments, he gave descriptions of the high civilization of Atlantis in "life readings" for some seven hundred people over a period of twenty-one years although he had read nothing on the subject. His readings detail a series of catastrophes that gradually destroyed the continent, during which its inhabitants migrated to the Pyrenees, Yucatan and Peru, Egypt and other lands, carrying their cultural arts and religious forms.³ One of the last waves of Atlantean emigrants to Egypt helped the existing population to create an advanced civilization and to erect the Great Pyramid in order to preserve their knowledge and history. The date of its building is given as 10,490 B.C. For the several catastrophes, Cayce sets the date of 28,000 B.C. for one that broke up Atlantis into islands; and 10,000 B.C. for the final cataclysm that sank the last vestige. This period generally coincides with the Ice Age culture of the Cro-Magnons.

The origin of Cro-Magnon man remains a mystery. Neanderthal man had existed for some 100,000 years, possibly evolving from the Heidelberg "ape man." An ungainly, brutish hunter of bison, mammoth, woolly rhinoceros, reindeer, and wild horse, he either died out during a period of glaciation or was killed off about 30,000 years ago by migratory waves of Cro-Magnon man who replaced him. The Cro-Magnon was tall, well-formed, and possessed a larger brain case than that of present man. Already culturally advanced when he arrived in Europe at the beginning of his Aurignacian period somewhere between 35,000 and 30,000 B.C. he fashioned many different tools of chipped stone and bone, weapons and figurines, made engravings, and painted polychrome animals on the walls of some two hundred caves. The superlative and sophisticated art of his cave paintings, notably at Lascaux in southern France and at Altamira in northern Spain, achieved its fullest expression during his last, Magdalenian period ending about 10,000 B.C. It is now believed that these glorious figures of animals represent ceremonial rites, being abstract depictions of ancestral myths utilizing symbols as a means of communication; and that certain marks are calendric notations. The eventual interpretation of these symbols and archetypal images may well link the prehistoric past and present of mankind in one integrated process of intellectual development. For Cro-Magnon man spread throughout all Eurasia. He was the first *Homo sapiens*, the direct ancestor of modern man.

But where did he come from? What spiritual source impelled this sudden outburst of creative energy reflecting his meaning of myth and cognizance of time? Bringing with him this heritage of conscious evolution, his inexplicable appearance bridges the gap between the unconscious, cultureless Neanderthals and the peoples of Mesopotamia and Egypt who founded the first historic civilizations. Little wonder that behind the cultural span of the Cro-Magnons—between 30,000 or 35,000 B.C. and 10,000 B.C.—looms the specter of Atlantis.

Do these dates relate to geological history in any way?

4 THE FOUR GLACIAL AGES

Astrophysicists now venture that the Earth was formed as early as five billion years ago; geologists place the beginning of the Archeozoic Era at some two billion years. It is inconceivable that the configuration of the land masses on this small planet always has been as it is now. Shifts of the orbital axis, disruptions caused by the gravitational influence of other planets, diastrophism of orogenic or mountain-making—these and other causes of crustal unrest have periodically changed the surface of the earth since its mysterious genesis.

Many theories have been offered to explain the cause of these cataclysmic revolutions: Cosmic Hypotheses, Planetary Hypotheses, Geophysical and Volcanic Dust Hypotheses, and theories that they were caused by changes in the orbital paths of other planets or by the sudden shifting of the surface shell of the earth itself.

Carl A. Zapffe, an American metallurgist, a few years ago offered a new theory connecting these sudden cataclysmic revolutions with the advent of glacial ages.[1] That portions of the earth have been covered at various times by great ice sheets was generally unknown until Agassiz first broached the idea in 1837. His postulate was indignantly refuted, but has now been universally accepted. During the last billion years seven glacial ages are now known to have existed. Four of them occurred during the last million years, resulting in extensive ice sheets thousands of feet thick stretching across parts of North America, Europe, and Asia.

Within this period—the Pleistocene Epoch beginning 1,000,000 B.C. and extending down to about 10,000 B.C., the approximate time set for the sinking of Atlantis—the first man of our own genus, *Homo Erectus,* is believed to have appeared and developed into modern man, *Homo Sapiens.*

Zapffe's Submarine Vulcanism Theory suggests eruptions of molten rock from volcanos and earth fissures extending hundreds of thousands of cubic miles along the Mid-Atlantic Ridge. These eruptions filled the atmosphere to stratospheric heights with dust, decreasing absorption of solar radiation and volatizing water in the form of superheated steam, thus accounting for cataclysmic deluges. The excessive quantity of moisture then precipitated as torrential rainfall over temperate land areas and as snow upon encountered freezing isotherms, resulting in ice sheets.[1]

Zapffe believes discoveries by oceanography and nuclear physics support his theory that the Pacific Ocean floor is studded with immense volcanic cones; and that the Mid-Atlantic Ridge is a range of submarine vulcanism extending from Iceland to the Antarctic Circle.

This perhaps throws into focus the celebrated Piri Re'is map discovered in 1929 in the archives of the Topkapi Museum in Istanbul. The map was copied in 1513 from more ancient maps by Admiral Piri Re'is, a Turkish naval officer, as he stated in a marginal note. The area it covered was not known until 1956 when the cartographer Arlington H. Mallery and two other map authorities identified it as a map of the Atlantic from the Carolinas down the coast of South America. The map shows the correct longitudinal relationship of the east coast of South America with the west coast of Africa. Of more importance, the Piri Re'is map accurately delineated the shorelines and mountain ranges of Antarctica. This south-polar area has been so thickly covered with an ice cap for thousands of years that it was not known land existed beneath it until revealed by infra-red photography in 1952. Supposedly the original Piri Re'is map had been prepared by a people possessing a science of cartography long before Antarctica was covered by its glacial ice sheet.

During 1957, the International Geophysical Year, new evidence came to light: the discovery of fossil ferns and coal deposits in the

Transantarctica Mountains indicating that Antarctica once had been covered with dense tropical vegetation. Hence there are late conjectures that Antarctica once comprised portions of the land masses of both Lemuria and Atlantis.

Despite these interesting discoveries, Zapffe's major thesis is more pertinent: that a major cataclysm accompanied each of the glacial ages, and that they coincide with the cataclysms of esoteric theology which gradually destroyed Atlantis. There is no doubt of the carbon-dating of the four glacial ages that occurred during the million-year Pleistocene Epoch immediately preceding our own: the Nebraskan at 800,000 B.C., the Kansan at 200,000 B.C., the Illinoian at 75,000 B.C., and the Wisconsin at 9500 B.C. We can doubt his assumption that the first of the four catastrophes which overtook Atlantis and impelled migrations to other lands occurred as early as 800,000 B.C. But there is another way of interpreting his data.

The last Wisconsin glacial age is divided into four stages, each accompanied by a catastrophe: the Iowan, Tazewell, Cary, and Mankato. Their calculated time-span roughly covers the period from 30,000 B.C. to 10,000 B.C. Can these four later catastrophes, instead of the far earlier ones, be related to the series that broke up Atlantis into islands and finally sank the last one? In either case, the final catastrophe was the Mankato Maximum specifically dated at 9564 B.C., which coincides with the catastrophe recorded by Plato as occurring in 9500 B.C., and closely approximates the date of 10,000 B.C. set by the psychic Edgar Cayce.

So much for the myth of Atlantis. Whether Atlantis ever existed as an actual land mass is a problem that still engrosses researchers of all disciplines the world over. Yet its psychological significance is more important. For the myth of Atlantis cannot be separated from its larger context of four successive worlds—a primordial image stamped on the soul of mankind in the remotest times, an imprint that has never been erased, and which still influences our lives today. The existence of this archetype in mankind's collective unconscious cannot be questioned. Nor can its deep significance. For as it has risen into consciousness it has given rise to universal myths that reveal a hidden knowledge of secret processes working within us—a longing, a striving to achieve that psychic wholeness symbolized by its four-fold mandala form.

The meaning of this archetypal myth and pattern was of paramount concern to Mesoamerica. Hence this excursion into the four continents of esoteric theology, the four geological catastrophes and glacial ages, and the four suns, worlds, or ages of Mesoamerican mythology, brings us back to the creation of the Fifth Sun, the Sun of Movement, and the religious philosophy of the Nahuas and Mayas.

5 THE FIFTH SUN

The four sons of the supreme dual creative principle, Ometéotl, who created the universe, heavens, earth, and hells, were four primary forces representing the four quadrants of space. Represented as gods, they are pictured in directional colors in the codices.

They were the Red Tezcatlipoca (Tlatlauhqui Tezcatlipoca, also known as Xipe and Camaxtli) representing the east; the Black Tezcatlipoca (Yayauhqui Tezcatlipoca) of the north; the White Tezcatlipoca, commonly known as Quetzalcoatl, assigned to the west; and the Blue Tezcatlipoca of the south, whom the Aztecs called Huitzilopochtli. It is quite possible that they were but one force, one god, manifesting in four aspects, as did the Mayan deities. If so, he embodied the same dual principles of his divine Creator, Ometéotl. These opposite and conflicting dualities were symbolized in the Black Tezcatlipoca (the one commonly called Tezcatlipoca), the ubiquitous god of darkness and evil; and the beneficent White Tezcatlipoca (commonly known as Quetzalcoatl), god of goodness and light.

These two gods were in constant opposition from the start, each striving to become the sun and rule the world. One succeeded the other, the duration of their supremacy constituting one of the four worlds or ages.

Tezcatlipoca became the first sun, initiating the first era or world whose inhabitants were giants. While he was ruling the world, Quetzalcoatl struck him with a club, knocking him into the water. Changed into a jaguar, Tezcatlipoca devoured the giants, depopulating the earth and ending the era on the day 4 Ocelotl (jaguar). As the jaguar symbolized the earth-bound conscious-ness, Tezcatlipoca was often regarded as the symbol of the element earth. He was also seen as the constellation of Ursa Major, which the Aztecs pictured as a jaguar. That is why *tecuani,* "devourer of people," is a Nahuatl name for jaguar.

Quetzalcoatl became the second sun, enduring until Tezcatli-poca struck him down with his paw. A great wind arose, destroy-ing most of the world's inhabitants, the survivors being changed into monkeys on the day 4 Ecatl (wind). This era, as we have seen, was that of the element air.

Tlaloc was chosen as the third sun. Quetzalcoatl then sent down a rain of fire from which only the birds escaped. Tlaloc's wife, Chalchiuhtlicue, "She of the Jade Skirts," was selected as the fourth sun. Perhaps it was Tezcatlipoca who now again asserted his power, causing it to rain so long that the earth was covered with a flood, and its inhabitants were turned into fish.

Good and evil, darkness and light, the positive and negative forces of the cosmic duality—one after another in spatial succes-sion—ruled the world from each of the four quadrants. The cosmic stage was now set for the creation of the fifth sun, the synthesizing center. The watery sky had fallen upon the earth, so that it was necessary for the two opposing rivals, Tezcatlipoca and Quetzal-coatl, to lift it up. Hence Caso interprets a painting in the *Codice Vindobonensis* as Quetzalcoatl holding up the sky with his hands.

So now all the gods gathered to create a fifth sun. *The Anales de Cuauhtitlan* recounts what happened.[1]

"*Alla en Teotihuacan*" the gods assembled to choose which of them should be sacrificed and changed into the sun. Two volun-teered and made offerings. Tecuzistecatl, rich and powerful, offered five feathers, pellets of gold, copal, and thorns fashioned of coral and precious stones. Nanahuatzin, poor and scabby with sores, offered green canes, pellets of hay, and maguey thorns dyed with his own blood.

For four nights they fasted and did penance. On the fifth night at midnight all the gods arranged themselves in two rows in front of the divine hearth where a large fire had been burning for four days. The two chosen gods, standing between the ranks of the others, faced the fire. Into it one of them must cast himself as the supreme sacrifice, and so emerge purified to light the world.

"Tecuzistecatl, enter thou into the fire!" directed the gods.

Tecuzistecatl stepped forward, then hesitated. The heat was too great. He was afraid and turned back. Four times he tried, but failed.

Then spoke the gods to the scabby one. "Nanahuatzin, be thou the one to enter the fire!"

Nanahuatzin braced himself, closed his eyes. He then rushed forward and hurled himself into the flames. Tecuzistecatl, hearing him crackling and roasting, also rushed forward and threw himself into the flames.

Soon the sun began to rise, lurching from side to side, red in color, and shining so brightly none could look at it. Then the moon rose, shining as brightly as the sun. Angered by the audacity of the moon, one of the gods flung a rabbit in Tecuzistecatl's face, darkening it (which explains the pictorial representation of a rabbit in the moon in Aztec codices.) But still the sun did not move.

"How shall we live?" the gods asked each other. "The sun does not move on its course. Let us surround him that he move through our sacrifice."

"And then the air set to killing all the gods." Only one, a sorcerer named Xolotl, refused to die. He hid in the maize stalks, turning himself into a maize root with two stalks until he was discovered ... He hid himself among the maguey, changing into a double maguey or *mexolotl* ... He next threw himself into the water, turning into an *axolotl* or *ajolote,* a salamander. Here he was finally killed with all the other gods.

Still the sun did not move ... until "the wind began to blow with a strong blast, and made the sun move on its course."

We recall Xolotl—or his name—as the Chichimeca chieftain who swept down from the north, established his capital at Tenayuca, and finally reigned over a large *señorio* from Texcoco. But this was the legendary Aztec character who appeared long after the mythical convocation of the gods at Teotihuacan. There was also the historical priest-king of Tula often alluded to as Quetzalcoatl who cannot be identified with the much earlier, mythical god, Quetzalcoatl. Whether these are examples of Aztec names and ideas appropriated from much older Toltec myths, or whether these myths were given form and substance by Aztec thought, we do not know. Nor does it matter greatly. The enduring value of the myth of the creation of the Fifth Sun is contained instead in its hermetic meanings.

It is at once apparent that the Sun of Movement whose sign is 4 Ollin (movement) was created by purification and sacrifice. But what gave it movement and set it on its course was "air," the "strong blast of wind" which came from Quetzalcoatl as Ehecatl, the god of wind. Only he of all the gods could at last overcome the inertia existing at the beginning of the world and the new era.

The Fifth Sun, then, was created and set in motion. But to keep it constantly moving on its course, a specified period of time within the fifth era was allotted to each of the gods of the four directions. Hence within each period of 52 years, each of the four directions was given a 13-year period of predominant influence; and the *tonalámatl*, or sacred calendar year of 260 days, was divided into four 65-day groups of five 13-day weeks, each group carrying a sign relating it to one of the four cardinal directions.

The Nahuatl concept of movement as a fundamental motivation of all life is symbolized by one of the key hieroglyphs and day-signs, *ollin* (movement).

These are many variations, all taken from the *Borgia Codex*, the last one showing a serpent and a centipede entwined.

All symbolize the interlock polarities of earth and sky, light and darkness, male and female, good and evil, as typified by Quetzalcoatl and Tezcatlipoca. The conflict between them, and their reconciliation, is what gives movement, life, to man and the universe.

The Nahuatl concept is not unique. In Iran the Zarathustran teachings of the antithesis between the light and dark powers is portrayed in the struggle between Ormuzd and Ahriman. In Christianity the light powers of Christ oppose the dark powers of Lucifer, or Satan. The ancient Chinese represented the "great primal beginning" of all that exists as a circle divided into light and dark, the *yang* and the *yin,* illustrated by the symbol:

Out of the interplay of these opposite forces rose the world of being, change and movement being conceived as the continuous transformation of one force into the other.

The three-thousand-year-old Chinese classic, *I Ching or Book of Changes,* is based solely on the polarity of these positive and negative principles, its central theme being the continuous change through movement underlying all existence. The attribute of one of its trigrams, *Chen,* is movement. It asserts that "The inviolability of natural laws rests on this principle of movement along the line of least resistance. These laws are not forces external to things but represent the harmony of movement immanent in them. That is why the celestial bodies do not deviate from their orbits and why all events in nature occur with fixed regularity."[2]

The Fifth Sun, the Sun of Movement, held for the Nahuas the added significance of being the unifying center of the four directional suns which had preceded it. Thus is shown on the monumental twenty-five-ton Stone of the Sun, commonly called the "Aztec Calendar Stone," where it holds the center place surrounded by symbols of the previous four suns, the twenty daysigns of the *tonalámatl,* or sacred calendar, and on the outer circle by serpents which enclose the infinite and primordial *pleroma* of all space and time and creation. A grandiose conception, it has been aptly called "a finite statement of the infinity of the Aztec universe."

Yet within the Fifth Sun, world, or era, lay another synthesizing center—the soul of man. Writes Leon-Portilla: "The profound significance of movement to the Nahuas can be deduced from the common Nahuatl root of the words movement, heart, and soul. To the ancient Mexicans, life, symbolized by the heart (*y-ollo-tl*), was inconceivable without the element which explains it, movement (*y-olli*)."[3]

The meaning, the challenge, is plain. The movement taking place in man's heart between the two opposite polarities must be harmonized if man is to assume his greater role in the pattern of Creation. How? The myth of Quetzalcoatl may help to answer the question.

6 THE MYTH OF QUETZALCOATL

Of the many gods, Quetzalcoatl stands out alone as the most warmly human, divinely inspired, and mysteriously unknown.

Quetzalcoatl, says Spinden, was "the greatest figure in the ancient history of the New World." Writes Séjourné, "His image, the plumed serpent, had for pre-Columbian peoples the same evocative force as has the Crucifix for Christianity."

Certainly the myth of the god who helped to create the Fifth Sun and gave it movement, who as a white, bearded, culture-hero appeared among his people, taught them the arts of civilization and founded their religion, and then disappeared, was the basic religious theme common to all Mesoamerica.

Quetzalcoatl's Nahuatl name derives from two words: *quetzal* —a rare, brilliantly green bird found only in the highlands of Chiapas and Guatemala; and *coatl*—serpent; literally "the plumed serpent." But *coatl*, says Nicholson, is a combination of the generic Maya term *co*, for serpent, and the Nahuatl word *atl*, for water. Caso states that quetzal feathers were a symbol of something precious and *coatl* also means "twin brother," so that Quetzalcoatl may also be translated as the "Precious Twin," another of his names which may also allude to the fact that the morning and evening stars are the same planet, Venus.

His names were legion. Among the Nahuas he was known as Quetzalcoatl, the Plumed Serpent, Lord of the Land of the Dead, Ehecatl, the God of Wind, and the personification of the planet

Venus, the Lord of Dawn. As the morning star is often represented by Quetzalcoatl, and the evening star by Xolotl, his twin
brother, Quetzalcoatl takes on other names: Xolotl, Ce Acatl
from the time of his birth, and Tlahhuizcalpantecuhtli, who appears with two faces, one of a living person and the other that of
a skull. To the Mayas of Yucatan he was known as Kukulcan,
closely associated with Itzamna, the deity represented as a celestial lizard or serpent with two heads, and Gucumatz, the serpent
covered with green feathers.

There are two principal myths about Quetzalcoatl in the *Codice
Chimalpopoca*. According to the one recorded by Sahagún, he was
the ruler of the Toltec capital of Tollan. Deposed because he was
opposed to human sacrifice which was upheld by the followers of
Tezcatlipoca, he fled to the east coast and sailed away on a raft
of snakes after prophesying his return in the year of his birth, Ce
Acatl.[1] This is the most common myth about him and the reason
that Cortés was hailed as the returning Quetzalcoatl when he
arrived in the year of the god's prophesied return. This is the myth
so dramatically illustrated by the famous mural paintings of Diego
Rivera. It is still believed by thousands of Indians in Mesoamerica;
and his prophesied return from across the great salt water in the
direction of the rising sun, under his Hopi name of Pahana (from
Pasu–Salt Water), is still anticipated by the Hopis of Arizona.
This may illustrate the old belief that Latin America will fulfill
her true destiny only when the plumed serpent learns to fly.

This version of the myth is based on the assumption that
Quetzalcoatl was the historical Topiltzin, priest of Quetzalcoatl
and ruler of Tula. Deposed from his throne, he fled Mexico sometime in the twelfth century. Presumably he arrived in Yucatan
where he was known as Kukulcan, and initiated a renaissance of
Maya culture in Chichén Itza, duplicating that of Tula. It is doubtful that Topiltzin actually arrived there in person. More probably
Mexican migrations to Yucatan of warriors, merchants, artists,
craftsmen, architects, and religious missionaries occupied many
previous years. Also it seems quite true, as Thompson states, that
this Quetzalcoatl as Kukulcan was but a "late flash in the Maya
pan." But that his teachings were received and adopted so readily
may attest a long and previous knowledge of Quetzalcoatl's char

acter and meaning.

Who the original Quetzalcoatl was is not known. Volumes of conjectures have been written in attempts to identify him as an actual person: an errant Norseman, the Irish St. Brendan, a Buddhist priest from the Near East or from China as postulated by Mertz, St. Thomas or St. Paul the Apostle. The early Spanish historians Torquemada and Clavigero describe him as a man white-skinned, of ruddy complexion, with a long beard, clothed in black linen robes. He is reported to have appeared on the west coast of Mexico, at the Isthmus of Tehuantepec, on the east coast at the mouth of the Panuco, also in South America.

Attempts have been made to link him with concepts in ancient Greece and Egypt. He may have been indigenous, an early religious concept originating on the east coast of Mexico as suggested by Caso; elaborately carved "apotheosis" statues of him dating from about A.D. 1000 have been found among the Huastecs on the northern Gulf coast.

How many Quetzalcoatls there were! Their very number refutes all attempts to identify him as a legendary or semi-historical personage. One can only conclude that Quetzalcoatl was an archetypal figure which first emerged into consciousness at Teotihuacan, where he was given full form and meaning, and whose teachings virtually constituted the religion of the vast Teotihuacan empire and were spread throughout all Mesoamerica.

Hence the second principal myth about him is hermetic rather than historical, and it emerges as a Nahuatl expression of a universal truth impervious to time. Here briefly is the myth as best related in the textual *Anales de Cuauhtitlan.*[2]

As the ruler of the City of the Gods established after the creation of the Fifth Sun, Quetzalcoatl was wise, good, and chaste. Then his old heavenly rival and dual antithesis, Tezcatlipoca in the guise of Titlacaun, with two demons, Ihuimécatl and Toltécatl, contrived his downfall. Tezcatlipoca brought him a mirror "the size of a hand's span," and said to him, "Ce Acatl Quetzalcoatl, I greet thee and come to give thee thy body."

Quetzalcoatl, conscious of his divine origin, was perplexed. "My body? What is this concerning my body? Let me see."

And seeing his earthly form for the first time, reflected in the mirror, he was very frightened.

Tezcatlipoca then tempted Quetzalcoatl with a drink of pulque. Quetzalcoatl refused.

"Just taste it," insisted Tezcatlipoca.

Quetzalcoatl tasted it with his little finger and found it good. So he took a drink. He took four drinks and then a fifth, after which he called for his sister, Xochiquetzal, goddess of love and beauty. She too drank four pulques, a fifth, and then they slept together.

Upon awakening, Quetzalcoatl realized he had been induced to get drunk, forget his chastity, and commit incest. "Woe is me!" he wailed, singing a sad song of departure. "Acolytes, it is enough. I shall go away. Order a stone box to be made."

A stone coffin was made at once. In it Quetzalcoatl immured himself for four days. He then disposed of all his material riches, and went to *la orilla celeste del agua divina,* the shore of the divine sea. During his pilgrimage necromancers kept asking him, "Why hast thou left thy people? Whither goest thou?"

"I go to Tlillan Tlapallan. The Sun is calling me."

Arriving at the seacoast, he put on his feathers and mask, and built a great fire. Then he cast himself into the flames. When he burned, all the rare birds gathered to watch his ashes rise. And then eight days later his heart rose like a flaming star.

After his mortal manifestation died in the funeral pyre, Quetzalcoatl went underground to Mictlan, the Land of the Dead. He was accompanied by his twin or double, Xolotl, who took the shape of a dog. From Mictlantecuhtli, Lord of the Dead, he secured the bones of a man and a woman with which he escaped after many trials. He then sprinkled the bones with his own blood, thus redeeming them so that they could inhabit the earth.

Four days more he spent making arrows and on the eighth day he made his ascent, being transformed into the Lord of Dawn, the Morning Star. Thereafter, as the planet Venus, he astronomically repeated his ritual journey: first appearing in the western sky as the Evening Star, disappearing underground, and then reappearing in the eastern sky as the Morning Star to unite with the rising sun.

Laurette Séjourné through her interpretation of many graphic

Nahuatl symbols has given the most illumined presentation of the esoteric meaning of this myth—and as an archaeologist, she has been castigated for her views by her academic contemporaries.[3] The eminent analytical psychologist Erich Neumann suffered no such censure. Forthrightly and succinctly he asserted that Quetzalcoatl was a uniting symbol achieving the union of opposites: heaven and earth, morning and evening star, matter and spirit. In the Orphic Gnosis the winged serpent was the symbol of the Redeemer and Son of God. And Jolande Jacobi, another analytical psychologist, points out that the Serpilion or "serpent bird" (related to the Persian *semenda,* a combination of snake and bird) was a symbol illustrating the instinctive dual nature of the unconscious.

Certainly the transcendental meaning of this great myth is clear. It is an expression of the universal doctrine of sin and redemption, of death and resurrection, the transfiguration of man into god. But if Quetzalcoatl, one of the four sons of the supreme Creator, Ometéol, was already divine, how could he have succumbed to mortal sin? Simply because this myth, in the broadest possible terms, enunciates the principle of all Creation: the incarnation of divine light, purity, and spirituality into gross matter; and then the agonizing redemption of matter by spirituality—the immortal theme of all world religions. The Nahuatl dramatization of this cosmic principle gives Quetzalcoatl the same significance as the Christian myth gives its own redeemer who died on the cross, was resurrected, and illumined the way of redemption for all mankind.

The other chief characters in the myth also embody subtle meanings and relationships. Tezcatlipoca we know as the heavenly rival of Quetzalcoatl. Throughout the creation of the previous four worlds, one of them dominated and then the other. Their rivalry was continued on the mortal plane by their priests up to the time when Topiltzin-Quetzalcoatl was deposed as the ruler of Tula by the adherents of Tezcatlipoca.

Sahagún says of Tezcatlipoca: "He was considered a true god, whose abode was everywhere—in the land of the dead, on earth, and in heaven. When he walked on earth he brought vice and sin. He introduced anguish and affliction. He brought discord among people, wherefore he was called "the enemy on two sides.... All evils which came to men, all (these) he created, brought down, afflicting men and dividing them (one against the other). And sometimes he bestowed riches—wealth, heroism, valor, position of dignity, rulership, nobility, honor."⁴

Caso reports his many names: "The Smoking Mirror," attested by the mirror he wore in place of his amputated foot and the mirror he gave to Quetzalcoatl; Telepochtli, "He Who Never Grows Old" because sin never grows old; Yaotl, "The Enemy," because he was the enemy of Quetzalcoatl and the patron of warriors; Nezahualpilli, "The Prince Who Fasts"; and Tecpatl or Itzlacoliuhqui, "The Curved Flint Knife."⁵ He was the patron of the *telpochcalli,* the Aztec school of war, while Quetzalcoatl was the patron of the *calmecac,* the school for priests and nobles.

According to Spence, the name of Tezcatlipoca derived from the obsidian scrying stone of the seers, the *tezcat*; another "wizard-stone" being the *tepochtli,* another minor name for the god.⁶ Tezcatlipoca was therefore associated with the practice of black magic, as was Quetzalcoatl with white magic, being the supreme magician.

In Aztec Tenochtitlan the feast conducted in his honor, reports Sahagún, "was the most important of all feasts. It was like Easter, and fell near Easter Sunday."⁷ Its climax was the sacrifice of a young man in the image of Tezcatlipoca. He had been chosen the year before. Comely and well-mannered, he was dressed in fine robes and taught to play the flute. He walked through the streets carrying flowers and sounding his flute, accompanied by eight pages, and all whom he met bowed down and worshipped him.

Twenty days before the feast he was given four carefully selected virgins for wives, and his long hair was clipped like that of a war captain. During the five days before he was to die, many feasts and banquets were held for him. He was then escorted to a temple-pyramid whose steps he climbed alone. On each of them he broke one of the flutes which he had played all year. Reaching the summit, he was bound on the sacrificial stone where the priests slashed open his breast, tore out his pulsing heart, and offered it to the sun.

So too does Tezcatlipoca, his counterpart, give way to the

greater life of his voluntary death and resurrection after enjoying all earthly honors and pleasure.

The constant parallels between these opposites—including Tezcatlipoca's seduction of Xochiquetzal—suggest their basic unity. They are one and the same, Quetzalcoatl representing the "good," "light" aspect, and Tezcatlipoca the dark hidden side, his shadow self. Confirming this was the Aztec belief that Tezcatlipoca was invisible. Only the imprint of his hands and feet betrayed his presence.

Caso identifies him in the pictorial codices by the smoking mirror he wears at his temple, and by another which he wears in place of a foot torn off by the monsters of a previous world. He is painted black, as is Quetzalcoatl, but his face is striped with yellow and black horizontal lines. His hair is cut in the *tzotzocolli* style of warriors; and he carries the *chimalli* shield, the *atlatl* dart hurler, and the *tlacohtli* darts. All these proclaim him a god of war as reflected by the monumental warrior and Atlantean sculptures at Tula, in contrast to the peaceful and benign Quetzalcoatl as represented by the Plumed Serpent at Teotihuacan.

Xolotl is also related to Quetzalcoatl, being called his "double" or twin brother. During the creation of the Fifth Sun he was able to transform himself into double-maize and double-maguey because he was the god of twins. And from his transformation into an *axolotl,* a salamander, comes his name. Despite his attempts to escape, he was killed with all the other gods; and being Quetzalcoatl's double, he accompanied him to the Land of the Dead where he took the shape of a dog. Just as Quetzalcoatl symbolizes the daylight journey of Venus overhead, as Séjourné affirms, Xolotl symbolizes its night journey through the underworld. In this infernal region Quetzalcoatl suffered all the ordeals of a penitent. So Xolotl is often pictured with body sores and burst eyes.

The dramatic myth of Quetzalcoatl's apotheosis thus unfolds as a true Passion or Mystery Play rich with spiritual teachings. It is not yet ended, for its esoteric meaning is made still clearer in a pictorial codex depicting his underworld trials in the Land of The Dead before he rose triumphant as Venus, the Morning Star, Lord of the Dawn.

7 THE VOYAGE OF VENUS THROUGH HELL

The pictorial account of Quetzalcoatl's apotheosis comprises the most essential and strangest section of the *Codice Borgia*. Its theme, as termed by its commentator, is *El Viaje de Venus por el Infierno*—"The Voyage of Venus Through Hell" or "The Journey of Venus Through the Underworld." Venus here is equated with the figure of Quetzalcoatl who was transformed into the planet as related in the *Anales de Cuauhtitlan*.

The *Codice Borgia* is one of six codices in what is called the Borgia group which includes also the *Codices Laud, Fejervary-Mayer, Cospi, Vaticanus B,* and the *Mexican Ms. 20* of the Bibliotheque Nationale in Paris. All are screenfolds painted with glyphs or signs on animal skins, and deal only with religious or ritualistic matters, in contrast to other remaining codices which record historical events. The *Borgia Codex* came into the hands of Cardinal Stefano Borgia, for whom it is named, and at his death became the property of the Library of the Vatican where it now reposes. It was first reproduced in Lord Kingsborough's monumental collection, *Antiquities of Mexico,* London, 1831. The Duke of Loubat then financed in 1898 a reproduction in colored photoengravings at Rome. The great German scholar Eduard Seler was engaged to interpret it, his large two-volume commentary in German being published in 1904. Not until 1963 was this translated into Spanish and published with the reproductions in a handsome edition by

the Fondo de Cultura Económica, Mexico.[1] It has not yet been
translated into English.

The *Borgia,* as it will be abbreviated henceforth, is believed to
be of Nahuatl origin, perhaps coming from the Mixteca-Puebla
region. Its paintings, with their rich color, design, and composition,
are conceded to comprise the finest of all codices. Their religious
and ritualistic content makes the codex the most complex and esoteric of all those known.

Seler's voluminous commentary is itself a classic of its kind. His
original text in stylistic German, translated with evidently great
difficulty into Spanish, is laborious to follow. Also somewhat confusing is Seler's constant comparison of the *Borgia* paintings to
those of the *Fejervary-Mayer* and other codices in the group. Yet
with his remarkable scholarship and intuition, he painstakingly
identifies and interprets the hundreds of hieroglyphs, images, and
strange figures in the seventy-six full-page *laminas,* or paintings,
and gives captions to each series of related paintings, enabling us
to follow the development of the themes.

It must be remembered at the start that all periods of time from
hours and days to planetary phases of synodical revolutions, and
all divisions of space in sky and earth, were regarded as cosmic
forces directed by and represented as gods. So what we see here
is a great cosmic drama played by a cast of multitudinous gods
and goddesses. Their characters are not set and stylized for they
too are positive and negative, embodying the great principle of
duality. Nor do they remain in one period of time and one division
of space. They are forever moving about, interchanging positions,
following that other great Nahuatl principle of *movement.* And so,
in short, we confront in the *Borgia* the whole vast complex of
Nahuatl cosmography and religious belief.

The first part of the codex is a pictorial presentation of the
tonalámatl, the sacred calendar, with its twenty signs of the days
and their deities; the calendar divided in columns of five members,
showing the regions of the four directions; "the four times five
guardians of the periods of Venus"; the six regions of the world;
the five periods of Venus and their guardians; and other series
of paintings. These preliminary sections not only introduce us to
the cast and setting, they also confirm the importance of the *tona-*

lámatl, which Seler believed was built on the relation of the synodical periods of Venus and Earth.*

The priest-astronomers of the Nahuas and Mayas devoted special attention to the phases of the planet Venus. The synodical period of Venus, as Förstemann first pointed out in his study of the Mayan *Dresden Codex* in 1886, was known to be 584 days (583.92 by modern calculations), compared with that of Earth which took 365 days to revolve about the sun. Their relationship was thus based on the ratio of 5 to 8, for within a period of 2,920 days Venus made five synodical revolutions while the Earth made eight.

Each synodical revolution of Venus was observed to consist of four main phases. From its heliacal rising four days after inferior conjunction, its visibility as the Morning Star until it was lost to view in the light of the sun was assigned 236 days by Förstemann. For ninety days it was invisible, passing through superior conjunction to rise as the Evening Star. After 250 days of visibility as the Evening Star, it passed through inferior conjunction, becoming invisible for 8 days. These eight days, according to the Quetzalcoatl myth, represent the time he was in the underworld before reappearing as the Morning Star at the end of Venus' synodical cycle of 584 days.

Both Förstemann from the *Dresden Codex* and Seler from the *Borgia Codex* observed that these synodical phases were based upon a series of godlike images which traced the movement through space and time of Quetzalcoatl. But there are two differences between their interpretations. Seler concludes that the number of days in the four phases, corresponding to calculations derived from the *Borgia,* were not 236, 90, 250, and 8, but 243, 77, 252, and 12—Quetzalcoatl spending twelve days underworld, or in hell, instead of eight. The other difference is Seler's interpretation of five periods instead of four for Venus. He points out that the five Venus periods begin on five of the twenty signs of the *tonalámatl:* the first, fifth, ninth, thirteenth, and seventeenth. Moreover, the guardians, or representatives, of these initial days of five Venus periods are associated with the five regions of the world. This is beautifully illustrated by painting 25 in the *Borgia* which

*An explanatory discussion of the *tonalámatl* is given in Section III of the present text. To avoid repetition here, the reader is referred to it.

places Xipe Totec in the first period and west, Tlaloc in the second
period and south, Matlactli in the third period and east, and Mixcoatl in the fourth period and north. In the center, the fifth phase
is designated by the familiar hieroglyph *ollin,* movement. This
confirms the esoteric significance of the Fifth Sun, The Sun of
Movement, as the synthesizing center, and of movement as the
guiding force. In other paintings, Mictantecuhtli, the god of death,
designates the spatial center, the fifth region.

North is astronomically assigned to the disappearance of Venus
before superior conjunction, west to its appearance as the evening
star, south to its disappearance four days before inferior conjunction, and east to its reappearance as the morning star. Symbolically, the West represents the paradise of Tamoanchan, the
land of primordial origin and of corn, the house of birth, the region
of sanctified women. The East is the region in which dwell the
warriors killed in battle or immolated on the sacrificial stone.
North is the region of war, presided over by Mixcoatl; and the
deity of the South is Tlaloc, god of rain and of rain of fire.

In the first of the four series of *Borgia* paintings, "The Four
Times Five Guardians of Venus," are pictured the deities cutting
out an eye from a figure in front of them. In the second series the
guardians are making offerings of small effigies of themselves,
symbolizing the sacrifice of their own blood. First shown is Xochiquetzal, goddess of flowers and beauty and love. Next to her is
painted the same determining symbol shown with Quetzalcoatl:
the *nezahualli,* a ball which contains *chalchiuhatl* (blood), and
into which are stuck a bone punch, a sacrificial knife, and a flower
instead of a maguey thorn. Xochiquetzal we recall as the beautiful goddess who committed carnal sin with Quetzalcoatl before
his apotheosis. Thus she considers herself, as did Quetzalcoatl, as
a representative of self-sacrifice. For all she represents—pursuit
of pleasure, love, beauty—brings on self-sacrifice as an inevitable
consequence. Hence Seler interprets the actions in these first
two series as symbolizing human sacrifice and self-sacrifice.

In the third series, guardians are extracting from the belly of a
human figure a wavy strip of yellow skin or some precious thing, a
flower or precious stone. The actions symbolize procreation, the
birth of a child, and in a larger sense the birth or rebirth of nature

in spring. But birth and life must be paid for, as only by self-sacrifice and ritual exercises can women give birth to a child Hence we see as guardians the dread Tezcatlipoca; Xipe Totec, Lord of Flaying, in whose honor the skin of sacrificial victims was flayed from their bodies; Xochipilli, the god of flowers and procreation; and Macuilxochitl, god of pleasure, representing both the souls of dead warriors and of women who died in childbirth; and Tonatiuh, god of the Fifth Sun, who vanquishes the stars of night.

The fourth series is composed of female deities nursing a child. They include Mayahuel, goddess of the maguey plant, who with her four hundred breasts was metamorphosed into the maguey, the plant which exudes sweet juice for inexhaustible mouths. Here she suckles a fish, also known for its fecundity. Another is Chalchiuhtlicue, goddess of water, whose determining sign is the *chalchihuitl* from which issues a stream of "water of precious stone." This is not water, but "the liquid that cleans the filth of sin," the blood of self-sacrifice.

How confusing all this first seems, expressed in a medium of queer hieroglyphs, strange images, and barbarically frightening figures difficult to make head or tail of without Seler's acute guidance! But how simple really. These four series of remarkable paintings depict the fundamental cycle of procreation, conception, birth, and suckling of the childhood of all humanity under the auspices of the cosmic forces of the universe. It is not a bit different than the constant rebirth of humanity by the warriors who die in battle or on the sacrificial stone, for their blood too furnishes the sun its divine energy. Penitence, self-sacrifice, death, and rebirth or transfiguration. This cosmic cycle of life is the one great theme of the *Borgia,* epitomized now by the transcendent figure of Quetzalcoatl the penitent, who self-sacrificed himself in flames, journeyed through hell, and rose transfigured as the Morning Star.

His journey begins towards the East, towards Tlillan-Tlapallan, Land of the Black and Red, the Place of Burning, Tlatlayan. Here he climbed on the pyre and was burned to death, just as the Morning Star dies or disappears among the sun's rays. *Lamina 29* depicts his death. This painting is enclosed by a square in the form of a goddess of death whose open mouth provides an opening or exit to the frame. In the center is a circle painted deep black, representing a hole in the earth, the center of the subterranean kingdom. In it lies the goddess of death and a vessel or urn containing the ashes of Quetzalcoatl. Out of it they rise in a whirlwind, signifying that his ashes were scattered by the wind and transformed into flocks of beautiful birds as they rose to heaven. Six serpents wearing the heads of Quetzalcoatl in his aspect as the god of wind appear on the four corners of the painting. In the opening are two more serpents with the heads of Quetzalcoatl entwined to form the hieroglyph of movement. All these figures indicate that the heart or soul of Quetzalcoatl did not die in the fire but was resuscitated from his ashes, transformed into Venus, and now begins its journey through the underworld toward the West in the period of Venus' invisibility of 77 days.

In the next painting—one of the most beautiful—is shown his heart: a gorgeous red circle, the *chalchihuitl,* the precious stone placed by the Aztecs in the mouth of a dead king to represent his heart, the symbol of life. Within it, surrounded by the twisted cord of the *malinalli,* are two serpents of the wind and two entwined serpents with the heads of Quetzalcoatl, symbolizing his heart as Venus. This same hieroglyph of movement is repeated at the exit of the painting. Four figures of Tlaloc, god of rain, stand in the four directional corners, bearing in their hands a maguey or tree in flower, all signs of life. Clearly this is the region of the East. The heart of Quetzalcoatl then traverses the regions of the North and West, the regions of sin, as shown by two goddesses of sin, one robed in black and one in red. From their respective hearts are escaping the soul of the dead god.

The South is the Place of Thorns, of cutting, dismembering, and decapitating. So we see here as the principal figure the decapitated goddess of voluptuousness, Tlazoltéotl, whose legs and arms end in eagle claws. In place of her head are two huge flints between which emerges a small black figure of Tezcatlipoca. In the four corners four more representations of Tezcatlipoca appear: white, yellow, red, and blue, each carrying the decapitated head of a skeleton or human being. Tlazoltéotl wears on her breast a large and ornate flint, and from this emerges a small red figure of Quetzalcoatl. This same motif is repeated in the exit of the painting, showing that he has successfully emerged from this fifth region. If the decapitated goddess is the moon which is dismembered and destroyed in the phase of the new moon, as Seler asserts, the severed heads are those of the stars and Tezcatlipoca who holds them is the crescent moon which appears in the evening sky. Quetzalcoatl is analogous to Tezcatlipoca, for as the Evening Star he also now appears in the western sky for a period of 252 days.

The following paintings depict two pyramid-temples: the masculine House of the Black Serpent and the feminine House of the Red Serpent, the Tlillan and the Tlapallan, both of the West. Each is upheld by a great serpent. The figures in the first are men wearing the crests of heron feathers common to warriors. In the second are women, those who have died in childbirth. Quetzalcoatl, painted black and kneeling on a black eagle, presents himself to pay homage to Yohualtecuhtli, lord of the temple of the night. He is accompanied by Tezcatlipoca. On the platform of the temple is a bundle from which flames are shooting out. It is the *mexquimilli*, the bundle containing the ashes of Quetzalcoatl's father and the predecessor of Quetzalcoatl, that are interpreted as the ashes of the deity of the Evening Star which, resuscitated, appears in the evening sky. We are reminded of different versions of the myth. In one, Quetzalcoatl obtained the bones and ashes of dead men from the god of the underworld and sprinkled them with his own blood, creating a new race of men; hence Caso regards him as the father and creator of men.[2] In another version the bones were those of a man and woman with which he escaped after many trials to sprinkle with his blood. Thus he redeemed man from death, becoming, as Séjourné states, the Redeemer.[3] The meaning of all versions is the same, the redemption of man by sacrifice; and here in the *Borgia* Quetzalcoatl receives from Yohualtecuhtli the *mexquimilli* and with it continues his journey.

One sees him at the moment he is disappearing into the earth, into the open fauces of Cipactli, the earth dragon, for the twelve-day period of Venus' invisibility. But there appear now two Quetzalcoatls, one black and one red—the same that appeared earlier, emerging from the flints on the neck and heart of the decapitated goddess Tlazoltéotl. On the side of the black Quetzalcoatl are the black Tezcatlipoca; Mictlantecuhtli, a black skeleton with eagle

claws; and a blue Xochipilli or Tonacatecuhtli. Beside the red
Quetzalcoatl are the red Tezcatlipoca, Tepeyollotli, and Tlahhuizcalpantecuhtli, god of the Morning Star. Around them are twelve
goddesses, the *cihuatetéo* or *cihuapipiltin,* the women who dwell in
the West and represent Tlazoltéotl, goddess of the moon and of
birth.

The two Quetzalcoatls each carry large sacrificial knives, and
each is escorted by a figure of Cihuatéotl. Tlazoltéotl makes a
prisoner of the black Quetzalcoatl by grasping a lock of his hair,
and the red Tezcatlipoca similarly makes a prisoner of the red
Quetzalcoatl.

They enter now, in *lamina* 41, the region of the North, the dark-
est and lowest area of the subterranean world, Mictlampa, the
Realm of the Dead, Hell. Two roads lead into it. On one of them,
guided by the black Tezcatlipoca, comes the black Quetzalcoatl
carrying maguey thorns and a bag of copal. Along the other road,
led by the red Tezcatlipoca, comes the red Quetzalcoatl, really
bone-colored with dots of red, also carrying the maguey thorns,
huitztli, and the copal, *copalziquipilli.* The heart of this darkness
is pictured as a great vessel, the *chalchihuitl,* "well of the water of
precious stone," the blood of sacrifice. Within it a god and a goddess of water draw blood from the legs of the two Quetzalcoatls
with a bone punch. It gushes upward in two streams like baptismal
water, under which the red Quetzalcoatl kneels while Tlaloc, god
of water, pours water over him.

The division of Quetzalcoatl into two beings, the black destined
to live and the red destined to die, plunges into an esotericism
that can best be understood by a parallel in the Hindu and Tibetan
doctrine of *karma* and rebirth. This asserts that a man may have
consciously repressed or inhibited all his base instincts during his
lifetime on earth. Yet even these may unconsciously erupt, as
borne out by the erotic dreams and visions of many monks. Or
else they are carried by him into the after-death state. What is
necessary before a man emerges into full spirituality, then, is that
these karmic propensities or predispositions be extinguished on
the unconscious level as well as on the conscious level. And this,
in the *Borgia,* is the status of Quetzalcoatl. Of divine origin, a
"god" in his own right, he was not yet above the dictates of his

earthly self when he was incarnated as the ruler of Tollan. His sin of drunkenness and carnality he consciously atoned for by burning himself on the funeral pyre. But his predispositions are still unconsciously embodied within him when he reaches the land of the dead. And these too must be extinguished, expunged by sacrifice. So we see here the two aspects of Quetzalcoatl, the conscious one first shown in an earlier painting emerging from the head center of the decapitated Tlazoltéotl, and the unconscious one emerging from her heart center.

There follows the scene of sacrifice, the red Quetzalcoatl stretched out on the sacrificial stone, his heart being torn out. Appropriately, the one who executes the sacrifice is the black Quetzalcoatl, that enduring principle destined to live. Beside him, the black Tezcatlipoca, his dual opposite, drinks the blood which spurts out from the wound. The body of the sacrificed Quetzalcoatl is thrown down to disappear in the fauces of the *cipactli,* symbol of the earth, just as the Aztecs threw the bodies of their sacrificed victims down the steps of a pyramid. And here the sacrificed Quetzalcoatl kneels before Mictecacihuatl, wife of the god of death.

Now the black Quetzalcoatl, the enduring spiritual principle, must be resurrected, and this of course includes his fleshly twin or earthly double, Xolotl. But Xolotl also symbolizes the dualities of fire and water, being the fire that falls from the sky (lightning) and is born of water as lightning comes from the cloud, and so is associated with Tlaloc, god of water. It is necessary for him to immolate himself as did Nanahuatzin in the myth, who threw himself into the fire in order to be resurrected as the sun. So here, misshapen, with twisted members and a protruding eye, he is being cooked in a bowl in his form of Nanahuatzin—a pictorial variation from the narrative myth. Across the painting Xolotl appears again, this time coming out with lightning in his hand, showing that he is born of water as lightning from the cloud. Between these two pictures of Xolotl is shown an "eagle vessel," the *cuauhxicalli,* filled with a yellow liquid and surrounded by a sea of fire. It is the fire that burned Xolotl-Nanahuatzin, and the renewing water of life. Seated on the bowl are two Quetzalcoatls sucking the water through reed tubes. They are no longer the sacrificed red god and the living black god. Both are painted black, are living gods.

The meaning is clear. Quetzalcoatl has drunk the water of renewal, has been resurrected and transformed into the Morning Star. This takes place in the deepest underworld, Mictlampa, the realm of the dead, in the region of the North. But as North is the second of the directional underworld regions, he must still traverse the others before rising triumphantly in the eastern sky.

He now enters Cincalco, the cave that forms the entrance to the West, the land of the origin of corn. This is one of the caves to which Moctezuma was directed when he was thinking of committing suicide upon the arrival of the Spaniards. Here in the House of Corn are goddesses of corn and water kneeling before a *métatl*, the grinding stone. Quetzalcoatl is kneeling on a chair decorated with eagle feathers, and Tezcatlipoca on a chair covered with a jaguar hide. They represent the *cuauhtliocelotl*, the "eagle and the jaguar," first symbolizing the opposing principles of these two gods, and then the warrior orders of the Eagles and Jaguars who waged the Blossoming War or War of the Flowers.

The South is characterized as the House of Stone Knives, Iztcalli, and the House of Flowers, Xochicalli. It is also considered the region of destruction because in it are torn to pieces the great stars.

The four creatures that tear to pieces are the bat, jaguar, eagle, and *cipactli*, the aquatic monster, the last being replaced here by the quetzal bird. The bat, however, is offering a human heart, the symbol of life, to the familiar goddess Xochiquetzal. This suggests that, after her self-sacrifice, she too is transformed into "the young lunar goddess who shines in the first half of the night, the crescent moon beloved of the solar god." She is so shown in the center of the painting with a large rayed disk on her belly whose center is the hieroglyph of the *chalchíhuitl* drawn as a human heart.

From it issues a tree whose branches end in flowers, and on top perches Quetzalcoatl in the form of a hummingbird. The significance of the hummingbird is best explained by Fray Diego Duran, a Dominican missionary to Mexico in the late 1500s: "For six months of the year it is dead, and for six it is alive. And, as I have said, when it feels that winter is coming, it goes to a perennial, leafy tree and with its natural instinct seeks out a crack. It stands upon a twig next to that crack, pushes its beak into it as far as possible, and stays there six months of the year—the entire duration of winter—nourishing itself with the essence of the tree. It appears to be dead, but at the advent of spring, when the tree acquires new life and gives forth new leaves, the little bird, with the aid of the tree's life, is reborn.... Consequently the Indians say that it dies and is reborn.... I feel secure in writing this here, and I believe what the Indians told me."[4]

The *huitzitzilin*, the hummingbird, then, is a symbol of rebirth. Huitzilopochtli, the great god of the Aztecs, was often so represented, wearing a rich headdress in the shape of a hummingbird. And still today during the great Corn Dance at Santo Domingo, New Mexico the "flag" or standard carried is a long smooth pole— he *coatl*, the serpent-staff of Quetzalcoatl, which bears on top the *huitziton*, the crest of Huitzilopochtli with its bunch of macaw and hummingbird feathers, symbol of the new, reborn corn, as contrasted with the dried corn husks of last year's corn worn in the hair of the *koshares*.

Quetzalcoatl now has gone through all four regions of the underworld. He has been sacrificed, descended into the deepest pit of Hell, transformed into Xolótl-Nanahuatzin, resuscitated, and transformed into a hummingbird. Now he can ascend into the Eastern sky, the dwelling place of sacrificed warriors who have gone to the House of the Sun. Here we see the four *cuauhcalli*, "houses of eagles, houses of warriors," corresponding to the directions, and Quetzalcoatl portrayed as the stellar god.

But as the Morning Star comes out before the rising sun, the fire of its brilliance having been lighted in the underworld, the last painting depicts this underworld, integrating all its regions. This is the realm of fire. On the borders stand the gods of fire, West, South, North, and East, all representatives of the *atl-tlachinolli* symbolizing the union of fire and water. In the center a fire is burning in the belly of the goddess of fire, and above it is a *tlecuilli* or *tlecuatzli*, a firebox. Roasting inside it we see again a figure, not this time Xolótl-Nanahuatzin, but the god of air who is finally reborn from fire and water—the meaning of *atl-tlachinolli*.

And in the exit to the last painting, *lamina* 46, the door to heaven, we see Quetzalcoatl at last ascending in the eastern sky as the Morning Star, Lord of Dawn.

Seler keeps reminding us that the sun and moon also disappear in the underworld, but for shorter periods than Venus. With his ripe scholarship he develops at length the astronomical relationship of these three luminous bodies to each other and to the deities in the myth. Nevertheless the fundamental meaning of Quetzalcoatl's apotheosis is spiritual rather than astronomical. Death and transfiguration—this is the great theme, like the sound of deep running water, that runs through the *Borgia*.

There is only one comparable parallel to Quetzalcoatl's after-death journey through the underworld. It is related in *The Tibetan Book of the Dead,* similar to *The Egyptian Book of the Dead,* both of which may have derived from a more ancient source.[5] It is a treatise or guide to the art of dying, relating the experiences encountered by the soul on the *Bardo,* or after-death plane, before reincarnating in another body on this world plane, or achieving transformation into a higher spiritual plane above the polar opposites.

The *Bardo,* or transitional period, is divided into three main stages. In the first stage, the *Chikhai Bardo,* beginning at the moment of death of the physical body, the Knower—the subtle death-surviving element, the soul-entity, nexus, or whatever it may be called which suffers no breach of consciousness—is in a trance-state, unaware he is separated from the human-plane body. The second stage, the *Chönyid Bardo,* begins when he awakens to the fact that death has occurred. It is a "transitional state of glimpsing reality" during which he experiences hallucinations created by the karmic reflections of his actions in the earth-plane body. He encounters a series of comforting Peaceful Deities and then a series of frightening Wrathful Deities. None are real; they are but apparitions, personifications of his own human feelings and thoughts. During the third stage, the "transitional state of seeking rebirth," the *Sidpa Bardo,* his karmic predilictions or remnant desires for *sangsaric,* or earthly, fleshly existence, assert themselves. And in a fourth stage he is reborn in another human body. Or else, as an exceptional being, he is freed from the Wheel of Life and achieves liberation from the bi-polar opposites by reaching a higher spiritual plane.

These are the experiences Quetzalcoatl undergoes from his immolation on the funereal pyre and death of his physical body. Descending into the underworld Realm of the Dead, he encounters a frightening succession of *tzitzimimes,* Demons of Darkness, and of Wrathful Deities in the forms of gods and goddesses who would destroy him, and of Peaceful Deities who would preserve him. Passing through all the directional regions of the underworld, or all the stages of the *Bardo,* he is divided into two Quetzalcoatls; transformed into his twin or shadow, Xolotl-Nanahuatzin; allied with his opposite counterpart, Tezcatlipoca. No aspect of his psyche is ignored; he is divided and subdivided into all manifestations of his physical, mental, emotional, and spiritual components according to the karmic propensities of his being. He is a prism reflected in all this composite lights and colors. And his final transfiguration into the Morning Star confirms that Quetzalcoatl, in terms of the parallel Chinese Taoism, has found the Tao, the "Way," to supersede the bi-polar opposites of earth and heaven.

He has achieved that psychic or spiritual wholeness so difficult to put into words, but which has been represented from time immemorial by the numinous symbol of the mandala. The word in Sanskrit means a magic circle, symbolizing the fullness of divine creation, the boundless and immeasureable infinitude of all space and time, enclosed by the serpent swallowing its own tail. Geometrically, it is a design whose basic form is a combination of the circle and the square: a circle divided into four quadrants, a four-petalled lotus, a cross, a wheel, a flower or a square divided into four, but always with four as a basis of its pattern.

Mandalas have been found everywhere, in all ages. Egyptian mandalas show Horus in the center with his four sons at the cardinal points, as later Christian mandalas place Christ in the center surrounded by the four evangelists. The mandalas of Tibetan Buddhism are perhaps the most ornately beautiful, while the sand paintings of the Navajos and Pueblos are also superlative examples. The great Medicine Wheel of the northern Plains Tribes —Sioux, Cheyenne, and Crow—as ceremoniously expressed in their common Sun Dance, reflects the mandalic form. To the North is found wisdom. The South is the place of innocence. The West is the Looks-Within Place, which speaks of the introspective nature of man. And the East is the place of Illumination, its color the gold of the Morning Star. At birth each of us is given a particular Beginning Place on the Medicine Wheel. We must then grow by seeking understanding in each of these four directional ways in order to learn to be Total Beings, to achieve Wholeness.[6]

The gorgeous *Borgia* paintings are among the finest mandalas in the world. One after another, in brilliant color, they show a circle enclosed by a square, as in *laminas* 29 and 30, the square having an opening on one side as do the Navajo sandpaintings "to let the spirit escape." All of them have the basis of four as their structure with a synthesizing center, as *laminas* 25 to 28. Their form corresponds to the Nahuatl concept of the universe, the four directional worlds, and the four "continents" of esoteric theology. In this respect we may view the four directional underworlds in the Land of the Dead as forming a great psychological mandala wherein Quetzalcoatl sought the synthesizing center and achieved wholeness.

Jung recognized that the mandala reflected the psychic structure of man himself, and encouraged his mentally ill patients to draw their own as an unconscious aid to their recovery. For the mandala symbol is not only a means of expression, but it works an effect. This undoubtedly was one of the chief values of the *Borgia* hieroglyphic paintings; they created an effect greater than any literal language could have. And this today, so many centuries later, is what arouses our admiration, stimulates our imagination, and unconsciously re-evokes our conception of that spiritual wholeness which we too may achieve like Gautama the Buddha of the East, Christ of the Near East, and Quetzalcoatl of Mesoamerica. As Seler fittingly concluded, "Those bloody polytheists caught sight of an essential unity in the multiplicity and variety of their gods."

The feather and the flower of the Nahuatl concern with space, the spatialization of time itself, is the apotheosis of Quetzalcoatl.

8   VENUS-QUETZALCOATL

The importance of Venus to pre-Columbian Mesoamerica is
not too strange. In that latitude it looms up in the dawn sky big as
a snowball, shining with inexpressible brilliance. The ancient
Chaldeans, Egyptians, and Greeks regarded it with the same
veneration as the Mayas, Toltecs, and Aztecs. To the Babylonians
the planet was personified by the goddess Ishtar; to the Egyptians
by Isis; the Greeks, Aphrodite; the Romans, Venus. It was hailed
as Hesperus when it appeared in the evening sky, and as Phos-
poros when it later appeared in the morning sky. Venus was not
only regarded as a beneficent female body in the heavens. It was
also considered male and malefic, personified by Ahriman, Seth,
Lucifer, and Satan. Little wonder that Mesoamerican myth
assigned to Venus, personified by Quetzalcoatl, the role of medi-
ator between night and day, between good and evil, with the
power of transcending these opposites within man himself.

Pythagoras, who offered proof of the spherical form of the Earth
in the fifth century B.C., called it "Sol Alter," the "Other Sun,"
believing that as the "little sun in which the solar orb stores its
light" it received a triple supply of energy from the sun and transmitted one-third of this to Earth. Measurements now show that
Venus reflects seventy-six per cent of the sunlight that strikes it,
compared to Mercury's six per cent.

Yet long before these astronomical observations, Venus was
believed to be Earth's spiritual prototype. During the course of

man's early evolution, his original wholeness was represented by a circle ◯ . The symbol then became ⊖ when mankind was changed into androgynous beings, male and female. Later it became ⊕, the T, or *Tau*, then evolving into the cross ┼ . Hence the "Twin Sisters" were symbolized by one globe over and one globe under the cross: Earth ♁ and Venus ♀ . This latter is the astrological sign for Venus still used today, that for Earth being ⊕.

As we know now, Venus and Mercury are the only planets within the orbit of the Earth around the sun. Venus is nearest to Earth at a distance of 25 million miles, Mercury being 50 million miles away but only 43 million miles from the sun. All the other known planets lie outside the orbit of Earth, Mars being the closest at 34 million miles. Venus is moonless, the brightest heavenly body except for the sun and moon. With a diameter only seventy-nine miles less than that of Earth, Venus is still considered Earth's "twin sister."

The ancient peoples of both the eastern and western hemispheres developed a Venus calendar of five synodical years (2,919.6 days) equivalent to eight solar years (2,920 days) which can be equated with the 2,922 days of eight Julian calendar years of 365¼ days. Just when were these calendars developed, and how far back can the existence of Venus be established?

It is generally assumed that the Babylonians during the third millenium before the Christian era knew only four planets: Mars, Mercury, Saturn, and Jupiter; and that not until the first half of the second millenium was Venus observed. Why, if Venus was the nearest planet to Earth and the brightest?

Immanuel Velikovsky answers this with his famous theory in a book so original, erudite, and sensational that orthodox scientists attempted to suppress it.[1] His premise is simple and startling. Venus did not exist in the third millenium. It was born from Jupiter as a comet in the second millenium. In a near collision with Earth, it caused two terrestrial catastrophes fifty-two years apart, as recorded by the Flood of Deucalion in the time of the Exodus, 1516 B.C., and the Flood of Ogyges in the time of Joshua, 1568 B.C. These catastrophes may have caused the postulated sinking of Atlantis: not 9,000 years before the time of Solon, according to Plato, but 900 years before, or about 1500 B.C.

For seven centuries Venus remained a comet, a heavenly body dreaded by all peoples on Earth. Then it moved near Mars, causing two more world upheavals on February 26, 747 B.C. and March 23, 687 B.C. Mars was thrown out of orbit, Venus' orbit was changed from an elliptical to a circular orbit, and it became a planet.

Velikovsky's theory itself collides violently with the generally-accepted uniformitarian belief that the solar system always has been as it is now, without any such disruptions. First presented in 1950, his theory challenged the foundations of all established sciences: physics, geology, astronomy, paleontology, biology, and history. Vituperatively refuted, it has since proven its predictions of a high temperature on Venus and that the planet's atmosphere contains carbohydrates and hydrocarbons; that the "canals" on Mars are cracks; that Jupiter emits radio noises; that the Earth has a magnetosphere reaching to the moon; and many others. Today Velikovsky symposiums are being held throughout the country, courses in his theory are taught in many universities, scientists are giving it serious consideration, books and articles are supporting it. Hence it seems probable that his theory will be eventually accepted in the field of science. In his study, Velikovsky also documents the effects of catastrophism as reflected in world myths and history. In this field his theory is gaining slower credence, for if fully accepted it will revolutionize all present world chronologies. Without presuming to question his premise, let us inquire how it may affect the chronology of Mesoamerican myth and history as it is known now.

Its assertion that the two catastrophes fifty-two years apart, in 1568 and 1516 B.C., were the basis of the 52-year periods whose ends were so dreaded, runs counter to the fact that these periods are measured by the meshing of the 260-day Sacred Calendar and the 365-day Solar Calendar every 18,980 days or 52 years, called the Calendar Round, which will be explained later. It is now believed this permutation system was developed by the Mayas about the beginning of the Christian era. Its base was the Sacred Calendar whose origin is unknown, as is the reason for its time period of 260 days. Could it be possible, according to Velikovsky's theory, that it originated 1,500 years before? And if so, what was the reason for the choice of the *tonalámatl's* 260-day period?

That the earth was enveloped by darkness during a fifty-two-year interval is attested by myth. But that this darkness occurred in the fifteenth century B.C., marking the ending of the Fourth Sun and the beginning of the Fifth Sun, runs into many mythical contradictions. Nahuatl sources vary widely on the dates of the beginning of the various Suns or Worlds.

According to the *Leyenda de los Soles,* as interpreted by León-Portilla,[2] the First Sun began 2,513 years before the oral account was recorded here in writing in A.D. 1558. This would date its beginning in 955 B.C. The *Leyenda* gives the duration of each of the four preceding Suns in the Calendar Round multiples of 52—13 multiples of 52 years or 676 years for the first Sun; 7 multiples or 364 years for the second; 6 multiples or 312 years for the third; and 13 multiples or 676 years for the fourth. But as the total duration of these first four Suns adds up to 2,028 years, the present Fifth Sun would not have begun until 470 B.C.

Fernando de Alva Ixtlilxóchitl in his *Obras Historicas* presents another chronology. He gives the combined duration of the four Suns as 3,028 years, the date of the last Sun corresponding to 217 B.C. Assuming that this was the end of the Fourth Sun, this date corresponds to the founding of Teotihuacan where the gods assembled to create the Fifth Sun. Ixtlilxóchitl also concludes that the Nahua race was 5,768 years old as of the date of his work, A.D. 1570, which would place the origin of the Nahuas in 4198 B.C. And here we run into problems of interpretation.

The *Leyenda de los Soles* and the *Anales de Cuauhtitlan*[3] list four previous worlds, their number and order corresponding to those in the *Historia de los Mexicanos por sus Pinturas* and sculptured on the Aztec calendar stone. But while both Ixtlilxóchitl and Clavigero[4] give the same names to the four Suns, their names differ from those given in the above sources. Moreover, Clavigero includes the present Sun among the four, leading us to question whether there were four instead of five Suns according to their version. Ixtlilxóchitl enumerates the durations of each of them— 800, 810, 964, and 1,416 years respectively; and these add up to 3,990 years, not 3,028 years as he stated. Now if the "date of the last sun," 217 B.C., meant the ending of the 3,028-year duration of the previous Suns, then 3245 B.C. was the beginning of the First Sun. And this roughly corresponds to the Mayan date of 3113 B.C. for the beginning of the Fifth Sun. But if we accept the duration of the four worlds as 3,990 years as Ixtlilxóchitl has enumerated them, the First Sun began in 4207 B.C., which approximates his date of 4198 B.C. for the beginning of the Nahua race.

None of these different chronologies appear to be conclusive, possibly because the Aztecs confined themselves to the Calendar Round periods without adopting the longer calendrical periods of the Mayas. And these show a far different picture. According to the Mayas' more accurate reckoning, they projected the Long Count date of 3113 B.C. for the beginning of the present Fifth World. Its premise and its meaning will be developed later.

What we have then for the end of the Fourth World and beginning of the Fifth is a vast spread from the Mayan date of 3113 B.C. and from 217 B.C. to 470 B.C. according to ancient Nahuatl sources.

Hence there is a wide variance between Nahuatl and Mayan mythical sources as to the beginning of the present Fifth World, none of whose dates coincide with Velikovsky's assertion that the fifteenth century B.C. catastrophes marked the turning point.

Another moot question is whether the Quiché Mayas emigrated to Mexico during the darkness intervening between the catastrophes of 1516 and 1568 B.C. It is not known when and from where the Quichés emigrated. Did they emigrate from Guatemala to Mexico, only to return? Or did they emigrate across the Pacific from southeast Asia, as some anthropologists assert? It is only known from myth that they came in darkness from the four quarters of the earth to gather at legendary Tulán, commonly supposed to have been Tula, Hidalgo in Mexico. Still in darkness they then emigrated to their present homelands in Guatemala. But this emigration, according to conjectural history, took place sometime between the seventh and tenth centuries A.D. This supposedly historical emigration, as we have suggested, may have been only a mythical Mayan analogy for mankind's journey from the unconscious to consciousness.

Now for the two following world upheavals which Velikovsky describes. For the next seven centuries after Venus' near-collision with Earth, Venus was still a comet, described as a serpent with a tail, or a serpent adorned with feathers, "flames of fire." This aptly suggests a planetary origin for the Plumed Serpent, Quetzalcoatl. Then began a tremendous war in the sky when Venus nearly collided with Mars, lasting from 747 to 687 B.C. Now if Venus was revered by the later Aztecs as Huitzilopochtli, this was the genesis of the war between the two gods and their ideologies. For this interpretation, Velikovsky mentions that the name of the war god Huitzilopochtli was "Tetzateotl or the raging Tetzahuitl," apparently referring to Tezcatlipoca, who was far from being a by-name of Huitzilopochtli.

As we recall from the *Codice Chimalpopoca,* the heavenly wars were waged between the Black Tezcatlipoca, the ubiquitous god of darkness and evil, and the beneficent god of goodness and light, the White Tezcatlipoca commonly known as Quetzalcoatl, from the beginning of Creation and throughout the first four worlds. Not until far later did the Aztecs identify Tezcatlipoca with their war-god Huitzilopochtli. Hence if the creation myth is to be brought into conformance with Velikovsky's theory, creation of the First World and the beginning of the war in heaven took place in the seventh century B.C.

The celestial conflict between Venus and Mars was symbolized assertedly by wars between the Toltecs and Aztecs. There is no record of wars between the original Toltecs of Teotihuacan where the myth of Quetzalcoatl took form, and the Aztecs who did not arrive in Mexico until centuries after the city had been abandoned. The Toltecs referred to are undoubtedly the later Toltecs of Tula in Hidalgo, established in 968 A.D. Here there was a conflict between the adherents of Tezcatlipoca and Quetzalcoatl. It was won by the first faction, the high priest of Quetzalcoatl and ruler of Tula being forced to abdicate his throne and leave Mexico.

This of course is in direct opposition to the ending of the planetary war in heaven between Venus and Mars seventeen centuries earlier. Mars was thrown out of orbit. Venus became a planet, no longer menacing, but a beneficent heavenly body with two aspects as the Morning and Evening Stars. Was this then the origin of Quetzalcoatl's transformation? If we accept this planetary thesis as the basis of the myth, the first concept of malign Quetzalcoatl-Venus must have occurred in the fifteenth century B.C., and that of his transformation into the beneficent planet in the seventh century B.C. This is some four centuries earlier than the archaeological dating of the founding of Teotihuacan where the myth of Quetzalcoatl first took form.

Myth assures us that the tribal deity of the Aztecs was Huitzilopochtli, the god of war. "He was not like Mars, he was Mars," asserts Velikovsky. "They were one and the same planet-god." But to the Aztecs, whose myth will be developed later, he was sired by the sun, personified the sun. Hence the Aztecs regarded themselves as "People of the Sun" with the divine mission of supplying it with nourishment—human hearts—for its constant battle over the stars and the forces of night. The Aztecs carried an image of Huitzilopochtli during their migration into Mexico. But, according to present historical records, their arrival as the last wave of barbarian Chichimecas occurred not earlier than the eleventh century A.D. If Velikovsky is right, we must push back the arrival of the Aztecs about eighteen centuries if we believe they identified Huitzilopochtli with Mars from the start.

Velikovsky's theory runs parallel to Mesoamerican myth in general outline. Only the chronology erupts from their common context in different time-faults. These few variations suggest the vast amount of new research necessary if Mesoamerican history is to be brought into conformance with his theory. The great problem posed is the relation of history to myth. Mesoamerican historical dates and events may never be equated precisely with those in its myths, for myth is impervious to time. It originates not on a conscious, temporal level, but on the lower level of the unconscious where arise the archetypes that give it psychological meaning.

Man from Earth has landed on the moon, carrying his golf clubs. A future astronaut will no doubt reach Venus, perhaps also carrying his golf bag. But it is extremely doubtful that he will carry the spiritual capacity of Quetzalcoatl. Venus for each of them represents an entirely different goal.

9   COSMIC CATASTROPHISM

Somewhat similar to Velikovsky's theory was one offered by
Hans Hoerbiger, an Austrian inventor and cosmologist.[1] It was
first proposed in 1913 as a glacial cosmogony, and in 1927 expanded
as a Theory of Satellites. Briefly, it postulates four geological
epochs brought about by Earth's capture of four successive satellites or moons. Each approached nearer and nearer to Earth, disrupted, and was transformed into a frozen body which then began
to revolve about Earth as its moon. This caused a world catastrophe which destroyed large portions of Earth and mankind.

During the second epoch the world was inhabited by giants, as
reflected in world-wide mythology. The third, or tertiary, age saw
the rise of the great civilization of Atlantis, a world-wide maritime
power. One of its chief centers was Tiahuanaco on the shores of
present Lake Titicaca, high in the Andes of Bolivia. Another center was situated in a land mass in the North Atlantic, the postulated area we now call Atlantis. When the third satellite or moon
disrupted, this first Atlantean civilization was destroyed although
there remained in the North Atlantic a remnant of its civilization
on the last central portion.

About twelve thousand years ago Earth acquired a new satellite, our present moon, which caused another great catastrophe,
sinking the last remnant of Atlantis—the catastrophe recorded
by Plato. There now began the rise of a new civilization built

150

on the learnings and teachings of Atlantean refugees. Yet everywhere throughout the world isolated groups still perpetuated in gigantic monuments, like the Celtic menhirs and the Easter Island statues, the mythical memory of their ancient ancestors.

The Hoerbiger theory was enthusiastically endorsed by Hitler and adopted into the National Socialist activities of the Nazi Party, as enunciating the perpetual conflict between ice and fire throughout the universe—*Wel* (*Welteilehre*, the doctrine of eternal ice.) With Hitler's fall the Hoerbiger theory collapsed.

If it has no basis in astronomical fact, it does have many curious parallels to other theories and mythological beliefs. Hoerbiger postulates that ice ages are accompanied by catastrophes, as does Zapffe; that these are caused by the sudden advent of celestial bodies, as does Velikovsky; and that great world changes occur about every 6,000 years which roughly corresponds to the 5,200-year cycle of changes observed by the Mayas. Moreover, he postulates in his "ice and fire" premise that every 700 years there is an uprush of fire in mankind—an assimilation of fire into spiritual energy, which results in man becoming more religious, more conscious of his cosmic role. This 700-year period curiously corresponds to the aeonian lifetime of major cultures as we have previously discussed.

On the basis of Hoerbiger's theory, Bellamy and Allen in England later postulated three great civilizations separated by two world catastrophes.[2] The first civilization was that of Tiahuanaco, Bolivia which was destroyed 22,000 years ago. The second civilization was that of Atlantis. It was destroyed 11,500 years ago when another satellite, Luna, came within gravitational attraction of Earth and was captured as our moon. This drew great masses of water from the higher latitudes of Earth to the lower latitude of Atlantis, submerging it. The third great civilization is our own, which developed in Sumeria and Egypt about 7,000 years ago. Bellamy and Allen date the existence of Tiahuanaco by their readings of astronomical markings on its monolithic Great Idol and the celebrated Temple of the Sun.

And there is still another parallel. Professor and engineer Arthur Posnansky, by a lifetime of independent research, not knowing Hoerbiger's theory and far earlier than Bellamy and Allen, fixed the founding of Tiahuanaco thirty-five thousand years ago when the city, now high in the Andes, was a seaport; Lake Titicaca now being a suspended body of ocean water.[3] The present ruins represent Tiahuanaco's second period, dating from 15,000 B.C. Posnansky bases his calculation of the time on the change of obliquity of the ecliptic; i.e., comparison of the ecliptic marked on the Temple of the Sun and that of the present time, the temple having been a true solar observatory located on the astronomic meridian and a great stone calendar. Moreover, he believes that Tiahuanaco was the mythical Aztlán of Aztec mythology.

"The Americas," he writes, "were not populated through the arrival of a miserable contingent coming across the Bering Strait . . . as the learned and industrious men so assiduously allege. Mankind has the same length of residence in America that it has in Europe and Asia. Mankind emigrated to the Americas from the same point whence it emigrated to Europe and Asia . . . from the point where the two primordial races—Mongoloid and Middle Eastern—were engendered from one or more prehuman groups. . . . The fable concerning the immigration of American man through Bering Strait must be completely rejected. . . . Man came to America from the same place of origin whence he populated Europe, Asia, and Africa, and at precisely the same time."

All these theories are of course regarded as preposterous by archaeologists, who maintain that the ceremonial center of Tiahuanaco was built between A.D. 150 and 370—a revealing measure of the distance between these two modes of thought. Is there any meeting ground between them?

It is undeniable that there were two focuses of ancient civilization in the Western Hemisphere: Teotihuacan in Mesoamerica and Tiahuanaco in South America. Jorge E. Hardoy of Buenas Aires, Argentina, an authority on both modern and ancient city planning, asserts that Tiahuanaco was the first large, planned complex in South America.[4] He points out its marked similarity with Teotihuacan not only in its orientation to the cardinal points and the rectilinear direction of its composition, but many common architectural features. The main structure in its ceremonial center, a truncated pyramid, is similar (although smaller) to the Pyramid of the Moon in Teotihuacan; and the sunken courtyard on the main axis of the Kalasasya group, which contains the Gateway of the Sun, is similar to the Citadel at one end of the main axis, the Street of the Dead, of Teotihuacan. If it is difficult to believe there was any intercourse between these first two metropolises continents apart during the first centuries of the Christian era, it is still more difficult to believe that their marked similarity happened by mere chance. Could their basic plans and functions as religious centers both have stemmed from a common source long before their present archaeological dating, as Posnansky asserts?

Whether any of the tenets of all these theories are acceptable in their present form, they pose to modern science the great problem of cosmic catastrophes and historical cosmogeny. Collin refutes all such theories which regard the solar system as a vast machine liable to breakdowns which hurl its parts through space. According to him, if the solar system is a living macrocosmic body informed with life by its central sun, its planets cannot be violently displaced any more than the organs and glands of our microscopic human bodies. Order is inherent in them both, and their constantly reordered forms take place in the continuing mysterious process of all Creation. The theories of Velikovsky, Hoerbiger, Bellamy and Allen, however sound or implausible any of them may prove to be, reflect a growing belief that planetary rearrangements have occurred, perhaps not haphazardly but according to yet unknown cosmic laws. The theories differ widely on what may have happened and how, but agree that planetary disruptions did happen. When? By what time? World time? Cosmic time? Or psychological time? This seems to be the dimension lacking in all the present cosmological theories—the dimension embraced by myth which records the psychical changes in the soul of man.

II

Images and Symbols

1 THE MAYAN TWINS

THE MAYAN PARALLEL to the Nahuatl myths of Quetzalcoatl and the creation of the Fifth Sun is recorded in the *Popul Vuh*, the sacred book of the Quiché Mayas, the oldest book in America.[1] The story is long and involved, and it begins when the world was still in darkness, before the sun, moon, and stars had appeared.

It relates that there were two men, Hun-Hunahpú and Vucub-Hunahpú, who did nothing but play dice and ball all day long. The Lords of Xibalba in the underworld were disturbed. "What are they doing up on Earth? Who are they who are making the Earth shake, and making so much noise? Go and call them! Let them come here to play ball. Here we will overcome them!"

So Hun-Hunahpú and Vucub-Hunahpú descended to Xibalba by some very steep stairs. Here they were killed. The head of Hun-Hunahpú was cut off and placed in a calabash tree, where it immediately became a calabash or gourd.

To it came a maiden named Xquic, stretching up her hand to the miraculous fruit. Immediately it spat into her palm. "In my saliva and spittle I have given you my descendants," said the voice in the tree. "Now my head is nothing but a skull without flesh. So are the heads of all great princes. The flesh is all that gives them a handsome appearance, and when they die men fear their bones. So too is the nature of the sons, which are like saliva and

154

spittle. They do not lose their substance when they go, but they bequeath it to the daughters and sons whom they beget. I have done the same with you. Go up, then, to the surface of the Earth, that you may not die. Believe in my words that it will be so."

So the maiden, made pregnant by the spittle, returned to Earth and gave birth to two sons, Hunahpú and Xbalanqué. Grown into youths, they discovered the rubber ball used by their fathers and resolved to go down into the underworld and avenge their deaths. It was still darkness, before the sun, moon, and stars had appeared. But there was a certan being, Vucub-Caquix, who claimed to be the sun, the moon, and the stars for all mankind because he was vain and wanted to exalt himself and to dominate the earth. He had two sons: Zipacná, a giant who carried mountains on his back, and Cabracán, "a double giant" who symbolized the power of great earthquakes. Descending into the underworld, the twin brothers were subjected to trials in the House of Gloom, the House of Knives, the House of Cold, the House of Jaguars, and the House of Fire, defeating the Lords of Xibalba in all games of ball. But in the House of Bats the Lords cut off the head of Hunahpú and hung it in the ballcourt.

Coming at the call of Xbalanqué, all the animals arrived, and the turtle assumed the head of Hunahpú. Then Xbalanqué directed the rabbit what to do when he played the next game of ball. So when the ball bounced over the ballcourt and went toward an oak grove, the rabbit hopped after it, followed by all the lords. This gave Xbalanqué time to take possession of the real head of Hunahpú, who was restored to life.

Now the wicked lords, determining to kill them both, built a great fire in order to burn them. The two boys embraced and willingly jumped into the flames and died together. The Lords of Xibalba promptly ground up their bones and cast them into the river. Whereupon Hunahpú and Xbalanqué were restored to life, appearing five days later in the guise of fishermen to dance, to perform miracles, and finally to kill the wicked Lords.

Their grandmother up on the earth was filled with joy when she saw them. She called them the Center of the House, *Nicah* the Center, and Green Reeds because they had resprouted.

The two boys honored their fathers whom they had avenged,

saying, "You shall be the first to arise, and you shall be the first to be worshipped by the sons of the noblemen, by the civilized vassals. Your names shall not be lost. So it shall be!"

And "instantly they were lifted into the sky. One was given the sun, the other the moon. Then the arch of heaven and the face of the earth were lighted. And they dwelt in heaven." Then four hundred youths previously killed by the giant Zipacná also ascended and were changed into the stars in the sky.

This Mayan myth lacks the direct spiritual theme of the myth of Quetzalcoatl, but it is a close parallel to the Nahuatl myth of the creation of the Fifth Sun. Hunahpú and Xbalanqué descend into the underworld, overcome the pride, vanity, and power of the wicked lords, cast themselves into the fire, are regenerated, and finally transformed into the sun and moon as were Nana-huatzin and Tecuzistecatl.

J. Eric S. Thompson, the Maya scholar, reminds us that the *Popul Vuh* was first reduced to writing in Latin script from Quiché oral traditions in the middle of the sixteenth century; and thus probably reflects a degeneration due to Spanish influence in identifying one of the twins with the moon. He could not have been transformed into the moon because the Mayas regarded the moon as a woman, the wife of the sun. Also they considered the sun and Venus as brothers. Hence Thompson believes the two Maya twins were the sun and Venus. As Hunahpú was the Quiché equivalent of the day 1 Ahau, the day sacred to Venus, and a name for the Venus god in Yucatan, it was he who was transformed into Venus. Hunahpú thus was the ancient Maya equivalent of Quetzalcoatl.[2]

Both the Nahuatl *Borgia Codex* and the Mayan *Dresden Codex* associate gods with the five appearances of Venus as the Morning Star in the eight-year period; and of the five shown in the *Dresden,* three are Nahuatl in origin, one being Quetzalcoatl. It seems clear there was a close similarity between the concepts of Venus in both areas.

The sacred twins or hero brothers of Mayan myth, Hunahpú and Xbalanqué, have many parallels in Pueblo and Navajo myths. Among the Navajos they are known as Nayenezganí, Monster Slayer, the elder brother who was bold and active, and Tobadzhistshini, Child Born of Water, the younger, weak and shy. They were born from the union of the Sun Father and Changing Woman, the Earth Mother. When grown they journeyed to the House of the Sun. Here their father gave them his wisdom and the power to destroy the great monsters killing the people who had just emerged to the First World.

In the Zuni myth Uanam Achi Piahkoa—the Beloved Twain, the Twin Brothers of Light, the Elder and the Younger, the Right and the Left—were born shortly after the Sun Father impregnated a Foam Cap on the great waters, near the Earth Mother. To them, Uanam Ehkona and Uanam Yaluna, the Sun Father imparted his knowledge-wisdom. The Twin Brothers then descended to the Mountain of Generation in the First Underworld and led all created beings up into the Second Cave-World.

These are beautiful myths, tales of high adventure, recounted in solemn ceremonials. All have the same basic symbolism. They take place at the beginning of Creation. The twins are born from the primal union of sun and earth. Like the antipolar Nahuatl gods Quetzalcoatl and Tezcatlipoca, they are primeval images representing the dual forces that created the world itself—positive and negative, left and right, light and darkness, good and evil. These archetypes assure us that human duality was implanted in man from the beginning; and from the Nahuatl conception of Ometéotl it may be ventured that the supreme Creator embodied in himself the bipolar opposites. Later we shall understand that all his manifestations, the destructive cataclysms of nature as well as the psychic transformations within man, reveal the necessary interplay of both these forces.

The Hopi myth of the creation of the sacred twins, also by spittle, is the closest literal parallel to the Mayan myth.[3] It happened just after creation of Tokpela, the First World, when *Kókyangwúti*, Spider Woman, was directed to produce the first beings.

So Spider Woman took some earth, mixed with it some *túchvala*, saliva or spittle from her mouth, and molded it into two beings. Then she covered them with a cape made of white substance which was the creative wisdom itself, and sang the Creation Song over them. When she uncovered them, the two beings, twin brothers, sat up. The one on the right was named Pöqanghoya and was di-

rected to go all around the world and put his hands upon the earth
so that it would become fully solidified. The twin on the left was
named Palöngawhoya, and his duty was to go about all the world,
sending out sound. When this was heard he would also be known
as "Echo," for all sound echoes the Creator.

Traveling throughout the earth, Pöqanghoya solidified the
higher reaches into great mountains. The lower reaches he made
firm but still pliable enough to be worked by those later beings
who would call it their mother. Palöngawhoya sounded out his
call as he was bidden, all the vibratory centers resounding to it.
Thus he made the world an instrument of sound, and sound an
instrument for resounding praise to the Creator of all. When they
had accomplished their duties, Pöganghoya was sent to the north
pole of the world axis and Palöngawhoya to the south pole, where
they were jointly commanded to keep the world properly rotating.

After her creation of the sacred twins, Spider Woman gathered earth of four colors, yellow, red, white, and black; mixed
with them *túchvala,* or spittle from her mouth; molded them; covered them with her white-substance cape of creative wisdom; and
sang over them the Creation Song. Thus were the first four human
male beings created. Then she created four *wúti,* female partners,
for them. This too is similar to the *Popul Vuh* version of the creation of the first four human beings from different colored ears
of corn.

The *Popul Vuh's* accounts of the game of ball attests its antiquity. The Game of Ball, *Juego de Pelota,* the *Tlachtli,* seems to
have been played throughout Mesoamerica. In almost every ruin
is found a ball court. The one at Chichén Itzá is perhaps the largest and best restored. It is in the shape of a rectangle 272 feet long
and 200 feet wide, flanked on each side by high stone walls, with
a temple or stand at each end and platforms for spectators. The
acoustics are remarkable; a person speaking in a normal voice
from one end can be heard at the other. In the center of each
flanking wall is imbedded a large stone ring, the *tlachemalácatl.*
The game was simple and dangerous. The opposing members of
each team played a hard rubber ball back and forth, the object
being to knock it through the stone ring. The use of their hands
was not permitted. They could strike the ball only with their

elbows, knees, and hips and over these they wore protective
covers. Death was the reward of the loser. This is dramatically
shown in a low relief sculpture on the lower side of one wall.
Players of both teams are facing each other, separated by a disc in
which is carved the head of death. The first player on the losing
team has one knee on the ground and his head has been cut off.
Opposite him is standing one of the winning players, holding in
one hand a large stone knife and in the other the decapitated head.
From the neck of the headless loser a stream of blood is spurting
in the form of serpents, while the central stream becomes the stem
of a plant bearing fruit and flowers. Surely this scene portrays the
symbolism embodied in the Game of Ball.

Its meaning is astronomical, according to Seler: the sudden
changes in the moon that alternately loses and wins in the game.
"It loses when it begins to approach the morning, the Sun, and
then dead, it ends up by becoming the new moon; it wins when
it appears in the western sky changed into a young god, when it
recovers a form which gets rounder and rounder until it at last
shines in all the splendor of the new moon."[4] There is justification
for this interpretation in the *Borgia* where there are depicted
structures resembling ball courts, notably in paintings 35 to 40;
and figures which he identifies as Quetzalcoatl and Yohualtecuhtli
wearing protective hide on their hips and putting out their but-
tocks to catch and bounce the ball.

How far back among the Nahuas the game stems is problematic.
Ball courts have been found in the ruins of major cultures like
the Zapotecs of Monte Alban, the Totonacs of El Tajin, and the
Toltecs of Tula. Those of both Monte Alban and Xochicalco show
unmistakable Mayan influences, and the one at Xochicalco is almost identical with the largest at Tula.

The notable exception is the great ruin of Teotihuacan where
no vestige of a ball court has been found. This is strange. Can we
account for it by the fact that this birthplace of Mesoamerica's
greatest civilization was almost wholly concerned, not with the
moon, but with Venus' identity with Quetzalcoatl, whose mythical
meaning did not require a structural and astronomical illustra-
tion? But how then do we account for the depiction of ball courts
in the *Borgia Codex* which so superbly and pictorially recounts the

Quetzalcoatl myth? Perhaps because the *Borgia* paintings may have been made far later by artists in the Mixteca-Puebla region, based on the religious beliefs of Teotihuacan.

2 THE PYRAMID

If there is another structure of Mesoamerican civilization that most stimulates the imagination it is the pyramid. In only one other place in the world can one see its perfect, unique, and mysterious shape. What does it mean, and why does it appear only here and in Egypt, hemispheres apart?

The Great Pyramids of Egypt have mystified the world for centuries. Their construction, purpose, and significance have been explored by hundreds of scholars. Schools of pyramidology, cults of superstition, and esotericism have been founded upon them.

Egyptologists believe that the first, the Step Pyramid at Saqqara, was built in the Third Dynasty, about 2600 B.C., as a gigantic tomb for King Zoser. Kings before him had been buried in flat-topped mud buildings called *mastabas*. Imhotep, King Zoser's architect, built a square *mastaba* of stone, and on top of it built five more, creating the step pyramid and the first great stone structure in the world.

King Sneferu for his own tomb later commanded erection of the first true, straight-sided pyramid. His son King Khufu, known in Greek as Cheops, then built at Gizeh what we call today the Great Pyramid. Numerous other pyramids were built by following kings up to the end of the Sixth Dynasty in 2181 B.C. The general conclusion is that the pyramids were built as monumental tombs to satisfy the megalomania of their pharaohs.

William Mullen presents another purpose for the erection of the Great Pyramid of Cheops.[1] Basing it on his reading of the Pyramid Texts of the Old Kingdom, he posits that the unification of Upper and Lower Egypt under the first human king, Menes, who is identified with King Narmer, and the first wide-scale attempt at cultivation, occurred soon after the Deluge. The date for this has not been established but Mullen believes it may have occurred sometime between 3400 and 3200 B.C. which roughly corresponds to the beginning of the First Dynasty about 3200 B.C. Hence the Great Pyramid was built as a symbol of the first mound to rise out of the watery abyss: a symbol of the body of Atum, the omnipotent Egyptian god, "the One who has been completed by absorbing others," the One who re-absorbs all created being into himself whenever he destroys the world. Mullen's interpretation of the king's tomb as an extension of his spiritual body thus presents a metaphysical basis for Egyptian mythology.

The third belief, once held by ancient Arab historians and still held by some contemporary Egyptologists, esoteric schools, and parapsychologists, is that the Great Pyramid was built as a precise scientific record by an unknown people before the Egyptians, far more advanced than we now believe existed, in order to preserve their knowledge for posterity. These are generally identified with immigrants from Atlantis who constructed the Great Pyramid about 10,000 B.C.

Tompkins in his massive study of the history of its measurements, establishes dozens of astounding facts.[2] Standing on a base covering 13 acres, the pyramid rises 485 feet to its missing capstone. Its height is equated with the distance between the center of the earth and its pole, from which the distance to the sun can be accurately computed. The length of its base in the units of measurement employed by its builders is exactly 365.24 which is equivalent to the length of the solar year. The perimeter of its base represents the circumference of the earth at the equator. And this divided by twice its height equals *pi,* or 3.1416, the ratio of the circle to its diameter. The value of *pi* is also incorporated in the measurements of the King's Chamber, and in the sarcophagus. The perimeter measures a half-minute of longitude. The apothem—the slant height—represents one-tenth of a minute of latitude at the

29th parallel, the position of the pyramid. And the sum of the diagonals in the base equals the number of solar years in the great period of the precession of the equinoxes ... From all these figures it is obvious that the builders of the pyramid knew the size and shape of the earth to a surprisingly accurate degree.

Designed on the basis of a hermetic geometry, the Great Pyramid incorporates scientific knowledge attributed to the Greeks a thousand years later. Academic historians assert the value of *pi* was not known until 1700 B.C.; and Pythagoras' theorems of geometry, attributed to the fifth century B.C., seem to have been derived from knowledge he obtained while studying with the priesthood in Egypt. The Great Pyramid has been proved to be a geodetic marker; a theodolite, or surveying instrument; an almanac by means of which the length of the year could be measured as accurately as with a modern telescope; and a celestial observatory from which maps and tables of the stellar hemisphere could be accurately drawn.

Livio Catullo Stecchini, a specialist in the history of measurement who has contributed to Tompkins' study, concludes that the pyramid is an exact scale model of the Northern Hemisphere projected on four triangular surfaces, the apex representing the pole and the perimeter the equator. Both he and Tompkins agree that it is a highly developed scientific instrument incorporating the basic formulae of the universe, designed to help man orient himself in the cosmos and to apply finite measurements to time and space.

Was the emblem of the pyramid adopted for the seal of the United States because it represented the structure of the world? What dictated its choice? Certainly it is validated by the pyramids of Mesoamerica. They are as unique here in the western hemisphere as they are in the eastern hemisphere.

Pyramid-building in Egypt apparently ceased about 2200 B.C. and began in Mesoamerica some two thousand years later. How comparable are their structures?

The Great Pyramid of Giza stood on a base of thirteen acres. The Great Pyramid of Cholua in Mexico is less than half its height, but its base covers forty-five acres and by cubic content it is the largest in the world. There is a tradition about it, according to the

Codex of Cholua, that it was built shortly before the Deluge so men could climb up it to escape destruction. It too is a step pyramid composed of four superimposed truncated pyramids, and precisely oriented. Some of the oldest mural paintings in Mesoamerica are those found on the walls of its innermost pyramid. An outstanding motif is that of a mythological insect. Can this be compared with the insect painted on the mask of the Mastop Kachina who appears during the contemporary Hopi ceremonial of *Soyal,* symbolizing the appearance of man on Earth after the Deluge? Mastop, according to tradition, had come a long, long way. His black helmet mask suggests the interstellar space he has traveled, the three white stars on each side of his head representing the three stars in Orion's belt. His very name signifies, and the symbol for his mouth and nose represents, a gray fly or insect which brought to Earth the germ cells of mankind.

Most of the pyramids in Mesoamerica, like the first Step Pyramid in Egypt, are stepped pyramids; one step or structure being constructed on top of another. The great four-step Pyramid of the Sun at Teotihuacan, already described, has a base whose sides measure less than a yard shorter than those of the Cheops Pyramid, although its height is much less. It is also precisely oriented, being set approximately sixteen degrees east of the astronomical north-south axis so that it faces the exact position at that latitude where the sun sets on the day it reaches its zenith. The great metropolis of Teotihuacan itself was laid out following its orientation. A base line of nine degrees north of west was established at Copan, Honduras with a sundial to give sunset coincidences at solstices and equinoxes. The axis of the Pyramid of the Magicians at Uxmal varies but a few minutes from the Copan base line. In Uaxactun the relation of its three temples and two stelae permits the precise orientation of the sun's position at the solstices and equinoxes. The Pyramid of Xochicalco contains a vertical shaft down which the sun shines without casting a shadow on one day each year, virtually serving as a telescope.

The so-called Castillo, or Temple of Kukulcan, in Chichén Itzá is a nine-step pyramid seventy-five feet high with a stairway on each of its four sides leading to the temple on top. Each stairway has 91 steps, adding up to 364 which, with the upper platform, makes a total of 365, coinciding with the number of days in the year. The fifty-two panels on the nine steps can be equated to the fifty-two year cycle; and as the nine steps are divided by a stairway, there are eighteen sections on each side, equivalent to the eighteen months in the calendar.

With all their similarities to those of Egypt, the *teocallis*, or truncated pyramids, of Mesoamerica show differences. Bearing a temple on top, they seem to have been more popularly functional. For access to the temple, Mayan pyramids were provided with a stairway up one side; Nahuatl pyramids with two stairways to two temples, as the central Aztec pyramid in Tenochtitlan. Another notable difference for long seemed to be that while Egyptian pyramids supposedly contained the tombs of their pharaohs, Mesoamerican pyramids did not entomb their rulers. This assumption was badly shaken in 1952 when the Mexican archaeologist Alberto Ruz Lhuillier discovered a loose stone slab in the floor of the Temple of Inscriptions at Palenque. Raising it, and excavating tons of rubble, he followed a steep corbeled stairway down through the interior of the pyramid to a crypt eighty-two feet below the floor of the temple and six feet below the base of the pyramid. Outside were the remains of five sacrificed Mayas. The walls of the crypt, thirty feet long and twenty-three feet high, were covered with stucco human figures in high-relief. Covering the tomb inside was a five-ton slab. Inside lay the skeleton of the ruler, buried twelve hundred years before. It was bedecked with a treasure of jade—reputedly 978 pieces—including a mosaic mask placed over the face, ear spools, bracelets, necklaces, finger and toe rings, a jade in each hand, and another in the mouth, as was also customary in China. Two jade figures, one representing the Sun God, lay at the side.

Carved in the immense lid of the sarcophagus was the head of a serpent whose simulated body in the form of a tube extended up through the pyramid to the tail carved on a panel in the temple above. Was this, as previously mentioned, the path by which the spirit escaped the body? If so, the concept might be compared to that of the Egyptian metaphysical belief. As explained in detail by Mullen from the Pyramid Texts, the spirit of the king escapes the tomb, moving upward in space and backwards in time. Ascending to heaven first in the form of a bird, the soul reaches the pole star to which the pyramid is oriented. From there he wanders to other planets and stars. The gods of the four directions supply him with a raft, and then a ladder for him to ascend to the sun, the manifestation of Atum, the omnipotent One. Finally he is bade to stand on the mound rising out of the primeval waters where Atum stood when he created the world; and here he enters into a "state of quiescence indistinguishable from that in which all matter existed before creation," entering into the arms of the "One who has been completed by absorbing others."

This in essential is the Buddhist allegory of the drop of water finally absorbed into the cosmic ocean of all life. And it has a parallel in the Mesoamerican myth of Quetzalcoatl who also ascended out of fleshly matter into spirit, assuming the potencies of the planets and the four directions, and being finally united with the sun in his aspect of the Morning Star.

In the bedrock below the great Pyramid of the Sun at Teotihuacan Jorge Acosta discovered in 1971 a complex of seven caves: the four major ones arranged like a four-petalled flower, a lotus; two leading out from the stem; and the stem forming the seventh. The four-petalled pattern instantly recalls the archetypal structure of the universe as held by Hindu and Tibetan Buddhist metaphysics, the four "continents" of esoteric theology, and the mandala form of Navajo sandpaintings. The possible historical significance of this recent great discovery will be outlined in the following chapter.

The structural parallels of Mesoamerican pyramids to Egyptian pyramids have never been established. We only know they were erected with astronomical and mathematical precision according to a scale unknown to us, for they have never been accurately measured. Stecchini makes a revealing statement: "All the measures of length, volume, and weight of the ancient world, including those of China and India, constituted a rational and organic system, which can be reconstructed from a fundamental unit of length. I have not yet completed the gathering of data concerning the units of pre-Columbian America, because these are difficult to obtain, since the metrology of the American continent has received meager attention; but the figures that I have succeeded in establishing so far suggest that the American units agree with those of the Old World."[3]

If this astounding postulation is substantiated by accurate measurements of Mesoamerican pyramids, the results may establish their definite relationship to the pyramids of Egypt, or possibly indicate a common prototypal source.

3   THE SEVEN CAVES

As related in the *Popul Vuh*, the first four men, forefathers of
the Quiché Mayas, were created from corn and named Balam-
Quitzé, Balam-Acab, Mahacutah, and Iqui-Balam. Wives were
created for them, and from them sprang all the tribes, all the
people of the Quiché. This was in the East where they had their
beginning and multiplied, and from which they came.

The world was still dark when they went to Tulán-Zuivá (Cave
to Tulán), Vucub-Pec (Seven Caves), or Vucub-Ziván (Seven
Ravines). There they received help and guidance from their gods.
While they awaited the coming of dawn, they left Tulán-Zuivá,
taking turns watching the Great Star *Icoquih* (Venus), the herald
of the sun. This sign of the dawn they carried in their hearts when
they came from the East, and with the same hope they left there.

"It is not quite clear, however," continues the poetic text, "how
they crossed the sea; they crossed to this side as if there were
no sea; they crossed on stones, placed in a row over the sand. For
this reason they were called Stones in a Row, Sand Under the
Sea, names given to them when they [the tribes] crossed the
sea, the waters having parted when they passed."

Finally they arrived at their future homeland and there dawn
came to them. Great was their joy. They burned incense and
danced, turning their gaze toward the East whence they had come.
And being together, the light shone on all the tribes in the order
of the names of the gods of each of the tribes.

Shortly afterward, Balam-Quitzé, Balam-Acab, Mahucutah, and Iqui-Balam died, being the first men who came here from the other side of the sea, where the sun rises. Their sons when grown then crossed the sea to the East, whence had come their fathers, to receive the investiture of the kingdom. Lord Nacxit, King of the East, promptly gave them the insignia of the kingdom and all its distinctive symbols.

This Quiché origin myth is paralleled by that of the Cakchiquels, another powerful Mayan tribe, in the *Memorial Cakchiquel*.[1] A total of seven Mayan tribes arrived at Tulán-Zuivá, the Seven Caves: the Quichés, Cakchiquels, Rabinals, Zutuhils and others, with all their clans and houses. But significantly the Cakchiquels assert, "From the West (not from the East as claimed by the Quichés) we came to Tulán where we were engendered and given birth by our mothers and fathers." Moreover they assert there were four Tuláns, "one in the East, another in Xibalbay (the underworld), and another where God is," the fourth not being mentioned. Along with the geographical, this myth introduces a psychic factor as well.

From where could these tribes have come before they gathered at Tulán and dispersed?

Let us recall a few suppositions about the origin of the Mayas. Orthodox anthropology holds to the theory that the Mayas, like all the Indians of America, derived from the immigration of a homogeneous people from across Bering Strait who built up their civilization from scratch, without any later contacts from overseas. Gladwin, in pointing out physical characteristics of the Mayas found nowhere else in Mesoamerica, suggests they may have come directly by boat across the Pacific between 300 B.C. and A.D. 500. Velikovsky, in presenting his theory of two world catastrophes in 1568 and 1516 B.C., asserts that the Mayas migrated to Mexico during the intervening darkness—the darkness so dramatically recounted in the *Popul Vuh*. He does not venture to say from where they emigrated.

The origin myth of the Hopis of Arizona, so similar to that of the Mayas, recounts how they came to this present Fourth World on reed rafts paddled from one "stepping stone," or island, to another as they crossed the sea.[2] In one of their nine great cere-

monies in the annual cycle, the Flute Ceremony, this Emergence
is still dramatically enacted today. In a muddy spring the Gray
Flute leader straddles a small reed raft which he paddles around
with a blue wooden paddle, while the Blue Flute people standing
around the pool sing how the rising water destroyed the Third
World, the escaping people paddling on reed rafts from one stepping stone to the next, finally landing on the shore of this new
Fourth World. At the conclusion of this ritual there is a long procession to the village. Two Flute Maidens carrying rods on which
are strung small reed rings, deftly toss the rings upon cornmeal
cloud-terrace symbols drawn on the ground in front of them. The
small reed rings, *pangwöla* (water shell or ring), symbolize both
the reed rafts and the stepping stones at which the people stopped
as they crossed the great water. Finally, at the village a full
ceremony of song, dance, and recital affirms the arrival of the
Hopis to this new Fourth World. It then recounts that upon their
arrival the Hopis first lived in seven *puesivi,* or caves. Migrating
northward they established seven successive villages named after
these seven original caves or womb-caverns. These are specifically
named and located, the third being near present Mexico City.
What sea the Hopis crossed is unknown.

According to the *Popul Vuh,* the Quichés crossed on stepping
stones placed in a row over the sand, the waters having parted
when they passed. According to the *Memorial Cakchiquel* this
tribe had been given a red staff which they thrust into the sands
under the surface of the sea, whereupon the waters parted, pro-
viding a pathway.

Now according to Recinos, Spanish translator of the *Popul Vuh,*
this crossing of the sea, ostensibly the Gulf of Campeche between
Mexico and Yucatan, took place *after* the Mayan tribes left Tulán-
Zuivá, which he identifies as Tula. The exodus was composed
of the Quiché, Cakchiquel, and other tribes accompanied by adherents of the deposed priest-ruler of Tula, Topiltzin Quetzalcoatl.
The combined groups of Tula Toltecs and Maya tribes journeyed
overland to the east coast where they were joined at Champotón
by the Itza Mayas. Recinos calculates that the exodus from Tulán
or Tula began in the seventh century A.D. and concluded with the
beginning of the Quiché dynasty in 1054. But even he doubts

whether Yucatan and Guatemala were uninhabited by Mayas before the eleventh century. Surely, he writes, there must exist a former tradition of their origin.

The bear in this tangled chokecherry patch is the Itza Maya tribe. Historically, its origin and history are uncertain. Interpreting the *Books of Chilam Balam,* Willard reports that the Itzas first occupied Cozumel Island.[3] Moving into the mainland of Yucatan, they occupied Chichén Itzá sometime between A.D. 456 and 534. The original name of the city was Uucyabnal, and it had been a center of pilgrimage for hundreds of years before the Itzas arrived. The Itzas abandoned the city in 633 to migrate to Champoton, returning in 987. The date agrees with that of Recinos, who states that the Itzas joined the Toltecs of Tula at Champoton on the Gulf of Campeche and moved into northern Yucatan to reoccupy Chichén Itzá in the Katun 4 Ahau period 968-987, establishing the religion of Quetzalcoatl under his Mayan name of Kukulcan (*kukul* "feathered", and *can* "serpent").

Thompson believes that the Putun or Chontal Mayas on the Mexican gulf coast were the sea traders of Mesoamerica, controlling all sea routes around the peninsula of Yucatan. A branch of them, the Itzas, established a beachhead on the island of Cozumel. They then invaded the mainland from the east coast and seized Chichén Itzá in 918 during a Katun 8 Ahau period. A second invasion from the west coast, comprised of Tula-Toltecs under Quetzalcoatl-Kukulcan, followed in the Katun 4 Ahau period 967-987.[4]

The Maya archaeologist Coe, on the contrary, believes this reoccupation is confused with the later occupation of Chichén Itzá by the Itzas in the next Katun 4 Ahau period 1224-1244, after the city had been abandoned by the Toltecs of Tula.[5] During this time Yucatan was filled with Tula Toltecs, Xius, and other tribes, all seemingly despising the Itzas as "those who spoke our language brokenly."

Many devious methods were used to convert them to the new belief. The *Chilam Balam of Tizimin,* a history of the Xiu and Chel tribes written in 1593, reports the priestly exhortation: "These sacramental objects of yours, O Itza, these holy things of yours, derive from *ku u kul canele,* God the holy one of heaven." This,

as Makemson, the translator, points out, is a play on the name
Kukulcan, the priest evidently trying to ally the Itzas and Xius in
their worship by identifying Kukulcan with Hunab-ku, the one
supreme and incorporeal god. The identification may have seemed
natural as the Xius were believed to have come from Suiva or
Zuiva, corresponding to the Toltec Zuiven, the uppermost heaven
which was the abode of the Creator, the father of Quetzalcoatl;
the name *sui vah* meaning "everlasting life." Also the Xiu tribe
was known as the "people of Ix Toloch," a Maya-named Toltec
goddess, and regarded as descendants of the Tula Toltecs.

In 1263 the Itzas founded the nearby city of Mayapan, which
became the new capital of Yucatan. Then in the Katun 8 Ahau
period 1441-1461, Mayapan was utterly destroyed by a revolt and
the Itzas migrated to Lake Peten Itza in northern Guatemala. Here
in 1697 a small force of only 108 Spaniards dispelled the 5,000
Itzas who fled without giving battle because it was only 136 days
before the last Katun 8 Ahau period prophesied as the end of
Mayan rule.

All these varying accounts and contradictory dates revolve
about the time when the militaristic regime of the Toltecs of Tula
introduced the cult of Quetzalcoatl in Yucatan, and the unre-
solved time of Topiltzin Quetzalcoatl's reign in Tula—either
from 873 to 895 or from 1031 to 1063, a difference of three Calendar Rounds of 52 years each. We have previously related Chadwick's postulated accounting for this time difference: that there
were two ruling priests of Quetzalcoatl whom he equates with
two Mixtec rulers of Tilantongo.

The Itzas were the first to occupy the northeast tip of Yucatan.
They were known as Itzas because their deity was Itzamna, the
Serpent of the East, personification of the rising sun. Another
name for him was Kabul, the Skillful Hand, as he was able to
heal by the touch of his hand. He was said to be an incorporeal god
without shape or form. His symbol was a human torch bearing the
symbol resembling the Tau or Greek letter "T".

The *Madrid Codex* pictures him in a boat rowing away from a
Mayan glyph denoting the East. The *Perez Codex* shows him
seated in a celestial band, a serpent's body on which are pictured
the sun, moon, Venus, and other planets. Stone carvings depict

him with a long nose and toothless mouth or deformed teeth.

Itzamna first landed on the island of Cozumel. One of his leaders was Zac-mutul, said to mean "white man." His company then moved to the mainland of Yucatan, "the first ones who, after the flood, populated these provinces." On the shore, almost opposite the lower end of Cozumel, still lie the ruins of an ancient walled city now called Tulum, its modern name meaning "wall" or "fortification." Its original name was Zama. The earliest inscription is A.D. 564, but there may have been earlier settlements, for the Itzas founded Chichén Itzá a century before. Here for the first time, reports Hardoy, are found evidences of an urban layout with rectilinear streets bordered by temples and palaces. Once established, Itzamna distributed lands, gave names. According to Father Bernardo de Lizana's 1633 *History of Yucatan,* he was "a ruler of benevolent character, like Christ. He came from the East and founded the Itza civilization."[6]

Thompson has a great deal more to say about him. He translates "Itzam Na" as "Iguana House," meaning the universe within which is set our world, four Itzams or Iguanas forming the walls and roof, each with its own world direction and color. The god is often referred to in old records as Hunab Itzam Na, suggesting that he was not the son of Hunab-ku but identical with him, the all-powerful Creator. The T-symbol associated with him is the identifying element of the day Ik, representing wind, breath, life, and germination. As such, Itzamna controlled all aspects of life under many different aspects and names, all lesser gods like those of the sun and moon and the Chacs serving as his manifestations or servants, as shown by their heads set within his open jaws. Worship of him as the one great god, concludes Thompson, approached close to monotheism.[7]

Excepting the Itzas then, all the other seven Maya tribes wandering in darkness gathered at Tulán-Zuivá, the Seven Caves, to await the dawn before dispersing to their separate homelands.

So too does the origin myth of the Aztecs relate that they came from Chicomoztoc, which also means Seven Caves, in their homeland of Aztlán. Here, according to Clavigero, the seven tribes of the southward-migrating Chichimecas gathered for nine years before dividing. The location of Chicomoztoc has been postulated as being the site of the present ruins of La Quemada or Chalchihuites in Zacatecas north of Mexico City. The recent important discovery of seven caves in the bedrock below the great Pyramid of the Sun at Teotihuacan, already alluded to, prompts another interpretation. Doris Heyden of the National Institute of Anthropology and History of Mexico, in a paper presented in 1973 at the 38th Annual Meeting of the Society for American Archaeology, under the title "A Chicomoztoc in Teotihuacan? An Interpretation of the Cave Underneath the Pyramid of the Sun at Teotihuacan," suggests that these seven caves were the mythical Chicomoztoc. If so, the site was sacred before the pyramid was built over it, extending the founding of Teotihuacan back beyond 150 B.C. and establishing it as the original Tollan of the Nahuas and the Tulan of the Mayas, rather than the historical Tula founded in the ninth century A.D.

But there are other allusions to the mythical seven origin caves or tribal wombs.

The Yaquis of Sonora name seven legendary origin villages. The still primitive Tarahumaras of Chihuahua believe the maze of seven great *barrancas,* or canyons, now collectively known as the Barranca de Cobre, was their place of origin. The Zunis of New Mexico also had seven original villages which were strangely connected with a coincidental European myth. In fifteenth century Spain and Portugal there was current a belief that in A.D. 734, the year Spain was conquered by the infidel Moors, seven fleeing Christian bishops had sailed westward into the Sea of Darkness. In it they discovered an island on which each prelate founded a city that shone with golden radiance. It was this myth of Antilla, or *Septe Citate,* the Island of the Seven Cities, that in 1540, soon after the Spanish conquest of Mexico, prompted the expedition of Coronado to seek the golden Seven Cities of Cibola far to the north, only to find the adobe villages of the Zunis.

We have then the seven ancestral womb-caverns—caves, ravines, barrancas, villages, or golden cities—at which mankind converged in the darkness of the unconscious to await the dawn of consciousness before laying the foundations of their early civilizations. We can only conclude that they have a common psychological meaning, and that these early Mesoamericans used the world without as a mirror reflecting what was hidden within themselves. So we must seek the meaning of the Seven Caves in the universal and esoteric myths about it.

As I have suggested in a previous publication, these Seven Caves are allegories for the seven psycho-physical centers within man himself.[8] To these *chakras,* Tibetan and Hindu religious philosophy assigns names and functions as they ascend upward in order from the *muladhara chakra* at the base of the spine, which governs the primary physical forces of reproduction. Each *chakra* in turn becomes less gross and more spiritual in function, the last and highest at the crown of the head being regarded as the seat of universal consciousness. As in Hopi belief, it is the *kópavi,* the "open door" through which man receives his life and can communicate with his Creator. Through these successive psychophysical centers he makes his migratory journey from gross physical functioning to complete cosmic consciousness. It is the ascending path of *Kundalini,* the Serpent Power.[9] This is what is pictured in the *Perex Codex* as a celestial band in the shape of a serpent's body on which is pictured sun, moon, and planets. This is the esoteric interpretation of the Ah-canule as the People of the Serpent, the significance of the serpent throughout all Mesoamerica. Yet we all, all humanity, are following the serpent path of evolutionary comprehension from the gross to the divine. In this sense the great allegory, the universal myth of the Seven Caves, belongs to us all.

4 PEOPLE OF THE SUN

It is easy to condemn the Aztecs as barbarians who distorted the meaning of the Quetzalcoatl myth for their own totalitarian ends. But behind their warlike facade they too possessed a body of symbolic myth.

They believed their place of origin was Chicomoztoc, an island in the middle of a lake, the "Place of Herons," located in their mythical homeland of Aztlán. Wandering south, they were guided by their tribal god Huitzilopochtli. Miraculous events had accompanied his birth. His mother Coatlicue was a widow with four hundred sons and one daughter, Coyolxauhqui. While she was sweeping what was apparently an abandoned Toltec temple, a ball of feathers descended upon her which she tucked in her bosom. From this she became pregnant. Upon discovering this, her four hundred sons and daughter resolved to kill her. But just as they attacked her, Huitzilopochtli was born full grown and armed with the serpent of fire. He beheaded his sister with this and killed all his brothers.

Now, wandering on south, Huitzilopochtli, sometimes in the guise of a hummingbird, kept urging the people on until they should reach another island in another lake which would reveal the same magical properties of their original homeland. Renaming his Aztecas the Mexicas, he put a sign on their foreheads, gave them bows and arrows, and promised that they would become lords of the earth.

And so in time, on a marshy island in the Lake of the Moon, ritually known as Mextliapan, they saw the signs promised them: an eagle perched upon a cactus, holding a serpent in its beak. The trees and the water turned white. A fountain gushed forth two streams, one red and one blue. Here Huitzilopochtli gave commands to his people, as quoted by Caso: "The first thing to adorn thee shall be the order of the eagle, the order of the jaguar, the sacred war, arrow, and shield. . . . In like manner was I sent on this mission, and I was charged to bring arms, bow, arrows, and shield. My principal purpose in coming and my vocation is war. . . . Behold, Mexicans, here is to be your responsibility and your vocation, here you are to watch and wait, and from all four corners of the earth, you are to conquer, earn, and subdue for yourselves . . ."[1] So here they founded a scrubby settlement that later became resplendent Tenochtitlan on an island in Lake Tezcoco, capital of the Aztecs, lords of their earth.

The full meaning of the myth is not clear. Many commentators interpret it strictly in astronomical terms. Coatlicue was the Earth Mother of all life, the sun, moon, and stars. After giving birth of Coyolxauhqui, the moon, and the stars who resented the miracle of light, Huitzilopochtli, the sun, sprang forth from her womb and vanquished them as the sun daily puts to flight the moon and the stars. Hence Huitzilopochtli was often called "Brother of the Four Hundred Southerners." From this, Caso derived his thesis that the Aztecs, identifying themselves with their god Huitzilopochtli, regarded themselves as "People of the Sun" with the divine mission of supplying it with nourishment—human hearts—for its constant battle over the forces of the night.

The phrase is similar to the "Children of the Sun" which Fray Diego Durán, a Dominican missionary in the sixteenth century, believed was applied to the Tula Toltecs. The four hundred stars or brothers whom Huitzilopochtli killed is paralleled in the Maya myth related in the *Popul Vuh*. It recounts, as we remember, that the four hundred youths killed by the giant Zipacna were changed into stars to be the companions of the two twins who were transformed into the sun and the moon: the "Four Hundred Southerners" who appeared in the southern sky.

Durán describes the image of Huitzilopochtli, "Hummingbird

from the Left" because he was left-handed, as seated on a blue
bench indicating his abode was in the heavens. Also painted blue
was his forehead and a band above his nose running from ear to
ear. "His headdress was shaped like the head of a hummingbird,
whose beak was of brilliant gold. In his left hand he carried a white
shield with five tufts of white feathers placed in the form of a
cross.... Extending from the handle were four arrows. These
were the insignia sent from heaven to the Mexicas, and it was
through these symbols that these valorous people won great vic-
tories in their ancient wars.... In his right hand the god held a
staff in the form of a snake, all blue and undulating. He was girdled, a shining gold banner set against his back. On his wrists he
wore golden bracelets. He was shod in blue sandals. Each of these
ornaments has its significance and connection with pagan beliefs."[2]

Durán also shows a variant color painting of the signs Huitzilopochtli promised the Aztecs on the site of Tenochtitlan. A great
eagle is perched on a nopal cactus on the island in Lake Texcoco,
devouring the tuna fruits red as human hearts. Above the eagle
appears the shield with its four arrows and tufts of white feathers.
The insignia on the shield shows four circles surrounding a fifth.

All these symbols, as indeed the whole myth, have given rise
to many other contradictory interpretations. It is possible that
the main pyramid in Tenochtitlan with its two temples, one blue
and white and one red and white, was built on the spot where the
fountain gushed forth its two streams of blue and red. Also that
the four arrows were later represented by the causeways leading
across the lake from Tenochtitlan to the mainland and to the
four corners of the earth which the Aztecs conquered as bidden.
The shield with its five tufts of feathers arranged in the form of a
cross and its insignia of four circles surrounding a fifth, is the
quincunx, emblematic of the Fifth Sun. And the Order of the
Eagles and the Order of the Jaguars were formed, as Huitzilopochtli commanded, as the prime military organizations to prose-
cute the Blossoming War for sacrificial victims. Nicholson suggests that the Order of the Eagles may have signified the day
sun, and the Order of the Jaguars or Tigers the night sun during
its journey underground.[3]

Mme. Laurette Séjourné, the archaeologist who has made major excavations at Teotihuacan, interprets the iconography on a deeper level. Her perceptive writings have not been well received in academic circles. For one thing, she has been a vociferous champion of the Quetzalcoatl myth and proponent of the belief that Teotihuacan was the original Tollan, not Tula as is now officially accepted. For another, she has been accused of basing her conclusions upon psychological and psychical grounds rather than upon currently acceptable archaeological and anthropological facts. In her studies she demonstrates that the quincunx is the most frequently occurring symbol throughout Mesoamerica.[4] It consists simply of four points placed about a center point. The points may be circles or petals, or they may be enclosed in a square or a circle:

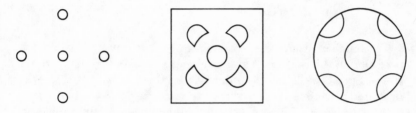

Or it may show the form of a cross:

The symbol appears on the shield of Huitzilopochtli, the Stone of the Sun or Aztec Calendar Stone, on the headdress of the old Fire God, the image of Tlaloc, the cheeks of Coyolxauhqui, Huitzilopochtli's sister, and on the Aztec Sun Eagle. More importantly, it marks the facial structure of the image of the deity of the planet Venus.

Hence its myriad meanings: the four quadrants of the universe, the four primordial elements, and the four worlds or suns, with the Fifth Sun as their unifying center. As the Fifth Sun is the Sun of Movement, the hieroglyph for movement, already pictured, is a variation of this in the shape of a cross, its two crossed lines forming four poles and uniting at the center. The synodical revolutions of Venus, as already discussed, occur in a series of five. So the number five is another symbol for Venus and for Quetzalcoatl. Sketched below are decorative forms of the hieroglyph for Venus:

Teotihuacan itself was astronomically laid out with geometric precision in the shape of a great quincunx oriented to the Pyramid of the Sun. Simple as the quincunx is, then, it is impacted with profound meaning. It symbolizes the four previous worlds or suns and the present Fifth Sun as their unifying center. But reconciliation of the bi-polar opposites during this era must take place within the human heart. So the quincunx also symbolizes Quetzalcoatl who by penitence and self-sacrifice made a final ascent out of matter into spirit, and was transformed into Venus. The quincunx, in short, is a mandala, and thus evokes a psychic effect from all its impacted meanings.

Sahagún characterizes Huitzilopochtli as "only a common man ... a sorcerer, an omen of evil; a madman, a deceiver, a creator of war, a war-lord, an instigator of war".[5] These also appear to be the attributes of Tezcatlipoca. This raises the question of how Huitzilopochtli usurped these qualities from Tezcatlipoca and was enthroned instead as the Aztecs' supreme god of war. But we must recall that the four sons of the divine Creator were the Red Tezcatlipoca, or Xipe, assigned to the East, the Black Tezcatlipoca of the North, the White Tezcatlipoca or Quetzalcoatl of the West, and the Blue Tezcatlipoca of the South. From Huitzilopochtli's blue colors—of his temple on the main pyramid in Tenochtitlan, the bench his image sits on, his face markings, his sandals, and his blue serpent staff—we know that to the Aztecs he was synonymous with the Blue Tezcatlipoca.

One other point. The jaguar was the ancient symbol of the earth as the eagle was of heaven, so we may suspect that the two military orders named for them symbolized the meeting of earth and sky through their conduct of the Blossoming War. Yet the jaguar does not appear with the eagle and the serpent among the symbols at the founding of Tenochtitlan. One wonders why Huitzilopochtli named the jaguar as one of the two orders that he commanded to be formed. But the jaguar was the *nahual,* the animal form of the spiritual guardian of Tezcatlipoca, and this too indicates the close connection between Huitzilopochtli and Tezcatlipoca.

The formation and meaning of the two Orders of the Eagle and the Jaguar lead still farther into an involved symbolism beginning when the Aztecs arrived at the Lake of the Moon—at the white seminal lake of life, the deep pool of the unconscious where all is one, undifferentiated. In this ethereal white purity they see the eagle, the Sun, holding Time, the serpent, in its beak. It is perched on a nopal cactus whose tuna fruits are blood-red and shaped like human hearts. The human heart, "the precious eagle-cactus fruit" of sacrificed captives lifted to the Sun, the soaring eagle. The human heart, the synthesizing center of the Fifth Sun. The flower that "buds and blossoms" in the "war of flowers" or the "blossoming war," the external Aztec representation of the internal war in the human heart to reconcile the two opposites. Nicholson compares it with the "Heavenly Heart" of the ancient and esoteric Chinese "Book of Life," *The Secret of the Golden Flower,* of the T'ang dynasty. "Here is the place whence Heaven and Earth derive their being," it states. "When students understand how to grasp the primordial spirit, they overcome the polar opposites of Light and Darkness. . . . All belonging to the dark principle is entirely destroyed, and the body born into pure light. When the conscious spirit has been transformed into the primordial spirit, then only can one say that it has attained an unending capacity for transformation . . . and has been brought to the present golden spirit."[6]

And so the arriving Aztecs also see a fountain gushing forth two streams, one red and one blue, symbolizing the re-uniting of the two opposites streaming from the one primordial unity. This gives rise to the hieroglyph *atl-tlachinolli* (*atl*–water and *tlachinolli*–burned) which shows two streams uniting, one of water and one of fire. Here are two variations:

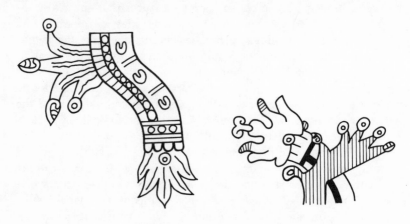

Seler in his commentary on the *Borgia Codex* points out that the gods of fire are the representatives of the *atl-tlachinolli*, that is, they are the gods of war. Following his lead, most commentators agree that the hieroglyph "burning water" is the symbol for the Blossoming War during which Aztec warriors captured prisoners for sacrifice.[7]

But it may be noted that Quetzalcoatl appears with the god of fire in the *tonalámatl* as representative of the *atl-tlachinolli*, symbol of war—a war which in his case was not a temporal one. We are also reminded by the *Borgia Codex* of the dualities of fire and water as expressed in the figure of Xolotl, Quetzalcoatl's twin. For Xolotl, being the fire that falls from the sky, is born from water just as lightning comes from the clouds, and hence is closely associated with Tlaloc, god of rain. Quetzalcoatl partakes of both these elements, as shown in the *Borgia Codex* where Xolotl and Nanahuatzin are being cooked in a bowl and Quetzalcoatl is transformed into both in order to be resurrected.

All this indicates the Aztec belief that the human heart blossomed only when it was torn out by priests and offered to the sun. Or in Séjourné's interpretation, when the internal war in the human heart was resolved by reconciliation of the two opposite forces symbolized by water and fire, for only then could the body "bud and flower" from fleshly matter into spirit as man finally freed himself from duality.

The gruesome Aztec ceremony of flaying captives taken in war was held at a spring ceremony in the month of Tlacaxipeuliztli and was sanctified by the god Xipe-Totec, Our Lord the Flayed One. Sahagún describes the gladitorial sacrifice in detail.[8] Each captive taken in battle was escorted to the sacrificial stone, "round like a grindstone," to which he was tied with a rope around his waist. He was then given a wooden sword or war club edged with feathers instead of obsidian blades, and four pine cudgels, with which to defend himself. One at a time four Knights Eagles and Jaguars armed with battle weapons engaged him in combat. A few captives lost consciousness or threw themselves upon the stone without taking up their arms, and were sacrified at once. Others were brave and stout enough to wear out their four adversaries. Then would come a fifth, left-handed, who was able to vanquish him and throw him flat upon the stone. Quickly the priest, in the guise of Totec, tore out the victim's heart and offered his blood to the sun. "Thus he giveth the sun to drink." The skin of the victim was then flayed and the body cut up, various parts being distributed to friends to be eaten. The head was cut off and dressed in the skins of the sacrificed; the people danced "the dance with severed heads."

On one level, considering the spring planting time of the ceremony, the dancers who wore the flayed skins may be viewed as symbolizing the renewal of vegetation, and the skins were used to forecast a wet or dry year, agricultural work being so directed. According to Durán, the bloody ceremony was instituted in the reign of Moctezuma the Elder. If so, it may indicate how the Aztecs distorted its original meaning for their own ends. Another deeper level of interpretation is suggested. For the left-handed warrior who finally vanquished the captive represented Huitzilopochtli, "Hummingbird from the Left," who was also left-handed, his name and headdress denoting the hummingbird, symbol of resurrection. The flaying of the captive's skin thus symbolized the shedding of man's earthly clothing and freeing his spirit from his mortal body.

Sahagún enumerates the "gifts" which Xipe-Totec, the god who sanctified the ceremony, dealt out to the people: "blisters, sores, smallpox, opthalmia, maladies causing watery eyes, infected eyelashes, lice about the eyes, fogging of the eyes, filling of the eyes with flesh, withering of the eyes, cataracts, glazing of the eyes. . . . Men thus sickened would thereupon vow to him, saying thereupon we would keep on, having donned it, his skin, on the celebration of the Feast of the Flaying of Men. . . . All wrapped in skins [of men], [blood-] stained, dripping [blood], gleaming [with blood], so that they terrified those whom they followed. . . . imitating and pretending to be warriors unafraid of death . . ."[9] The ills of mortal flesh, especially the diseases of mortal eyes preventing the sight of man's immortality—this was the earthly clothing that must be flayed to free the spirit for its ascent to the sun.

Details of the ceremony seem to bear out this interpretation. The Aztec warrior who had captured a prisoner in the Blossoming War did not kill him, but offered him as a tribute to the priests at home. The down of birds was applied to his head; he was given flowers, tobacco, rich cloaks. Hair was taken from the crown of his head at midnight. This was called "the sending upward of the eagle man" because he was recognized as an "eagle man." The captive usually went to his death with fortitude, "strong of heart and shouting, not without courage nor stumbling, but honoring and praising his city." For he knew that his heart, the "precious eagle-cactus fruit," would be lifted to the sun, the soaring eagle, and placed in the stone "eagle vessel." He knew that he would not go to the Land of the Dead, but into the presence of the sun.

Bringing him to the offering stone, his captor offered him wine. The captive raised the wine four times as an offering, then drank it from a long hollow gourd. After he was killed and flayed, his captor could not eat of his flesh. "Shall I, then, eat of my own flesh?" For when he had captured the prisoner he had said, "He is as my beloved son." And the captive had said, "He is as my beloved father."

The myth surrounding Huitzilopochtli cannot be isolated and separated from the myth surrounding Quetzalcoatl any more than

the Sun and Venus can be viewed apart in their common journey
overhead and underground. Too many of their elements fuse, if
only in a maze of apparent contradictions. There are many attributes common to both gods and the same mystery concerning their
birth. A variant of the myth relates that Quetzalcoatl was born
of Coatlicue, another that Huitzilopochtli was sired by the sun and
born of Coatlicue. As Huitzilopochtli was the sun, this would make
Coatlicue both the wife of the sun and the mother of the sun. It is
easy to accept Séjourné's conviction that the Aztec myth originated long after the Toltec-Teotihuacan myth, but not her corol-
lary that the Quetzalcoatl myth was so distorted by the Aztecs as
to be completely devoid of spiritual meaning. For the two myths
with all their contradictions seem to blend into a harmonic whole
with dual halves. Coatlicue, the cosmic earth-mother, mysteriously
gives birth to a son. As conceived by the Aztecs, he is Huitzilopochtli who assumes the sun's power and strength in putting to
flight the moon and stars and vanquishing darkness, and is himself the sun. To the Toltecs he assumed as Quetzalcoatl the mercy
and gentleness of a son who through penitence and self-sacrifice
reascended to union with the divine father as the Morning Star.
Both conceptions are complementary, representing the opposite
poles of the cosmic duality ever present to the Nahuatl mind.
Spirit must descend into matter in order to imbue it with life, and
matter must in turn be transmuted back into spirit to complete
the cosmic cycle in accordance with the one great law symbolized
by the hieroglyph *ollin*, "movement."

The colossal Aztec statue of Coatlicue fuses in one image the
dual functions of the earth which both creates and destroys. In
different aspects she represents Coatlicue, "Lady of the Skirt of
Serpents" or "Goddess of the Serpent Petticoat"; Cihuacoatl, "the
Serpent Woman"; Tlazolteotl, "Goddess of Filth"; and Tonantzin,
"Our Mother," who was later sanctified by the Catholic Church
as the Virgin of Guadalupe, the dark-faced Madonna, *la Virgen
Morena, la Virgen Guadalupana*, the patroness and protectoress of
New Spain; and who is still the patroness of all Indian Mexico. In
the statue her head is severed from her body, and from the neck
flow two streams of blood in the shape of two serpents. She wears
a skirt of serpents girdled by another serpent as a belt. On her

breast hangs a necklace of human hearts and hands bearing a human skull as a pendant. Her hands and feet are shaped like claws. From the bicephalous mass which takes the place of the head and which represents Omeyocan, the topmost heaven, to the World of the Dead extending below the feet, the statue embraces both life and death. Squat and massive, the monumental twelve-ton sculpture embodies pyramidal, cruciform, and human forms.

As the art critic Justino Fernández writes in his often quoted description, it represents not a being but an idea, "the embodiment of the cosmic-dynamic power which bestows life and which thrives on death in the struggle of opposites."

5 JAGUAR, EAGLE AND SERPENT

The Aztec orders of the Knights or Warriors Eagles and Jaguars suggest another set of symbols—animal, bird, and serpent.

Perhaps the oldest symbol in Mesoamerica for the earth and earth-bound matter is the jaguar, the Mexican *tigre*. As already mentioned it was the religious motif of the mysterious Olmec culture which reached its apex at La Venta. From there it spread into the Maya region, being represented in temple friezes and in the gorgeous red jaguar throne in the interior of the Castillo in Chichén Itzá. Among the Nahuas it became the god Tepeyollotl, Heart of the Mountain and one of the Lords of the Night, responsible for causing earthquakes. In the murals of Teotihuacan the jaguar is portrayed in many forms: jaguars and jaguar priests, jaguars sounding conch shells, jaguars with speech scrolls issuing from their mouths, and jaguars devouring human hearts.

But also in Nahuatl symbology emerges the feathered jaguar; one sculpture dated between the second and third centuries A.D. was found at the foot of the Pyramid of the Sun in Teotihuacan. What has happened is that the jaguar now has been linked with the symbol of heaven, the quetzal from the Maya highlands of Guatemala or the eagle from the central plateau of Mexico. Their combination in the winged jaguar thus represents the union of the two opposites, heaven and earth. At the same time the serpent, which is the symbol of the earth's energy, begins to sprout feathers. So the plumed serpent rather than the feathered jaguar finally emerges as the unifying symbol.

Nowhere is the relationship between these three prime symbols —the jaguar or tiger, the eagle or quetzal, and the serpent—more dramatically expressed than in the main temple of Malinalco.

The present village of Malinalco is one of the most primitive, remote, and difficult to reach in Mexico. In a car provided by the government's *turismo* agency, we climbed slowly up the Montes de Mixtongo. Tomás, the driver, was too accustomed to driving passengers over paved highways to see the tourist sights near the capital. Deathly afraid of the narrow dirt road, groaning and cursing at the deep ruts, protruding stones, sharp curves, and high centers, he crept along at ten miles an hour. At the crest of the mountains he refused to go farther. In a house there, he said, lived a man who owned a jeep. We would have to transfer into that. But the adobe was abandoned; there was no sign of a jeep. So from the pine-forested summit we snaked down the twisting road into the village far below. It lay in a subtropical valley almost hidden by profuse growths of bananas, mangos, grapefruit, papaya, tangerines, and coffee, and enclosed by high mountain walls with steep escarpments of volcanic tufa.

Almost at once Malinalco exploded into life. The day was December 12 and the fiesta of Guadalupe was in progress. One might have thought the village was under bombardment. Great rockets burst overhead with sharp explosions, their smoke blue against the mountainsides, accompanied by the clatter of firecrackers. The lower, rock-paved street was strung with paper streamers. Beneath them children were dancing to the music of three fiddlers. They were followed by a great parade: a huge turtle and an alligator, each mounted by several passengers, a devil dressed in a red suit, a masqueraded skeleton, and old women in masks.

Viva Guadalupe, our Guadalupana!

Far up above, the ancient ruins of Malinalco lay in deathly stillness, the silence and mystery of prehistoric Mexico. From the village a narrow trail twisted up one of the enclosing mountains, the *Cerro de los Idolos,* to a cleared level which overlooks the tiny village and green valley below. Here stand the five temple ruins of ancient Malinalco.

The main temple is carved out of the solid rock of the mountain wall. The facade has the shape of a small pyramid whose stairway of thirteen steps supports in the center the remains of a carved anthropomorphic figure. On one side is the sculpture of a serpent's head upholding an Eagle Knight. On the other side is a *tlalpanhue-huetl* drum representing a jaguar and supporting a Jaguar Knight. The doorway itself presents the open jaws of a serpent, the tongue protruding like a mat to the platform.

The inner sanctuary is a great circular chamber like a Southwest kiva with a low seating ledge. In the center of this, carved out of the solid rock, is the skin of a jaguar, flanked on each side by the skin of an eagle. In the center of the floor lies the outspread skin of another eagle with a hole behind it, probably used as a receptacle for offerings. And on the walls on either side are six openings.

Adjoining this great temple lie other temples. The Temple of the Sun was oriented so that the sun passed through its front section to the higher back section. Here there remain two rectangular altars, with a hole like a *sipapu* before them; possibly an image of the sun was mounted on the wall behind them. It is believed that in this solar temple on the day "Four Movement" was celebrated the annual feast of the sun when one of the warriors was sacrificed. In the adjoining *Tzinacalli,* or "Temple of Incarceration," the bodies of the sacrificed Knights were supposedly cremated. It consists of a large rectangular chamber connected with a circular chamber, each provided with altars, and the latter with another *sipapu,* or hole in the floor. Mural paintings, now obliterated, showed the souls of the warriors standing on a sky-belt fashioned of jaguar and eagle skins. There are remains of other temples in the complex, and more unexcavated ruins on top of the mountain.

There are many references to Malinalco in Aztec codices and early Spanish writings indicating that the Matlatzincas were conquered by the Aztecs during the reign of Axayacatl. His successor ordered work to continue on these monolithic rock temples; work never completed as there is still a large structure left unfinished due to the Spanish conquest.

Interpretations of the great temple and its symbols vary greatly. The official guidebook of the Instituto Nacional de Antropologia e

Historia of Mexico quotes Gómara, an early Spanish historian, who described a temple within the great plaza of Tenochtitlan as "one dedicated to the Wind-god, called Quetzalcoatl; and because the wind circulates around the heavens, so they made the temple round; and its entrance was like the mouth of a serpent, and it was painted diabolically. The fangs and teeth were in relief and it staggered all those who entered, especially if they were Christians, who thought they were facing the doors of hell . . ." The guidebook asserts that Gómara was wrong in considering that the symbols represented the Wind God Ehecatl-Quetzalcoatl. Likewise it flatly denies that the similar round temple at Malinalco and its symbols have any relation to the myth or cult of the Wind God Quetzalcoatl, but definitely connect this great sanctuary with the military organizations of the Eagles and Jaguars "which might be likened to the European Military Orders."

Furthermore, the official guidebook refers to the great *tlalpanhuehuetl,* the drum of Malinalco, now in the museum at Toluca. Magnificently carved, its upper section shows an eagle with outstretched wings and the face of a human being emerging from its beak. On each side are representations of an eagle and a jaguar; and behind, the date *Nahui Ollin* (Four Movement). In the lower section are figures dancing. Around the center of the drum is a band of fire interwoven with a band of water, the *atl-tlachinolli,* "which in this case means that the eagles and tigers were singing a war-song. We also see this sign once again at the feet of the eagles and tigers implying that they were not only singing, but engaged in a war-dance."[1]

Despite this astounding interpretation, it seems more probable that this remote complex of rock-hewn sanctuaries was dedicated to initiation rites embodying the religious beliefs of the Quetzalcoatl doctrine even as late as the period of Aztec domination. The similarity of its circular chambers and the holes in the floor in front of the altars to the Pueblo underground kivas, or ceremonial chambers, and their *sipapus* representing the openings from the previous underworld is too striking to be ignored. It raises the question of how far north, as well as south, the Quetzalcoatl cult spread.

The great Serpent Mound in Ohio, the largest serpent effigy

in the world, attests the significance of the serpent throughout much of the United States. The plumed serpent was a primary symbol throughout Alabama, Georgia, and Oklahoma where it has been found on stone discs, shell gorgets, and pottery. In the San Francisco mountains of Baja, California has been discovered a plumed serpent rock-painting sixteen feet long, surrounded by black and red men and six deer. The black and red remind us of the two colored streams of water springing from the site where the Aztecs founded their capital, the same two streams of fire and water that form the *atl-tlachinolli* symbol. The association of the deer with the serpent also suggests the close association of the snake and antelope in the ceremonialism of the Hopis in Arizona.

The now famous Hopi Snake Dance in which priests dance with snakes in their mouths is the most dramatic ritual still emphasizing the serpent. The complete Snake-Antelope ceremonial embodying it is one of the most complex and esoteric of all the Hopi ceremonials.[2] It cannot be reported here in detail. In brief, two religious societies, two kivas, participate in it: the Snake and the Antelope. The bowels of the earth in which the snake makes it home are symbolically equated with the lowest of man's vibratory centers, which controls his generative organs. In Hindu mysticism this is the *muladhara chakra,* corresponding to the *sacral plexus* and *plexus pelvis* which stand for the realm of reproductive forces, within which the serpent-power, *kundalini,* lies coiled. The antelope, conversely, is associated with the highest center of man located at the crown of the head. Tibetan and Hindu mysticism also use the antelope to symbolize the highest psychical center, as shown by the horned antelope pictured on Buddhist temples. Hence the snake and the antelope symbolize the opposite polarities of man, the gross or physical and the psychic or spiritual. The fusing of these two is the hermetic theme of the Hopi ceremonial.

Ritual after ritual in the sixteen-day ceremony develops the theme. Throughout all of them the higher spiritual self takes precedence over the lower physical self. Every day the Snake chief dutifully presents himself at the Antelope kiva; during the races the Antelope Race comes first; and the Antelope Dance is given the day before the Snake Dance. There comes at midnight on the eleventh day, in the Antelope Kiva, the mystic marriage of the Snake Maiden and the Antelope Youth, symbolizing the union of man's two life-forces, the physical and the spiritual. And this is followed on the sixteenth day by the combined Snake-Antelope Dance, the consummation of the union which releases the rain which recharges all the psychic centers of the individual body and the stream of life in the earth itself.

As this ceremony is structured on the symbolism of the antelope and the snake, the previous ceremony features the eagle. The *Niman Kachina* or *Kachin-nima* means simply the "going home of the kachinas" to their spiritual realm after residing on earth for six months. It is a major ceremony of many rituals, culminating in the great, last dance of the kachinas before they depart. To accompany them, eagles are bloodlessly sacrificed by wrapping a blanket around their heads and snuffing out their lives. Each bird is laid down with its head to the west, and beside it are laid cornmeal and a prayer feather. When the body becomes cold, the first and most perfect feather is pulled out as an offering to the sun. Others are then plucked for future use. The body is then carried to the eagle burying ground where it is buried, head to the west, with cornmeal, *piki*, tobacco, and prayer feathers. Stones are piled over its head, and into them is stuck a stick symbolic of the ladder by which its spirit may ascend to its high realm with the departing kachinas.

This was the great proud bird who first welcomed mankind to this Fourth World. No bird flies higher; so to the Hopis the eagle is a symbol of height, of the spirit of the sun, of the spiritual principle. The frequent depiction of an eagle holding a victim in its beak—as the Aztec eagle holding a serpent on the site of Tenochtitlan—is symbolic of the sacrifice of lower beings, forces, and instincts to the higher spiritual powers.

There seems little doubt that the cult and the symbol of the Plumed Serpent spread northward from Mexico to the Southwest. Representations of the plumed serpent, known as *Awanyu* among the Tewa, appeared in now abandoned pueblos of Galisteo Basin, central New Mexico, as early as A.D. 1250. In Zuni, the largest pueblo in New Mexico, the "tufted serpent" holds prime importance in its ceremonialism. Ruth L. Bunzel whose basic studies of Zuni ceremonialism were published in the *Forty-Seventh An-*

nual Report of the Bureau of American Ethnology, 1929-1930, stated: "Nowhere in the New World, except in the ancient civilizations of Mexico and Yucatan, has ceremonialism been more highly developed. . . . It pervades all activities. . . . The Zunis may be called one of the most thoroughly religious peoples of the world."

They are also one of the most secretive about their religious ceremonialism, particularly the worship of the tufted or winged serpent Kolowisi. Fray Estevan de Perea, visiting the Zunis in 1629, reported seeing numerous rattlesnakes confined in wooden cages. He was told they were being kept so that their venom might be used for poisoning arrows, not that their main purpose was for use during rituals. Not until the nineteenth century did patient anthropologists begin to sound their symbolism and meaning.

One of the first was Mrs. Tilly E. Stevenson who in 1883 described a procession of an effigy of Kolowisi, the Plumed Serpent. It was made of hide, about twelve feet long and eighteen inches thick. The belly was painted white, the back black, covered with white stars. The neck rested on "a finely decorated kind of altar" carried by two attendants. The tail was held by a priest who constantly blew through a large shell. Passing through the village, the head of Kolowisi was thrust down into all the kivas and finally deposited in the Earth Kiva, *He-tka-pa-que,* between the heads of two other painted Kolowisi whose serpent bodies extended around the walls of the room. Here at sunrise were initiated young boys, signifying their entrance into the greater world of the spirit.

Small effigies with stylized turquoise rattles adorning them from head to tail are still kept in jars in most households where they are fed with sacred corn meal. So even today the Hopis of Arizona and the Zunis of New Mexico still perpetuate in dramatic ritual, dance, song, and symbolism the belief of the Nahuas and Mayas in the Plumed Serpent. It is the universal doctrine of the reconciliation of the opposite polarities (Jung), the transformation of fleshly matter into spirit (Buddhism), and the resurrection of man into god (Christianity).

6 THE GODS

Tlaloc, god of rain, seems to have been the most commonly worshipped deity throughout Mesoamerica for the reason that rain was so important. One of the two temples on top of the great pyramid in Tenochtitlan was dedicated to him. Sculptured heads of him alternate with those of Quetzalcoatl on the inner temple at the Ciudela in Teotihuacan. Among the Olmecs his image appears with the mask of the jaguar; among the Mayas he was known as Chac, among the Totonacs as Tajín, and among the Zapotecs and Mixtecs as Cojido. He was usually pictured, according to Sahagún, with his face painted black with liquid rubber; his mask, adds Caso, gives him the appearance of wearing eyeglasses and a mustache. His body was painted black to represent storm clouds, while his white heron-feathered headdress, *aztatzontli,* symbolized white clouds.

Durán describes his great image in the temple at Tenochtitlan.[1] The stone body was that of a man. His face was that of a horrendous serpent with huge fangs, bright and red as flaming fire, symbolizing the brilliance of the lightning cast from the heavens when he sent tempests and thunderbolts. His head was crowned with a panache of shining green feathers. From his neck hung a necklace of *chalchihuitl,* or green jade, with a gold pendant set with a round emerald. In his right hand he carried a purple thunderbolt "curved like lightning which falls from the clouds, wriggling like a snake toward the earth". In his left hand he held a leather bag filled with copal. "No other idol was more adorned or enriched with stones and splendid jewels than this."

His name was given to a high mountain bounded by Coatlichan and Coatepec on one side, and by Huexotzinco on the other, where storms of thunder, lightning, thunderbolts, hail, and rain were formed. It was called *Tlalocan,* Place of Tlaloc. Here on the twenty-ninth of April, when all the maize had sprouted, was placed the statue of Tlaloc, as described by Durán. To it came the great king Moctezuma, Nezahualpilzintli, king of Acolhuacan, the rulers of Xochimilco and Tlacopan, the lords of Tlaxcala and Huexotzinco, and all their princes and nobles.

One after another they presented to the image rich garments worked in feathers, and exquisitely fashioned necklaces, bracelets, wristbands, and earplugs. Then was brought an array of sumptuous food: turkeys, hens, and game, stews, breads, and chocolate, all in pottery never used before. Moctezuma fed the idol himself. Finally there was brought a child of six or seven years who was sacrificed by priests to the sound of trumpets, conch shells, and flutes. When the ceremony was over, the lords descended the mountain to the celebration and sanctification of the lakes, streams, springs, and cultivated fields below.

They then hastened back to the same feast of the waters in Tenochtitlan. A small artificial forest had been set up in the courtyard in front of the temple of Tlaloc. In the middle was set the most beautiful tree that could be found on the Hill of Colhuacan, the Cerro de la Estrella, Hill of the Star. After it had been felled, its branches were tied carefully and bound to the trunk so that not a branch nor a leaf would touch the ground. While it was being carried, it was not allowed to rest on the ground. Brought to the courtyard with songs and dancing, it was planted with four smaller trees around it in the form of a square. Twisted straw ropes were stretched between the four small trees and the large central tree. They resembled the cords which penitents used to chastize their flesh. "Nezahualcoyotl and his son Nezahualpilli took their names from these ropes," affirms Durán, "because Nezahualpilli means 'Penitent Lord' or 'Fasting Lord'. And I affirm that he took the name from these ropes because they were called *nezahualmecatl* which means 'cords of penance' ..."

The ceremonial planting of this tree has modern parallels. *Los Voladores,* the Flying Pole Dance, is still performed by the Huastecas of San Luis Potosí, the Otomis of Pahatlan, Hidalgo, and by the Totonacs who stage it before the ancient pyramid of El Tajín near Papantla, Veracruz. Before cutting the tree in the jungle, the Totonacs dance around it, asking its permission to cut it down. After the first few blows the tree is given a drink of *tepache* so it won't feel pain. Stripped of branches, the pole is carried home without letting it touch ground and it is sprinkled with brandy whenever a stop is made for rest. At home in the plaza a hole has been prepared for it, being fed with a live chicken, food, and brandy. The *palo volador* is then planted in the hole to the accompaniment of fireworks and the ringing of church bells. The spectacular "dance" is performed by four *voladores,* or fliers, who ascend to a small platform on top of the pole with a musician. While the musician plays his simple melody on flute and drum, the *voladores* tie to themselves the ends of four ropes wrapped around the pole. At the end of the music the four fliers fling themselves into space—four sacred birds, or *tocotines,* dressed as eagles dedicated to the sun, flying with the four winds to the four sacred directions. Traditionally each makes thirteen revolutions around the pole as the ropes unwind, their total number of flights symbolizing the calendar cycle of fifty-two years.

The Hopis in former times performed a somewhat similar ceremony known as *Sáqtiva,* the Ladder Dance, and still today the climbing of the pole is a feature of the San Geronimo fiesta in Taos Pueblo, New Mexico. A tall, straight pine in the mountains is selected. Prayers are said, and its permission is asked before it is cut down. Ceremonially stripped of branches and bark, it is then brought down to the pueblo and planted in the great plaza. On the day of fiesta, el Día de San Geronimo, a dozen weirdly painted clowns, the Chiffonetas, attempt to climb it. The pole is too large, too smooth, too high. So with tiny bows and arrows of straw they attempt to shoot down the fruits of harvest suspended from the top—a deer or sheep carcass, squash and corn, a bundle of groceries. Finally an accomplished climber shinnies up the pole, lets down the treasure to the shouts of the crowd below, the honking of automobile horns. He then balances on top of the pole, singing his eagle song of triumph...

To return to the ancient Aztec ceremony in Tenochtitlan. When the great tree or pole had been set in place with the four smaller ones and the penitential ropes, the high priests carried forth a little girl seven or eight years old dressed in blue to represent the great lake and other creeks and springs. She was put in a canoe and taken to a great whirlpool where the lake had its drain. There her throat was slit with a small spear, and her blood was allowed to flow into the water before her body was swallowed by the whirlpool. At the same time the great tree was thrust into the waters. And after them the sovereigns flung many riches of gold, silver, precious jewels, and feathers.

There were many myths and legends about Tlaloc. He was believed to reign over the Terrestrial Paradise, Land of Water and Mist, *Tlalocan*, for which the mountain was named. It is pictured in the well-known mural covering a wall in the excavated palace of Tepantitla in Teotihuacan. In the center rises a mountain from which gushes forth a stream that divides into two rivers flowing in opposite directions. Along their banks tiny human figures sing and dance, play ball and leapfrog, and chase butterflies. It is a scene of merriment and delight set in a paradise described as a land with a perpetual abundance of corn, squash, chile, beans, and flowers. Completely and unusually earthy and human, as contrasted with the weird scenes depicted in the *Borgia*, it may be interpreted from its analogy with the realm described by Tibetan Buddhism. Here, as there, the souls of the dead who warrant heavenly happiness are granted a brief sojourn before they are reborn on earth to resume the eternal round. Not having risen beyond the completely human state of fleshly desires, they are unfit for *Tlillan-Tlapallan*, Land of the Black and Red, or for the still higher realm of *Tonatiuhcan*, the House of the Sun, reserved for those who achieved full spiritual illumination, as did Quetzalcoatl.

There is some support for this comparison. Nicholson mentions a four-year sojourn of earthly souls in Tlalocan,[2] and Séjourné offers the hypothesis that the inhabitants of Tlalocan still enjoying earthy delights were the uninitiated who had died unredeemed.[3]

The appearance of the twin temples of Tlaloc and Huitzilopochtli on top of the great pyramid in Tenochtitlan indicates the close affinity of water and fire. If the pyramid were indeed erected on this ancient site where a fountain gushed forth two streams, one red and one blue, forming the basis for the hieroglyph *atl-tlach-inolli*, "burning water," the affinity between these two primary elements is further established by the respective colors of the two temples. Also we may recall from the myth of the creation of the four preceding suns that the third sun over which Tlaloc reigned was *Quiauitonatiuh*, Sun of the Rain of Fire, whereas the fourth sun, *Chalchiuhtlicue*, was ruled by the goddess of terrestrial water.

Dr. Thelma D. Sullivan asserts that Tlaloc may also have been an earth god, basing her belief on an etymological interpretation of his name. She points out that the name Tlaloc, "He Who is Made of Earth" or "He Who is the Embodiment of Earth," is related to the adjective *tlallo* which means "full of earth, covered with earth, made of earth." Its plural is *tlalloque* which also is the plural of Tlaloc and the name of his multiple extensions who sent down types of rain corresponding to the four directions or sectors of the universe. She concludes that he may have been first conceived either as an earth god or dual god of earth and water, and with his evolution into the rain god his abode was transferred from Tlalocan in the earth to the mountain tops. Her interpretation will no doubt stimulate more research into the essence and nature of this most important deity.[4]

With these Nahuatl deities representing the forces of earth, water, and fire, and all those we are already familiar with, there were countless others. One of the most important deities of vegetation was Chicomecóatl, "Seven Serpent," also called Chicomolotzin, "Seven Ears of Corn." Caso explains that calendar names having the numeral "7" signified seeds, "Seven Serpent" being the esoteric name of corn, and "Seven Eagle" that of the squash seed.[5] Corn, especially important, was deified as Centéotl—literally *centli*, "corn," and *téotl*, "god." The stages of development in an ear of corn were also represented by deities. Xilonen was the tender ear of green corn, represented by a young girl whose head was cut off to signify the ear of corn cut from the stalk. Ilamatecuhtli, "Lady of the Old Skirt," represented the matured ear covered by wrinkled shucks.

The Hopis also venerate corn as a sacred entity embodying both the male and female principles of Creation which are reflected in its stages of development. When the plant begins to grow, the leaf curves back to the ground like the arm of a child groping for its mother's breast. As the stalk grows upward the first tassel appears, which is male. Then appears an ear of corn, which is female. This stage of growth corresponds to the halfway span of a man's life. The female element, the ear, is now ready to be fertilized by the male element, the tassel. Then the silk appears and pollen is dropped on the "life line" to mature and season it to fullest expression. When finally the tassel begins to turn brown and bend downward, male and female have reached their old age and the end of their reproductive power.[6]

Someone, somewhere, has said there were 65 gods in the Aztec pantheon, although he might well have said 165. To the mass of common people it was enough to have gods of earth and sky, of all the elements, to worship. Only the *tlamatinime*—the wise men, priests and nobles trained in the *calmecac* school of religion—speculated endlessly on their interconnecting relationship, a possible synthesis of so many diverse manifestations of the one divine principle that created the gods themselves, the world, and man.

The gods of the Mayas are far less known than those of the Nahuas. There are many reasons for this. The Maya deities are generally impersonal; few of them are in completely human form, most of them blending human and animal features, particularly those of the serpent family. This is wholly in accord with the Maya preoccupation with time, as the serpent is a symbol of time. Hence the most important Maya gods are deifications of various time periods. If the Nahuatl gods had two dual aspects, benevolent and malevolent, so do the Maya gods. But also they had four aspects, each assigned to one of the four world directions and colors. As each of them was assigned a different name, the total number of Maya gods has been estimated to number 250. In fact, it has been so difficult to identify them that most of them have not been given names, being distinguished only as god A, B, C, D, etc. Nevertheless there are many parallels between Nahuatl and Mayan gods.

The supreme being, Hunab Ku, creator of the universe and ruler of the thirteen heavens and nine underworlds, is the parallel of

Ometéotl. Omnipotent and invisible, beyond human conception, he was not worshipped as an individual deity.

This divine principle had a son, like Quetzalcoatl, who assisted in the creation of the world, introduced corn, invented writing, and established the culture pattern. In the *Popul Vuh* he is given the name of Gucumatz, the Quiché translation of the "Feathered Serpent," Quetzalcoatl. But he seems to be identical with Itzam, the god of heaven, also claimed to be the son of Hunab Ku or identical with him.

Itzamná or Itzam Na is translated by Thompson as "Iguana House," meaning the universe wherein is set the world. Four celestial *itzams*—lizards, alligators, iguanas, or serpents—one assigned to each world direction and color, form the walls of the *na,* the house or the world. This is one of four scenes shown on pillars in the Temple of Inscriptions, Palenque.

There were four Bacabs, each with a separate name and all with the generic name of Balam, presiding over the four quarters of the world and the 260-day sacred calendar periods. Their Nahuatl equivalents are the four Tezcatlipocas. There were also four benevolent Chacs, or rain gods, which, taken together, are a parallel to Tlaloc.

Kinich Ahau, Ah Kinchil, or simply Kin (sun) is the sun god; Ixchel, Ix Ch'up, or Ix (moon) the moon goddess.

And now for the alphabet: God A is Ah Puch, god of death, often pictured with a dog, a moán bird, or an owl, who ruled over Mitnal, similar to the Nahuatl hell, Mictlan. He gives rise to the still prevalent Indian saying, "When the owl cries, an Indian dies." Another name for him is Cumhau, which ended series of time periods. God B is Kukulcan-Quetzalcoatl, pictured with a long nose and serpent fangs, who occupies the center of the four directional points or quincunx, like Quetzalcoatl. He never appears associated with death symbols, being the god of resurrection and rebirth. God K, with his long nose extended into an elephant trunk, may be another variant. God D, an old man with a toothless mouth, is remindful of the Nahuatl "old god" or god of fire. But as he wears a conch shell, symbol of birth or rebirth, and never appears with death symbols, he too may be associated with Hunab-ku or Kukulcan-Quetzalcoatl. God E is Yum Cax, the maize god, the most beautiful Maya god as represented in the stucco panels of Palenque and the mural paintings of Bonampak. He is the equivalent of Cinteotl. God F resembles Xipe, the Nahuatl god of flaying...⁷ And so through the alphabet, through 250 gods.

It seems likely from so many similarities and parallels that the Nahuatl and Mayan gods stemmed from one archetypal source; the difference being that the Nahaus emphasized the humanized personalities of the gods, while the Mayas were preoccupied with their manifestations as representing periods of time. As they rose from man's collective unconscious into consciousness, these primordial images representing divine universal forces took on the shape and color, the rainment and adornment of the different peoples.

Fundamentally they are duplicated today by the kachinas of the Hopis and Zunis; more than 250 have been identified. As their name denotes (*ka*—respect, and *china*—spirit), they are "respected spirits" of the mineral, plant, bird, animal, and human kingdoms; of mountains, clouds, stars, the elements, and color-directions; spirits of all the invisible forces of life. For "the universe is endowed with the same breath, rocks, trees, grass, earth, birds, all animals, men." This breath, as we know, is the breath of life. It is the immortal component which at death separates from the body, returns to the one cosmic lake of life, and then reactivates another material form to continue the evolutionary journey of the Road of Life. Hence the kachinas are the inner forms, the spiritual components of the outer physical forms, whose benign powers may be invoked so that man may be enabled to continue his journey.

So they appear here on earth as primordial images impersonated by men wearing strange anthropomorphic masks who have lost their personal identities, being imbued by the spirits they represent. How barbarically beautiful, how wonderful they are! To see these kachinas come dancing into the plaza, each masked and garbed differently, each uttering his own distinctive cry, suggests what it may have been like in Tenochtitlan when images of the Aztec gods appeared for the great ceremonies and sacrifices. The name kachina is also given to similar small figures of carved wood, like dolls, presented to children so they may become familiar with their masks and names. Old ones for so long have been collectors' items, and new ones are being made in such quantity to supply museums and the general public, that there now exists a virtual kachina cult far exceeding that among the Indians themselves. Their popularity is not surprising, for as archetypal images they appeal directly to our own unconscious. It seems strange that Mexican artists and entrepreneurs have not followed suit by promoting the sale of such replicas of Aztec gods to museums, schools, and student anthropologists.

Duplicating in essence the images of Nahuatl and Mayan gods and Pueblo kachinas are the images of the saints of the Christian calendar—the *retablos* painted on flat slabs of wood and the *bultos* carved in the round in Spanish Colonial times, and which in plaster-of-paris are still manufactured for churches and homes. These Santos too are innumerable, one for almost every day of the year. If their separate blessings are also invoked by individuals on their Saint's Day, they do not invalidate a common belief in a supreme power above them all.

7 THE SUN

If in our attempts to peel the Mexico mystique onion we seem to have reached its core of religious belief, it is only to find that all its expressive symbols and images, even of the gods themselves, are but symbols of one great abstract whole whose completeness is beyond comprehension. The sun, above all other symbols, embodies this mystery.

To the People of the Sun, as to other ancient peoples, the sun was a visible, astronomical fact—the one immutable fact of existence, the source of all life on earth. It journeyed overhead from east to west by day, dipped into darkness, and by night traveled underground west to east to rise triumphant again at dawn. The present Fifth Sun, as we have seen, symbolized the synthesizing center of the four preceding directional suns or worlds and the elements of earth, fire, air, and water. Hence to insure its life and movement, man must contribute to it his own life-energy. The epitome of this transference of man's energy to the sun was, of course, the bloody wholesale human sacrifices of the Aztecs.

This *participation mystique* in a milder form is still observed in Taos Pueblo, New Mexico where ceremonial races are held to give the sun energy for his daily journey. So on El Dia de Santa Cruz in the spring and on El Dia de San Geronimo in the fall, Indian men, youths and boys naked save for breechcloths, their bodies painted and eagle-down stuck in their hair, hurtle down the long track, expending their utmost strength to the sun. These

ceremonial races, with other *kiva* rituals, are done not only for the
Pueblos themselves, but for the whole world. Otherwise the sun
would no longer rise and make his daily journey across the sky.[1]

To understand better this Aztec and Pueblo conception, let us
view the role of the sun through our own eyes. To us also the
sun is the ultimate source of life. It alone, says Collin, gives out
matter in *electronic* state—light, heat, radiation—which travels at
the highest speed known, some 186,000 miles per second. All the
other planets in our solar system reflect this divine energy in a
molecular state. The speed of transmission of molecular matter
is that of sound, about one-fifth of a mile per second, or nearly
a million times more slowly than that of light. Our Earth, consist-
ing of matter in a *mineral* state, has little motion and is largely
inert. These three—sun, planets, Earth—combine to produce matter in a *cellular* state, or organic life, on the surface of Earth.[2]

They and their kinds of life, further asserts Collin, are separated
by their speeds of rotation. The speed of the sun is the. fastest; therefore it embodies the highest or divine state. The planet
Mercury, on the contrary, does not rotate at all with respect to
the sun; hence it has no organic life but only matter in a mineral
state. On Earth, those parts moving slowly—close to the poles
and within its interior—show only matter in mineral states;
whereas in the equatorial zones, where the rotational speed is
fastest, are found the richest forms of organic life. Throughout the
solar system, then, the planets are in different stages of development depending upon their speed or movement. All contain solar
or divine energy which is more or less locked up in their various
forms. Regeneration of living entities consists in unlocking this
energy, accompanied by an increase of movement. This process
of regeneration is against nature; the inertia of matter must
be overcome; and for this, movement or acceleration of speed is
necessary.

And this, as we have learned, is precisely the meaning of the
Sun of Movement which symbolically posits the transmission to
human matter of the movement to overcome inertia and to trans-
mute it into the spiritual energy of the sun. Quetzalcoatl illustrated the process by his penitence and self-sacrifice. Huitzilopochtli used an easy short-cut by the sacrifice of captives taken

in the Blossoming War.

Too little is known about the sun, that great radiant body ninety-three million miles away, more than a million times larger than the Earth, and millions of years old. The temperature of its surface is estimated to be 6,000 degrees Centigrade; that of its interior is said to be 20 million degrees Centigrade. Across its surface whirl great vortices called sunspots creating magnetic fields of their own. Occurring in cycles of eleven years, like pulsations of the sun, they affect all forms of life on Earth. Their origin is unknown. Rose-colored mountains or clouds resembling sheets of flame, called prominences, project against the chromosphere. The average prominence is 30,000 miles high, 125,000 miles long, with a volume 93 times that of the Earth; one extending outward to a distance of a million miles.[3]

The composition of the interior of the sun we don't know. All our observations are based on the radiations from its envelopes, significantly four in number: the photosphere, the gaseous crust; the chromosphere; the translucent corona; and the radiant zodiacal light. The corona is an extensive gaseous envelope surrounding the sun, visible only during a total eclipse when it appears with great splendor. Its form varies with the sunspot cycle. It may appear, says Collin, like a double pair of wings, the trace of the field of force created by the sun's rotation. As such it resembles a four-petaled flower, the Buddhist lotus, the Aztec quincunx whose center is the sun itself. The zodiacal light simply forms an outer aura which extends to the Earth.

It is now believed that the primary element of the sun is hydrogen which is converted into light by some process which has been likened to that in a hydrogen bomb. This transformation, says the nuclear physicist Hans Bethe, presents a change of matter into a state in which it can be transmitted at long distance. Where all this cosmic background material for hydrogen comes from, no one knows. Says the astrophysicist Fred Hoyle, "It does not come from anywhere. Material simply appears—it is created."

Adds Collin: "The matter of the Sun, or electronic matter, is beyond form and beyond time. It is even beyond the recurrence of form and the repetition of time. In relation to our world, it is immortal, eternal and omnipotent." So too, he continues, is the life and light energy it emanates. The total amount of light received from it is exactly the same at a distance of a million miles as at ten yards. "No fraction of the light of a single candle is lost even when it reaches the outskirts of the Solar System. . . . Moreover, this process of diffusion of light without loss goes on indefinitely. . . . Light is *undiminishable, eternal and omnipresent* . . . So that we are forced to the conclusion that light—actual sensible light—is indeed the direct vehicle of divinity: it is the consciousness of God."[4]

From these considerations we return to the metaphysical implications in the Aztec concept by a brief detour through the writings of William Blake, the 18th century English artist, poet, and mystic.[5] The atom he regards not as a small division of matter, but as the point of intersection between time and the timeless. Such points or centers he asserts, possess "an essence and perfect power which pervades through all partible natures." These centers may be compared to the center point of the quincunx, the Fifth Sun. According to Blake, matter is activated by a spiritual principle that has been imprisoned in it and must be released. Hence his theme of *The Opening of the Centers*. How it is to be opened in the human being, he portrays in *Jerusalem* when the heart of Albion, symbol of universal man, is torn out with a "knife of flint"—the obsidian knife by which Aztec priests tore out the hearts of human victims. His character of Jerusalem, Mother of the souls of men, is of course the Great Mother, the *anima* of Jung, and Coatlicue, the Earth Mother of the Aztecs, the mother of Huitzilopochtli. For Blake, as for the Aztecs, the serpent symbolizes matter; also immortality, as it could shed its skin and so renew its life. His character Los embodied the solar principle, and through the "tyger" or lion, the jaguar and Jaguar Knight of the Aztecs, man enters his new incarnation.

Light, life, or matter in electronic state, then, is transmitted from the sun, reflected by the planets to Earth in molecular state; and this, combined with the Earth's mineral state of matter, produces cellular matter or organic life on the surface of the Earth. But when the organic bodies incorporating this energy die, asserts Collin, their energy is reconverted into light and returns to the sun. This is the meaning behind the Aztecs' sacrifices of victims to the sun.

But how bloody, gruesome, and numerous these wholesale sacrifices were! One has only to read Sahagún's record of the ceremonies to realize the slaughter of victims that accompanied each one. Little wonder that Aztec life, strong and vital as it was, was permeated by a profound sadness. Its poetry, beautiful as any ever written, echoes this melancholy tone, carrying the theme of the transience of life, of all mortal endeavor. It also reflects the conviction that the Fifth Sun, as the four Suns preceding, must perish at the end of its cycle and be replaced by another. A Sixth Sun embraced in a space-time continuum which may be equated, as we shall see, with the coming sixth zodiacal age.

8 MAYAN GOD-POTS AND CROSSES

Many similarities and parallels between ancient Mesoamerican
and contemporary Pueblo rituals and beliefs have been given
throughout these pages to point out how obdurately these still
persist as far north as the American Southwest. I have neglected
to mention, however, how deeply they are rooted in the soil and
people of Mexico and Guatemala themselves. The omission will
not be missed, for the subject has been covered by hundreds of
documented studies. But it comes very much alive in the highlands stretching from Chiapas in southern Mexico down into
Guatemala. Here and in Yucatan live more than two million descendants of the ancient Mayas.

In these relatively remote, mist-covered mountains, life follows
the old pattern with few adaptations to encroaching progress.
Even the dress of the people trudging down the trails to market,
with variations to distinguish each village, reflects ancient styles
and designs. The men wearing a cape (*capixaiji*) or blanket (*pon-
chito*), and carrying a *bolsa,* or bag of woven cloth. The women in
a *huipil* (blouse), a skirt secured by a *faja* (belt), with a *tapado*
or *rebozo* and *cintas* of colored ribbons. The brilliant colors of the
textiles range from deep purple and violet through red and orange to yellow, all made with native dyes. The round hole in the
neck of the *huipil* represents the sun, with its rays of colored
stitches. Of the embroidery designs that of the Plumed Serpent
is most common, the *huipiles* of the Quetzaltenango region carry-

ing two rows of serpents banded above and below by rows of small birds. The double-headed eagle, so noticeable at Chichicastenango, is another duality symbol. Lilly de Jongh Osborne also distinguishes designs of many *nahuales*.[1] A variation of the Aztec *ollin*, symbol of movement, appears. The cross is common, and deserves study.

The cross is so prevalent among the Chamulas and Zinacantecos of Chiapas that many observers refer to their "Cult of the Cross." Chamula, about ten miles from the town of San Cristobal de Las Casas, is not properly a village, although it has a huge church. It is a *cabecera,* or ceremonial center, for the forty thousand or more Chamulas living in *parajes,* or remote hamlets, around it who come here for the observance of great religious ceremonies such as that of San Sebastion on January 20. Thousands massed in the plaza in front of the church, in a cup of the forested hills, with milky white clouds rising from the pines. All wearing the *traje tipica.* The men wearing white or black woolen ponchos, knee length, belted by a *cincho* around the waist, their hands tucked inside against the cold; heads wrapped in white scarfs like Oriental burnooses, their hats hanging down over their shoulders with streamers of colored ribbons. The women dressed similarly in black *rebozos*, most of them barefoot. A vast somber landscape of land and people in stark black and white.

The usual horseplay of all Mexican fiestas takes place in the great courtyard: bursts of rockets and fireworks, followed by a parade of dancing men bearing the *toro,* a wooden framework covered with canvas in the shape of a bull. But inside the massive church all is oppressively silent.

Outsiders are rarely permitted inside. Occasionally, after a formal interview with the *presidente* and *principales,* one is accompanied inside by the *presidente* to insure safe conduct. The emotional impact of the eerie scene is overpowering. Immense, long, and lofty, the room is bare of furniture and decoration save for two streamers of colored cloth suspended overhead and a dozen life-size Catholic saints propped against the two side walls. The floor is strewn with fresh pine needles. On it are squatting a hundred or more women with candles mounted on flat stones and with braziers of burning copal. Presumably they are praying to the saints along the walls, their lips almost imperceptibly moving, but giving forth no sound. From time to time small groups of men arrive from other remote *parajes,* led by a *jefe* carrying the immemorial cane of office, his men carrying handmade guitars and curious triangle-shaped harps. Finding a place to stand, the musicians begin plucking their strings in monotonous, muted tones. The music is a part of the silence, the candle-lit clouds of burning copal.

Through the dim light wreathed by spumes of the sweet-smelling incense the *presidente* gingerly leads us through the mass of huddled women to a wooden box up front. In it we dutifully stuff a five-peso note. This, with the *presidente's* sponsorship, validates our presence. The flag-bearers standing at the altar do not seem to notice our presence. The flags they bear are simply large squares of colored cloth attached to long pine poles. The *presidente* leaves us to stand in the swiftly filling church.

The fireworks and horseplay out in front have ceased. Not a sound enters the great closed doors. The immense dimly-lit room is packed with people and filled with silence, the heavy Indian silence, impregnated with the ancient perfume of burning copal. There is nothing here suggestive of the patina of Christianity. There is no formal worship. Only the mute and eerie observance of the archaic mystery, the mystery of life itself.

Little by little the church empties, the Chamulas massing in front of a row of high crosses beyond the courtyard. All are decorated with crude designs of trees and branches. What is there in this ancient symbol that holds silently entranced so many thousands of people?

Some fourteen miles away the same fiesta is being observed by a crowd of the eight thousand Zinacantecos from fifteen outlying *parajes,* or hamlets, in their *cabecera,* or ceremonial center, of Zinacantan. It lies in a great open meadow in front of a church. In contrast to somber black-and-white Chamula, Zinacantan is cheerful pink and white in the bright sunshine. The color tone is given by the dress of thousands of Zinacantecos, the men wearing *serapes* or *ponchos* of fine-woven wool with narrow pin-stripes of pink and white, from which protrude their white shirt sleeves. Around their necks they wear a scarf of delicate blue, hanging down in back with brilliant red tassels tied to the corners. The woman's dress is similar, but in form of a *manta* fastened in front.

The cheerful scene belies the Nahuatl name of Zinacantan, "House of the Bat," given it because of the great stone bat once worshipped here. Everywhere in the meadow are huge piles of tangerines, sugar cane, peanuts. People are sitting on the grass eating tortillas and bits of meat purchased from a stall off to one side, or idly strolling about. Under a shelter sit older men, the new office holders, San Sebastion being the first major fiesta they have celebrated. The previous year's officers have visited the church to pray forgiveness for their misconduct during their term of office. Their wives are not exempt from censure. And this gives rise to a great deal of buffoonery.

Two men, faces painted black and wearing hats and tails of jaguar fur, appear. They are the *Bolometic,* the Jaguars. Each carries stuffed squirrels with genitals painted red, which he pokes with a stick and throws at persons in the crowd. They are said to represent wives of the outgoing office holders, shameless, oversexed women who interfered with their husbands' performance of duty. Late in the afternoon they climb a bare red tree, the Jaguar Tree, *Bolom Te,* and throw their stuffed squirrels and food to the crowd. More groups of masked clowns file in from a hamlet a mile away, indulge in horseplay, and vanish in the swelling crowd. Despite the church and modern innovations, one sees in both Chamula and Zinacantan vestiges of the ancient Mayan past. One is reminded of the great Navajo Sings of years ago: the tiny cooking fires, the massed crowd encamped on the snowy plain, the same Indian silence and absorption into the same mysterious spiritual realm.

As at Chamula, there are wooden crosses everywhere throughout these highlands—at the foot and on the summit of sacred mountains, beside springs and waterholes, in caves, and in the patios of houses. A most imposing array stands near the remote and primitive hamlet of Romerillo, high in the mountains above Las Casas. Rising starkly on top of a deforested hill stands a row of twenty-one huge wooden crosses some twenty feet high, with tree branches planted between them. On the barren hillside below lies the Campo de Santo with innumerable burial mounds. Each is marked by a foot-high cross and a planted twig.

From the appearance of all these crosses everywhere, as the anthropologist Vogt observes, one has the impression this is one of the most solidly Catholic communities in the world. "But while these crosses may look like contemporary replicas of the classic Christian cross on which Christ was crucified in far off Jerusalem, they have no such meaning to the Zinacantecos. . . . The Zinacantecos are not Catholic peasants with a few Maya remnants left in the culture, but rather they are Maya tribesmen with a Spanish Catholic veneer—a veneer that appears to be increasingly thin as we work with the culture."[2]

Some observers assert that the four-pointed cross represents the Maya four-fold rain god Chac. Others that the cross decorated with designs of trees, branches, and flowers is the Tree of Life, represented for the ancient Mayas by the sacred ceiba tree which is rooted in earth and tips the heavens, its arms signifying the four directions. Vogt offers another interpretation. The hundreds of *Kalvarios* at mountains, springs, and caves where crosses are erected are the meeting places of ancestral gods. The crosses are "doorways" or channels of communication with these gods, opened by processions of men offering prayers to the crosses, decorating them with pine boughs and flowers, lighting candles, burning incense, and depositing offerings of rum and black chickens. The *krus*, then, is an avenue of communication between the "essence" or "inner soul" of man and the gods.

Underlying all these interpretations is a common meaning. From the earliest ages of man, the cross has been a universal symbol. If the extension of its four arms in opposite directions represents conflict and division, their point of intersection signifies reconciliation and unification. It is the meeting point of the conscious and unconscious, the mystic center identical with the creative principle of the universe. Immemorially it has been shown surrounded by a circle, as often has been the entire cross. Now to leave the circumference of the circle for the center, as Cirlot reminds us, is equivalent to moving from the exterior to the interior, from multiplicity to unity, from form to contemplation. And it is here on these crosses that the Chamulas and Zinacantecos carve circles and hang flowers. The cross then is a Tree of

Life, for life develops only from the conflict and reconciliation of the opposites; the "doorway" of communication between men and gods; and between our unconscious and conscious selves. It was to its mystic center that Quetzalcoatl journeyed. And so it is in these multitudinous, stark crosses in the Chiapas highlands we see reconciled ancient and contemporary Indian belief.

One can journey still farther back in time by visiting the Lacandones. A surviving remnant of the ancient Mayas, the Lacandones refused to submit to the conquering Spaniards and hid in the depths of the tropical rain forest to carry on the life of their forefathers. Today, numbering only a few hundreds, they live in two small settlements on the Mexican side of the great Usamacinta River: one on the shore of Lake Naja, the other on the banks of the Lacanhá River.

They are difficult to reach except by a chartered plane which sets down on a narrow runway in the midst of the towering *selva,* the dense rain forest. At the edge of the clearing is a camp periodically occupied by a few guests (like ourselves) of Trudy Blom, widow of Franz Blom, the archaeologist. The compound comprises five *chosas* with palm-thatched roofs but without walls, the large one serving as a kitchen and the smaller ones provided with posts and hooks from which we can sling our sleeping hammocks.

From here two Lacandones, Old Chank'in and K'in, paddle us in a huge dugout canoe hollowed out of a mahogany across Lake Naja. Across this incomparably clear and beautiful jewel in its green setting lies the northern Lacandon settlement, or *caribal,* of Naja. It consists of some twenty or more *chosas* scattered at random in a clearing interspersed with small corn *milpas,* clumps of banana and orange trees. Life is still primitive. The men raise corn, fish in the lake, and hunt *cojolites,* the crested guan, the pheasant *curassow,* and an occasional deer with bows and arrows. The long bow is made of *guayacán* wood, the string of *ixtle,* or agave, fibers, and the arrows are tipped with parrot feathers. The women grind corn on stone *metates* and boil it in huge pots, and weave cotton cloth for their garments on small back-strap, horizontal looms. Each man has several wives, each wife having a separate fire in their common *chosa.* Men and women alike wear only one garment, a loose, white, knee-length gown down which hangs their long, uncombed black hair. Walking barefoot in file through the dank, dark jungle they resemble nightwalkers in nightgowns or pale, noiseless ghosts.

The Lacandones are said to be the most primitive Indians in all Mexico, although the Tarahumaras in their isolate Chihuahua canyons seem far more wild, shy, and secretive. But certainly the Lacandones with their short powerful bodies, broad feet, and childlike faces always breaking out in smiles, are true creatures of nature. There is a simple dignity about them; they are not abashed by strangers and meet them on equal footing. Their greeting is simple: *"Utz im pusical"*—"My heart is good." And no man enters another's *chosa* unless he is invited.

Their religious observances are simple. There are no chiefs or priests. The head of each family is responsible for conducting rituals, praying, and teaching his sons. Their common "church" is the God-house, an open thatched-roof hut like all the others save that on a shelf under the roof stands a row of God-pots. They are incense pottery bowls striped red, white, and black, and shaped on the rim into crude faces. Each represents a god, and holds a small stone effigy of the god or a bit of jade from an ancient temple ruin. Rituals are conducted for the birth of a child, to insure one's safety on a journey, to ask for a long life, to aid an ill patient. Old Chank'in permitted us to watch him conduct a healing ceremony for one of his wives. Making little palm wands, he squatted down in front of a God-pot in which he burned copal. Chanting and praying in a low tone for a long time, he blackened the wands in the smoke of the sweet incense. Then he left the God-house to touch them to the body of his ill wife.

Every spring there is held a long renewal ceremony during which all the people of Naja gather at the God-house. New God-pots replace the old ones which are carried away and hidden in caves. Women prepare *posole*, a corn gruel, and balché, a drink made from the bark of the balché tree mixed with water and sugar cane, and fermented. Copal is lighted in the new God-pots which are given food and drink while the men in unison pray and chant that the fumes of the incense may carry the essence of their offerings to the real gods above.

Remnants of similar God-pots have been found in ancient Maya

ruins, possibly indicating that the great mass of common folk may
have observed the same simple rituals, leaving the priests and
nobles to carry out the intricate temple ceremonies. The dwindling
Lacandones have forgotten the great religious structure of their
ancestors, but they still believe in three heavens—Chembeku, Ka-
poch, and Hachakyum, and one underworld, Yaralum, whose lord,
Kisin, is evil. Trudy Blom reports the names of four of their many
gods: Hachakyum who made heaven and earth; Akínchob, his
son-in-law; Itzanoku; and K'ak, god of fire.

The birthplace of all the gods was said to be Palenque, the loveliest of all Mayan cities. Price reports that the Lacandones knew
of the ancient tomb deep in the heart of the stone pyramid of the
Temple of Inscriptions long before it was discovered by archaeologists.[3] They also venerate Bonampak, now famous for its gorgeously colored temple murals, not far from Lacanhá. But the
holiest of all was Yaxchilán. It was built as a new city for the gods
of Palenque by Ak'inchob, the corn god, upon instructions from
Hachakyum.

Here the gods met and manifested themselves. On the Acropolis was the temple or earthly home of Hachakyum, where was
carved a great stone statue of him. To this now ancient ruin the
Lacandones used to make frequent pilgrimages. Old Chank'in and
one of his sons walked there a few years ago with offerings of
copal.

Their trip through the jungle must have been long and arduous.
Even for us it poses some problems in transportation. One takes
a small plane over the *selva*, so dense that from above it looks
like a solid growth of moss often obscured by a sea of clouds. This
makes plane travel uncertain; a jungle pilot has to wait hours for
the mist to clear before take-off, and may have to turn back if he
cannot see to land on the narrow strip at Aqua Azul. The three
buildings there lie on the high bank of the great Usamacinta River
which marks the boundary between Guatemala and Chiapas,
Mexico. In years past Agua Azul was a *centrál* for mahogany lum-
bermen and *chicleros* who gathered sap from the *zapote chico,* or
sapodilla, for chicle or chewing gum. From here the massive mahogany logs were floated downriver to Tenosique where they were
tied into rafts and floated on down to the Gulf of Mexico for

shiploading.

From Agua Azul a long mahogany dugout with an outboard motor takes the few of us downriver. The two or three hour trip, aided by the current, is magnificent. The great Usamacinta is flanked on each side by an almost impenetrable wall of rain forest: giant mahogany trees growing to a height of 150 feet; ceibas with tall straight trunks leaved at the top like umbrellas; sapodillas; the balché whose bark is used with sugar cane, honey, and water to make the Lacandon drink of balché; the *chechén* exuding a poisonous sap from its leaves; rubber, bamboo, palms. Orchids are everywhere. Begonias grow waist high. It is a glimpse of a virgin world just after Creation.

Then at the site of Yaxchilán the river makes a wide U-bend, the land jutting out like a peninsula with twenty-foot-high banks up which the river rises during the rainy season. There is a sandy spit for the dugout to beach, and up above a clearing containing a compound of a half-dozen *chosas* roofed with thatchings of palms. Two families live here, the headman being caretaker of the ruin. In two empty *chosas* we ate by lamplight, hung our hammocks, and lay listening to the howler monkeys.

The jungle begins a dozen yards away; one dare not go far alone. The ruins begin at once, but to reach them two men have to cut a path through the dense growth. Yaxchilán was one of the most beautiful and important of all Maya cities, and its ruins long have been famous. The Spanish saw them in 1696, Maudsley and Charney in 1882, Maler in 1895, and many late archaeologists have studied them and then left them to be eaten up by the jungle. Why Yaxchilán has not been preserved and restored, in preference to far later Chichén Itzá for one, is a mystery. Maler's map of 1897 shows an Acropolis Grande, an Acropolis Pequeña, and rows of majestic temples in front and behind, a total of some forty structures. Today it is impossible to detect the architectural plan. The encroaching growth surrounding the structures is so dense that the caretakers have to cut it every two months to make them visible. Even so, huge trees and tree-size roots extend down through roofs, walls, and subterranean chambers, tearing apart the cut stones.

Yaxchilán's pyramid-temples are not high, but their upper facades and roof combs are decorated with figures carved in stone. The stone here is said to be harder than at Palenque whose panel frescoes are so marvelous, so Yaxchilán's sculpture is among the best; it is famous for its carved stone lintels. Lintel 8 records a Calendar Round date of 755 A.D. The huge stelae are magnificent. Most of them have fallen and are covered by moss. Others that have been studied have been turned face down to protect them from the weather.

So it remains today, one of the jewels of classic Maya civilization, long abandoned and neglected save for venturesome pirates who have snaked out a stelae for sale to private collectors.

What the purpose was of the Lacandon pilgrimages to this holy city of their ancient culture, this place of brooding mystery, we did not realize until we saw the headless statue of Hachakyum in front of the middle doorway of the great temple. It had the shape of a humanized feline figure in a posture of worship that instantly recalled that of the Olmec semi-humanized jaguar sculpture in the museum at Villahermosa. Many years ago mahogany cutters had broken off the head which lay on the ground below. Here the Lacandones burn innumerable little pyramids of copal and offer their prayers to the time when the head and body will be reunited. It will mark the destruction of this world and the beginning of a new era, with the rebirth of the old gods, and a final flowering of the ancient Maya culture.

According to the precisely calculated, astronomical-astrological prediction made by their ancient forefathers, we shall see that that time is not far off.

III
Time

1 THE SACRED CALENDAR

T HE CALENDAR SYSTEM IN USE THROUGHOUT MESOAMERICA is
one of the most phenomenal achievements in the world. It
integrated in one vast complex, highly-developed methe-
matical calculations, astronomy, astrology, myth, and religion.
Wherever and by whomever it was first devised, the Mayas are
believed to have perfected it by the first century B.C.

There were several interlocking calendars involved within the
system. Its core was a cycle of 260 days popularly called the
Sacred Calendar, the Mayan *tzolkin,* or "Count of Days," and the
Nahuatl *tonalámatl,* said to mean the "Book of the Good and Bad
Days" or "Book of Fate." As such it was a sacred and divinatory
almanac and not properly a calendar corresponding to any natural
time-count.

The 260-day cycle consisted of groups of twenty days, each
bearing a name or day-sign combined with a number progressing
from 1 to 13, as shown in the first two columns of Table 2.

Thus to the first day-sign *cipactli,* "crocodile" or "water serpent," was assigned the number 1 and so on down to the thirteenth
day-sign *acatl,* "reed," which bore the number 13. The fourteenth
day-sign *océlotl,* "jaguar," took the number 1 again.

This permutation system of a name and number series has been
likened to that of two enmeshed wheels, one with thirteen cogs
and the other with twenty. The smaller wheel made twenty revolutions while the larger wheel made thirteen, at which time the num-

TABLE 2

No.	Nahuatl Name	Sign	Direction	Deity
1	Cipactli	Crocodile	E	Tonacatecuhtli, god of procreation
2	Ehécatl	Wind	N	Quetzalcoatl as the wind god
3	Calli	House or Temple	W	Tepeyollotl, heart of the mountain
4	Quetzpalin	Lizard	S	Huehuecóyotl, god of dance
5	Cóatl	Snake	E	Chalchihuitlicue, water goddess
6	Miquiztli	Death	N	Teciztecatl, moon goddess
7	Mázatl	Deer	W	Tlaloc, god of rain
8	Tochtli	Rabbit	S	Mayáhuel, goddess of maguey
9	Atl	Water	E	Xiuhtecuhtli, god of fire
10	Itzcuintli	Dog	N	Mictlantecuhtli, god of death
11	Ozmatli	Monkey	W	Xochipilli, god of flowers
12	Malinalli	Grass	S	Patécatl, god of pulque
13	Acatl	Reed	E	Tezcatlipoca
1	Océlotl	Jaguar	N	Tlacoltéotl, earth goddess
2	Cuauhtli	Eagle	W	Tezcatlipoca-Xipe Tótec
3	Cozcaquauhtli	Vulture	S	Itzpapálotl, obsidian butterfly
4	Ollin	Movement	E	Xolotl-Nanahuatzin
5	Técpatl	Flint Knife	N	Chalchiuhtotolin
6	Quiáhuitl	Rain	W	Tonatiuh, the solar god
7	Xóchitl	Flower	S	Xochiquétzal, goddess of flowers

ber cog and name cog appeared again in combination. Hence a
day with the same name and number could reoccur only every
20x13 or 260 days, beginning a new cycle. And this was repeated
endlessly without regard for the movements of the sun and planets which marked natural time periods.

Still another movement is implied in the *tonalámatl* as shown
in the fourth column of Table 1. For just as the previous directional four worlds held successive dominance in rhythmical order,
the day-signs were assigned directions rhythmically alternating in
groups of four: east, north, west, and south.

Each of the days was governed by a deity, as shown in the
fifth column of the table, who influenced it for good or evil. The
Mayas regarded the days themselves as gods, the glyphs for the
day names being stylized portraits or pictures of the attributes of
these gods. The numbers 1 to 13 were also personalized as the
heads of the gods they represented.

There were lesser cycles whose presiding deities were known as
the thirteen Lords or Companions of the Day, and the nine Companions or Lords of the Night, conforming to the conceptual structure of thirteen heavens and nine underworlds. Thompson interprets them as cycles of thirteen and nine days, while Seler believes they represented the division of the day into thirteen hours
and the night into nine hours.

The Sacred Calendar cycle of 260 days thus served ancient Mesoamerica—as it still serves many Mayan tribes—primarily as a "Book of Fate" or divinatory almanac. One had only to consult an astrologer or priest as to what a day name and number portended for a newborn child, when a marriage should take place, when crops should be planted. Its use by rulers and priests was more significant.

When, where, and how the Sacred Calendar originated is not known. Seler in his Commentary on the *Borgia Codex* believed that the *tonalámatl* was constructed upon the relation of the five synodical revolutions of Venus to the eight revolutions of Earth. Five Venus periods were represented in the *Borgia Codex,* associated with the five regions of the world. The first of the five periods begins on *cipactli,* the first of the twenty day-signs of the *tonalámatl,* the beginnings of the following periods falling on the fifth sign *coátl,* the ninth *atl,* the thirteenth *ácatl,* and the seventeenth *ollin,* as shown in column 2 of Table 2. In other words, only five of the twenty day-signs fall on the initial days of the five periods of Venus. On this basis the first part of the *Borgia Codex* is a pictorial presentation of the *tonalámatl* divided into columns of five members.*

Another, contradictory explanation is that the number 260 represents the interval between the two days when the sun appears vertically overhead at its zenith along the approximate latitude of 15 degrees north: on August 12 during its apparent passage southward, and on April 30 when it is returning on its northward course. The geographer Vincent H. Malstrom brings out the fact that at only two prehistoric sites within a narrow band along the 15th parallel could this zenithal interval have been measured. One was the astronomical center of Copan, Honduras which Malstrom believes was founded to precisely calibrate this measurement. The other was the far older site of Izapa just over the western border of Guatemala in Mexico where Malstrom postulates the Sacred Calendar originated far back in the pre-Christian era. Later it was developed by the Mayas into their complex calendar system, and adopted throughout all Mesoamerica.[1]

*See Section I, Part Two, for fuller discussion of this

This general idea was first proposed in 1928 and supported in 1945. The objection to it was that the function of the Sacred Calendar as a 260-day zenithal time-count does not hold true for all the area above and below the 15th parallel. In the central valley of Mexico where the *tonalámatl* was so important to the Nahuas, the interval was about 291 days, and among the Otomis the interval was about 311 days.[2] The recent development of the theory by Malstrom suggests that while the concept of the calendar was diffused northward to Mexico, only the Mayas developed it into a precise system for reckoning time and predicting celestial events.

Aside from these contradictory, astronomical theories of its origin, a deeper meaning of the Mayan *tzolkin* or Nahuatl *tonalámatl* can be deduced if it is regarded as a symbolic religious compilation.

Let us imaginatively view its structure as a five-step pyramid from which can be read the symbolized story of Creation as recounted in myth. Its full significance can be divined only by a thorough analysis of each of its twenty signs of the days, yet a brief summary reveals the structure.

The first day-sign is appropriately that of *cipactli*, the crocodile or water-monster immersed in a world-pool of water, on whose back rested the world. Its direction is East, the direction of the rising sun which lighted the world. The presiding deity is Tonacatecuhtli, the god of procreation. We know this is the Fifth World, for Quetzalcoatl in his aspect of the god of wind then breathed life into it, as related in the myth and shown by the second sign of *ehécatl*, wind. The third sign, *calli*, "house," is shown in the shape of an ascending pyramid with a quincunx on top. More precisely it indicates a temple, signifying a spiritual impulse imparted to the world. Its presiding deity is the oldest in Mesoamerica, the jaguar, symbol of Tepeyollotl, god of caves, the "Heart of the Mountains" or "Heart of the World." It was symbolized in historical times by a great emerald as large as a thick pepper pod upon which was delicately engraved a small bird surrounded by a serpent, and known as the "Heart of the World." This rare jewel, "so transparent it shone from its interior with the brightness of a candle flame" (Seler) was found in a sanctuary located on a high mountain near Achiotlan, the sacred city of the

Mixtecs. It was discovered by Fray Benedict Fernandez, a Spanish missionary, who ground it into powder, reports Clavigero, even though other Spaniards offered him huge prices for it. The fourth sign, *cuetzpalin,* "lizard," has no zoological derivation, being painted with the colors of all the phases of earth and sky, day and night. Its deity is Huehuecóyotl, the Old Coyote, god of the instinctive and sexual forces, god of the dance of life. He thus represents the creation of all forms of life from the invisible forces of nature.

On the four steps of the first terrace of this pyramidal structure of the *tonalámatl,* then, the world has been created; human life forms appear from the instinctive forces of earth; the first spiritual impulse has been given them. But man is not born from earth alone; he is born of water. So in the second group of four day-signs appear signs and deities associated with water. There appears *coátl,* the serpent, whose deity is Chalchihuitlicue, the goddess of water. Then *mizquitli,* pictured as the head of death, whose governing deity is Teciztecatl, goddess of the moon which controls the tides of all waters. *Mázatl,* the deer, governed by Tlaloc, god of rain. And *tochtli,* the rabbit, which as we remember is pictured in the moon, and whose presiding deity is Máyahuel, the multibreasted goddess of maguey.

The first sign of the third group is *atl,* water itself. It is no paradox that its regent is Xiuhtecuhtli, god of fire. For here is introduced the union of fire and water expressed by the hieroglyph *atl-tlachinolli,* "burning water." Water is not pictured here in a flowing stream, but by a small vase containing water in bands of red and white transformed into the hieroglyph *chalchihuitl* for the precious water or blood of sacrifice and self-sacrifice. The following three signs bear out the theme. With the tenth sign, *itzcuintli,* the dog, appears a heart—not because a dog was considered to have a heart, but because of its valor the dog could be substituted for man as the victim of sacrifice. *Ozmatli,* the monkey, the eleventh sign, has as its deity the young god of flowers and procreation, Xochipilli. In the twelfth sign, *malinalli,* a bunch of grass, the monkey destined for sacrifice is dressed in this grass. With the thorns of the *malinalli* Aztec penitents punctured their bodies to let blood in self-sacrifice. The great rock-hewn temple of Malinalco, as we recall, was named for this grass which grew in its remote valley. So here in this third group of day-signs, the steps of the third terrace, emerges the concept of the division of opposites, fire and water, and the necessity of uniting them through penitence and sacrifice .

The fourth set comprises the familiar symbols and regents associated with the Blossoming War. The day-signs *océlotl* and *cuauhtli* signify the military orders of the Knights Jaguars and Eagles, the warriors destined to die in battle or on the stone of sacrifice. The *ácatl*, or reed, used for their arrow shafts. And the *cozcaquacuauhtli*, vulture, bird of death. The deities are familiar: Tezcatlipoca and the red Tezcatlipoca, representative of Xipe Tótec, Tlazoltéotl, and Itzapapálotl, the Obsidian Butterfly goddess representing the *cihuateteo* in the underworld.

From here we mount to the last and fifth terrace of the pyramidal structure, and to the conception of the Blossoming War as taking place internally within man rather than externally on the battlefield. The last four signs begin with *ollin,* movement, the significant hieroglyph symbolizing the conflict between the opposite polarities which results in movement, life. Its direction is East, its deity Xolotl-Nanahuatzin, burned in a bowl in the underworld. *Técpatl* is the flint knife of sacrifice, the deity Chalchiuhtotolin, the bird-shaped goddess associated with the *chalchíhuitl*, the blood of sacrifice. *Quiáhuitl*, rain, signifies not rain of water—as does the ninth day-sign *atl* in the third group—but rain of fire such as destroyed the Third World, and represents the fiery torments of self-sacrificing penitents. Its deity is of course Tonatiuh, the solar god of the Fifth World. The twentieth and last day-sign is *xóchitl*, flower. The deity is Xochiquétzal, goddess of flowers. As the "House of Flowers" is the human heart, we understand that *xóchitl* here symbolizes the budding blossom of the human spirit at last freed from duality.

The *tonalámatl* may thus be seen as a four-sided pyramidal structure of twenty day-signs arranged in five terraces of four steps each, symbolically showing the process of creation—the birth of spirit in matter, death to the world of forms, and the ascent of the spirit to a higher plane as was exemplified by Quetzalcoatl.[3]

Many other allegorical aspects of the *tonalámatl* will be found when its full significance is thoroughly explored. For its inex-

haustible meanings, one can compare with it only the three thousand-year old Chinese *I Ching, or Book of Changes* whose origin
goes back to mythical antiquity.[4] Like the *tonalámatl*, it was and
is still used as a book of oracles. But it also was a book of profound
wisdom in which was rooted both of the branches of Chinese philosophy, Taoism and Confucianism. Like the *tonalámatl*, and as
its name implies, it was based on the universal law of change—the
beginning of movement, danger in movement, rest and completion of movement. Its eight trigrams and sixty-four hexagrams
were symbols of these constant states of change of all that happens on earth and in heaven. Everything constantly changes polarity from *yang* to *yin*, masculine to feminine, winter to summer,
according to the immutable law of *tao*, of movement.

Whether it be commonly regarded as the "Count of Days" or
the "Book of the Good and Bad Days," the *tonalámatl* amply jus-
tifies its name as the Sacred Calendar. It is the cornerstone of
the great calendar system and the wisdom of ancient Mesoamerica.

2 THE CALENDAR ROUND

The basis of practical time-reckoning was the Solar Calendar of 365 days. It is often referred to by meticulous scholars as the "Vague Year" because the actual length of the solar year is almost a quarter of a day longer, 365.2422 days by present calculations. The Mayas were not at all vague about it. According to their observations the orbit of the earth about the sun took 365.2420 days, closer than the 365.2425 days fixed by our later Gregorian calendar. Because of this difference we now intercalate one day every fourth year, Leap Year, to keep our calendar in time with the sun. The Mayas were not concerned about the difference although they kept records of the errors accumulated during the four thousand years since the projected beginning of their calendar.

They were more concerned with a year of 360 days corresponding to the 360 degrees in the circle or sphere, the *tun* or *haab*, divided into eighteen periods or months of twenty days each. To this was added an extra period of five unlucky days which they called the *Uayeb* and the Aztecs the *Nemontemi*. Each of the months as well as the days had its patron deity.

Of primary importance was the enmeshing of the Solar Year calendar of 365 days with the Sacred Year calendar of 260 days. Their relationship was based on the least common multiple of the two, 18,980 days. The first calendar was required to make 52 revolutions and the second 73 revolutions before they coincided: 365 x 52 = 260 x 73 = 18,980 days. This may be represented again by the analogy of two enmeshing cog wheels.

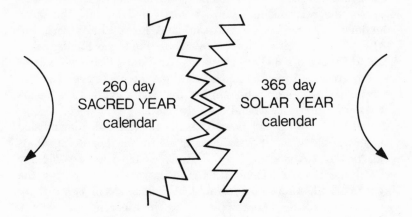

260 day
SACRED YEAR
calendar

365 day
SOLAR YEAR
calendar

This great cycle of fifty-two years was called the Calendar Round. The Aztecs believed that the world would be destroyed at the end of one of these cycles. As one ended, the people extinguished their fires, broke their cooking pots, lamented and fasted. When the calamity did not come on the last night, priests ascended to the temple on the mountain Huixachtecatl, Mountain of the Star, sacrificed a human victim, and kindled a new fire on his breast. From this, fire brands were carried to the great temple in Tenochtitlan and from there to other temples. From these householders in turn carried torches to light new fires on their own hearths. The Calendar Round of fifty-two years the Aztecs called *Xiuhmolpilli,* marking its beginning with the symbol of a fire drill.

The New Fire ritual of the Hopis, *Kokostawis,* still perpetuates this tradition every year. It is the first ritual in *Wuwuchim,* the first ceremonial in the annual cycle, dramatizing the dawn of Creation. Ritual kindling of the fire by flint and native cotton takes place in the *Wuchim* kiva at dawn before the sun rises, and brands from it are carried to light fires in the other kivas participating in the sixteen-day ceremony.

To these calendars was added a third, the Venus Calendar, based on the heliacal risings of the planet Venus as the Morning Star. It too had to be brought into agreement with the Solar Calendar and also with the Sacred Calendar.

The synodical period of Venus being 584 days, and that of Earth 365 days, the relationship of the Venus Calendar and the Solar Calendar was based on the ratio of 5 to 8. For within a period of 2,920 days Venus makes five revolutions while the Earth makes eight: $5 \times 584 = 8 \times 365 = 2,920$ days. As Venus years were computed in groups of five, compared to the synodical revolutions of Earth in groups of eight, the number five was a symbol for Venus as it was for Quetzalcoatl and the Fifth Sun.

To mesh the Venus Calendar with the Sacred Calendar offered a bigger problem, for it was necessary that the beginning of its cycle, the day 1 Ahau, the day of Venus, occur within the 260-day cycle of the Sacred Calendar. Hence it was necessary for the Mayas to calculate how many synodical revolutions of Venus there would be before the planet appeared as the Morning Star on the day 1 Ahau. The simplest method, Thompson explains, would be to find the highest common factor of Venus' 584-day cycle and the *tonalámatl's* cycle of 260 days, which is 4; divide this into the first —584 divided by 4 = 146; and then multiply this result by the second—146 x 260 = 37,960 days.[1] At this time 65 Venus revolutions and 146 cycles of the 260-day Sacred Calendar would coincide on the day 1 Ahau. Instead, the Mayas used the involved tables of calculations recorded in the *Dresden Codex* which took into account the fact that the synodical periods of Venus did not average exactly 584 days, but 583.92 days. This small accumulated error they balanced by a correction of eight days at the end of the fifty-seventh revolution in order to retain the day 1 Ahau as the closing or beginning of the cycle.

So precise were all these calculations that the cycles of the three calendars—Sacred, Solar, and Venus—coincided every 104 years or two Calendar Rounds of 52 years: $146 \times 260 = 104 \times 365 = 65 \times 584 = 37,960$ days. Hence every two Calendar Rounds or 104 years the cycles of the three calendars coincided on the day 1 Ahau, the sacred day of Venus. This was the great *lub*, or "resting place."

The expression derived from the Mayan conception of all periods of time, short and long, as burdens carried by relays of divine bearers. Each bearer was identified by the number distinguishing the period he carried on his back, its weight supported by a tump-line across the forehead. Thompson vividly describes this passage of time as pictured in elaborate hieroglyphic inscriptions: an end-less chain of bearers easing with one hand the strain on the tump-line; letting down their burdens at the ends of their periods, the resting places; each being replaced by another, endlessly, through-out all eternity. And each bearer-god, according to his burden, in-fluencing for good or evil the welfare of the people.[2]

In addition to these three major calendars the Mayas devised a Lunar Calendar, figuring a lunar month or lunation to be 29.5302 days (the modern calculation being 29.5305 days.) It was ritually important to correlate this also with the 260-day Sacred Calendar. Hence they adopted a cycle of 405 lunations, or 11,960 days, which exactly coincided with 46 Sacred Calendar periods. The Mayas determined that lunar eclipses could occur only within eighteen days of the node—the time when the sun crossed the path of the moon. So for any lunar cycle of about thirty-three years, they compiled tables predicting the dates on which eclipses would occur; such eclipse tables cover seven pages of the *Dresden Codex*.

Another table in the codex listing multiples of 78 appears to be a table of calculations for Mars whose synodical period is 780 days or three Sacred Calendar periods. There are indications that the Mayas were also interested in Mercury, and possibly Saturn and Jupiter.

It is useless to speculate how the Mayan priest-astronomers, without telescopes, measuring apparatus, computers, and the use of fractions, could have achieved with such remarkable accuracy this immense and complex calendar system. More incomprehen-sible is the fact that it combined the science of abstruse mathema-tics and astronomy with a metaphysical cosmology and myth-ology. For to them time was overwhelmingly meaningful. Every period, hour, day, month, year, and cycle, was a god. And so their great calendar system condensed into one cryptic unity all the space-time influences exerted on man. To this is given the name of astrology.

3 THE ZODIAC — THE "ROAD OF LIFE"

In Pueblo *kivas* the thin line of sacred cornmeal leading to the altar from the *sipapu,* or place of emergence from the underworld, is called the Road of Life. It symbolizes the evolutionary road of mankind, sustained by the life-giving sun.

The Hopis are more explicit, as shown below:

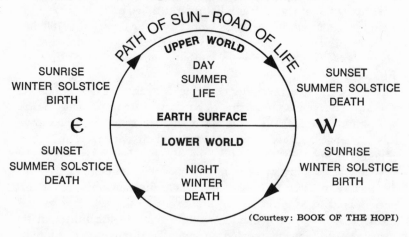

(Courtesy: BOOK OF THE HOPI)

Each morning the sun rises in the east, travels in a circular path above the surface of the Earth, and descends in the west at sunset. During the night the sun completes its circular journey, traveling west to east through the underworld. Day and night are thus re-

230

versed in the upper and lower worlds, the sun rising in the lower world as it sets in the upper world and setting in the lower as it rises again in the upper world. The same diurnal reversal takes place during the annual shifts of the seasons. Each year at the time of the winter solstice, December 21, the sun leaves his winter house and travels to his summer house where he arrives at the time of the summer solstice, June 21. Then again he returns to his winter house. Conditions are reversed in the underworld which experiences winter while the surface world enjoys summer, and summer during the winter period above.

Fundamental to the concept of the year's duality is the premise that life in the underworld duplicates life in the upper world. Whatever takes place during a certain month above also takes place during the corresponding month below, the important *Powamu* ceremony being held during February in the upper world and during September in the lower world. Because the corresponding ceremonies are held simultaneously, with the seasons reversed, the Hopis observe the rituals twice annually, first during the winter when the yearly plan of life is set up with ritual and prayer, and again during the summer when the winter's prayers are harvested. So too does man in unbroken continuity live in the upper world from birth to death and from death to birth in the lower world. The Path of the Sun thus coincides with man's Road of Life. They both describe the circular form of the perfect rounded whole of life, the pure pattern of all Creation.

Some three thousand years ago the Chaldeans in Mesopotamia, from their *ziggurats,* or watchtowers, in Ur, Urak, and Baylon, observed that the sun followed a similar route in the sky, the "Path of Anu." Along this path lay twelve "chiefs" of the constellations it passed through. The areas dominated by these chiefs the Chaldeans called "berous," giving them the names of strange unearthly monsters.[1]

The later Greeks gave to the Path of Anu the name of "Zodiac" which means the "Road of Life." They also gave in their language new names to the monsters or shapes of the constellations along its path.

This zodiac as we know it today is the Great Circle of the Ecliptic, an imaginary belt sixteen degrees wide, whose center line,

ZODIAC

SIGNS OF ZODIAC (dates of the beginning)
SYMBOL OF THE SIGNS
PLANETS (RULERS IN THE SIGNS)
ELEMENTS (▒ = Fire, ∷ = Earth ◈ = Air, ▨ = Water)
GENUS OF THE SIGNS (masculine or feminine)
ENERGY OF THE SIGNS (cardinal, fixed, mutable)
HOUSES (meanings)
SEASONS

Courtesy Dr. Verena Sequin
Zurich, Switzerland.

I–VI = ERAS OR AGES

1–12 = THE ASTROLOGICAL HOUSES

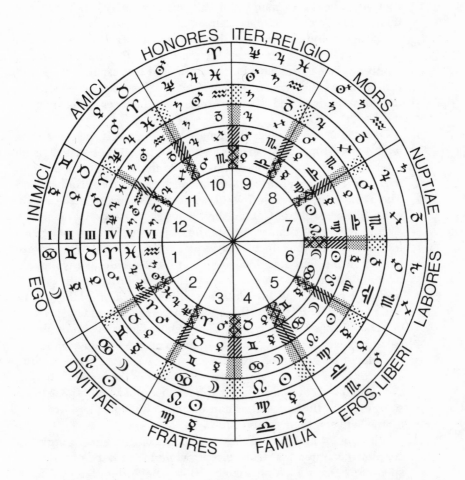

I = CANCER AGE	(from 8000 a. Chr. until 6000 a. Chr. Approximately)
II = GEMINI AGE	(from 6000 a. Chr. until 4000 a. Chr. Approximately)
III = TAURUS AGE	(from 4000 a. Chr. until 2000 a. Chr. Approximately)
IV = ARIES AGE	(from 2000 a. Chr. until 0 p. Chr. Approximately)
V = PISCES AGE	(from 0 p. Chr. until 2000 p. Chr. Approximately)
VI = AQUARIUS AGE	(from 2000 p. Chr. until 4000 p. Chr. Approximately)

Courtesy Dr. Verena Sequin
Zurich, Switzerland.

the ecliptic, is the apparent path of the sun, moon, and planets. It is divided into twelve sections of thirty degrees each. Every section or House is designated by a sign named from the shapes suggested by the constellations within it, the bull, scorpion, lion, goat, etc. The Greek names are still retained today; all but one of them are names of living creatures .

There are indications that the Mayas had a zodiac of thirteen sections or houses, a remnant of the *Codice Peresianos* showing the first three as the scorpion, tortoise, and rattlesnake. They and the Nahuas, like the ancient peoples of the East, believed that the constellations and planets exercised influences upon men on the Earth.

One of the most powerful planets was Venus. It was feared as well as worshipped, for it was believed that on its heliacal rising after inferior conjunction Venus cast malignant influences upon men and earth according to the day on which it rose. Nahuas and Mayas shut the doors and windows so that the rays of the newly risen planet could not enter their houses, causing sickness. The *Anales de Cuauhtitlan* recounts the objects of Venus' malignant influences according to the day upon which it rose. When it appeared in the first sign 1 *cipactli*, Venus cast baleful rays at old men and women; in the sign 1 *acatl*, the great lords; in the signs 1 *océlotl*, 1 *mázatl*, and 1 *xóchitl*, the children; in 1 *ollin*, the youths and maidens; and in 1 *atl* there was universal drought.

Five paintings in the *Borgia Codex* show Quetzalcoatl as Venus casting spears at various targets on earth on the five days on which the planet consecutively rose: 1 *cipactli*, 1 *acatl*, 1 *coatl*, 1 *ollin*, and 1 *atl*. Five sets of paintings accompanying the Venus tables in the *Dresden Codex* also depict the spearing of victims. All these sources show the same signs and targets, although there are variations between their relationships.

These paintings help to clear up an obscure point. A previous chapter recounted that Quetzalcoatl while in the Land of the Dead spent four days making arrows. Both the Nahuatl and Mayan paintings explain the purpose of the arrows or spears: they represent the rays or influences cast by Venus-Quetzalcoatl.

Comments Seler: "It is hardly possible to see anything else in these figures struck by the spear than augural speculations regarding the influence of light from the planet suggested by the initial sign of the period. . . . We shall have to accept this as true, not only for the representations in the Borgian Codex group, but also for the pictorial representations and the hieroglyphic text of the Dresden manuscript."[2]

If it is accepted that the various planetary bodies influenced different classes of people, it is not so clear how Venus influenced individuals in the groups. This is best illustrated in the *Codice Borgia* by a strange figure representing Camaxtli, the god of fate, with the twenty day-signs attached to different parts of his body, giving a detailed conception of their effect on parts of the human body.

According to Spence, whose information came from the *Codice Vaticanus*, "The sign of the wind was assigned to the liver, the rose to the breast, the earthquake to the tongue, the eagle to the right arm, the vulture to the right ear, the rabbit to the left ear, the flint to the teeth, the air to the breath, the monkey to the left arm, the cane to the heart, the herb to the bowels, the lizard to the womb of women, the tiger to the left foot, the serpent to the male organ of generation."[3]

From the vernal equinox, the start of the zodiacal year, there follow in chronological order the twelve periods of the solar year. By reference to our own current *Farmers' Almanac* or any popular astrological chart, we can read the astrological signs of the houses, their planetary rulers, and the parts of the human body we still believe they control (see Table 3).

There is some dispute whether the Chaldeans or Egyptians originated the zodiac. According to Fagan, the Egyptians invented the first or sidereal zodiac, the zodiac of the constellations, and carried it to Babylon where astrology developed as the "Chaldean science."[4] Its name reflects both influences: the Egypto-Babylonian zodiac. The later Greeks converted this into the tropical zodiac of the signs which spread to India, China, the Roman Empire, Europe, and to us today. The pertinent difference between them must be explained.

Because the great circle of the ecliptic has no beginning, being a circle, it was necessary to pick a point to mark the beginning of the zodiac. The point chosen by the ancient Egyptians was the

vernal equinox, the point at which the sun rose at the beginning
of spring, March 21. This initial point, asserts Fagan, was 0 degrees
in Taurus, whose prime star Aldebaron, the "Bull's Eye," occupied
the exact center of that constellation. This then was the first or
sidereal zodiac of the constellations.

TABLE 3

Signs	Symbol	Period	Planetary Ruler	Controls
Aries	Ram	Mar. 21 - Apr. 20	Mars	head
Taurus	Bull	Apr. 21 - May 20	Venus	neck
Gemini	Twins	May 21 - June 21	Mercury	arms
Cancer	Crab	June 22 - July 22	Moon	torso
Leo	Lion	July 23 - Aug. 22	Sun	heart
Virgo	Virgin	Aug. 23 - Sept. 22	Mercury	bowels
Libra	Scales	Sept. 23 - Oct. 22	Venus	loins
Scorpio	Scorpion	Oct. 23 - Nov. 21	Pluto	sex organs
Sagittarius	Archer	Nov. 22 - Dec. 20	Jupiter	thighs
Capricorn	Goat	Dec. 21 - Jan. 19	Saturn	knees
Aquarius	Water Bearer	Jan. 20 - Feb. 18	Uranus	legs
Pisces	Fish	Feb. 19 - Mar. 20	Neptune	feet

When Hipparchus in 139 B.C. discovered the precession of the
equinoxes, the Greeks placed the starting point or vernal equinox
at 0 degrees Aries. From this point the twelve signs of the zodiac
were reckoned. This tropical zodiac of the signs is the standard
zodiac of astrologers today.

Because the Greeks were convinced that the vernal or equinoctial point rose due east and set due west, they believed the vernal points were the only fixed points in the firmament. Hence in
their tropical zodiac the vernal point was fixed and the stars
moved. While in the ancient sidereal zodiac the stars remained
fixed, and the vernal point moved backwards along the ecliptic
circle. Not until Copernicus and Galileo discovered in the fifteenth
century A.D. that the earth revolved about the sun rather than
vice versa, was it confirmed that the stars were relatively fixed,

and that the vernal point retrograded along the ecliptic at the rate of one degree every seven-and-a-half years.

The dust kicked up by the resulting confusion is apparent in astrology today. The houses of the zodiac don't move, being merely sections along the ecliptic, but their order runs counter-clockwise from east to west. The signs and the planets move counter-clockwise from east to west, following the sun's apparent rotation around the earth. But the constellations within the signs move slowly clockwise from west to east. Hence the constellations cannot be paired with the signs as they move in opposite directions. The vernal point in Aries has moved into Pisces during the last precession; yet in our use of the tropical zodiac we are still placing it where the Greeks did. Fagan points out a simple method for reconciling the two zodiacs. As the present starting point of the tropical zodiac is twenty-four degrees in advance of the sidereal zodiac counted clockwise, a conversion from the first to the second may be made by simply subtracting twenty-four degrees from the tropical longitude.

Due to these inconsistencies, modern astrology has acquired its reputation as "the longest illness ever to have afflicted reason," and the "outcome of an infantile process of thought"—a fortune-telling game exploited by quacks and opportunists pandering horoscopes on the scale of a national industry.

At the same time a reaction has set in. The effect of the moon on the tides of the sea and menstrual periods of women has been long known. Scientists are now discovering more actual cosmic influences upon earth and man: the Venusian cycle of eight years reflected in the catch of salmon, the trapping of fur-bearing animals, the yield of crops; the Martian cycles of war; the correlation of accident peaks and the eleven-year cycle of sunspots; the reflection of the cycles of Jupiter, Mercury, and Saturn in the earth's cycles of crime, conquest, and healing; and many others.

These discoveries confirm the belief of the Mayas in the effect of planetary influences upon man. Of the three surviving Mayan codices, the *Madrid* is a divinatory almanac; the *Paris* deals with the divinatory aspects of certain time-periods; and the *Dresden* is a compilation of astronomical data and divinatory almanacs. They leave no doubt that the Mayas were less concerned with astronomy than with its derivative astrology; and more engrossed in the effect of cosmic influences upon long cycles of time than upon individuals. But long cycles of time are measured by the movement of the vernal point along the ecliptic, and have to do with the constellations rather than the planets. And this introduces a still larger scope of the zodiac.

The astrological signs or symbols of the constellations do not only represent the twelve periods of the solar year. They represent periods of more than two thousand years based on the precession of the equinoxes. This great cycle is due to the fact that the Earth in its annual circuit about the sun wobbles slightly like a spinning top, its axis describing a circle every 25,920 years.* As the zodiac is divided into twelve sections of thirty degrees each, it takes the vernal equinox one-twelfth of this cycle or approximately 2,160 years to move through one section. This period is commonly called an Age, designated by a sign representing the constellation which rules it.

Most astrologers use the rough figure of 2,000 years: Taurus the Bull covering the period from 4,000 B.C. to 2,000 B.C., Aries the Ram from 2,000 B.C. to 0 B.C., and Pisces the Fish from A.D. 1 to A.D. 2,000.

Fagan, however, defines an age as beginning and ending when the vernal point in its retrogression enters the thirtieth degree of one constellation and leaves it at the first degree.[5] On this basis he asserts that the Age of Taurus began in 4152 B.C. and ended in 1955 B.C. when Aldebaron, the "Bull's Eye," entered Aries. In these 2,197 years all the great nations of antiquity arose—Egypt, Sumeria, Babylonia, and Assyria. Taurus the Bull was an earthy sign and the cult of the bull was earthy, as attested by the great bull monuments erected in the palace of Sargon II of Assyria and the Egyptian Apis of Memphis, and by the Minotaur of Crete.

The Age of Aries beginning in 1955 B.C. similarly reflected, as Old Testament records attest, the symbolism of the ram. The following Age of Pisces apparently was long anticipated by Egyptian astrologers who portrayed two fishes on a decan about 2300 B.C.

---

*This figure is given as 25, 765, 25868, and many other variations. The one used here is based on the fact that man breathes 18 times a minute or 25,920 times a day, connecting him with the sun and the precession of the equinoxes.

Fishes are contents of the sea, symbol of the unconscious. Oannes, the Babylonian sage, came out of the sea in the shape of a fish; Vishnu saved the holy Vedas of India by diving into the flood in the form of a fish; and, with Christ, the fish emerged as the symbol of Christianity. Just when the present Piscean Age began is widely disputed, for the exact birthday of Christ ushering in the Christian era has never been established. This will be discussed later in connection with Mayan ages or eras.

The influence of directional space is explicit in Nahuatl religious philosophy. That of time is implicit in what the French astrologer Michel Gauquelin calls the "astrology which is outside time," that of the Mayas. Whatever the Mayas conceived it to be, they believed that time, with all its seeming sub-divisions, leaves its successive stamps like that of divisional space upon mankind. For if the planets exercise different influences upon man during the twelve periods of the solar year, the constellations dominant throughout the long ages of the precessional period must also exercise special influences upon mankind. Hence the Mayas projected great cycles of time far into the past, to the "resting places" of the bearers of the burdens of time. On the Tablet of the Inscriptions at Palenque is a date reaching back nearly 1,250,000 years. What was the purpose of such phenomenal calculations? Could it have been that by probing the way cosmic forces affected the previous worlds, they could predict the influences on this and future worlds?

Before inquiring into the validity of these projections, we must briefly outline two modern approaches to the same problem. Rodney Collin in England bases his theory on planetary forces progressively transmitted according to their spatial distances from the sun. The cosmologist Guenther Wachsmuth of Switzerland bases his study on the cosmic influences exerted in the different periods of time marked by the precession of the equinoxes.

4 SPACE-TIME INFLUENCES

Two centuries ago an arithmetical series of numbers called "Bode's Law" was discovered to give the distances of the planets from the sun with surprising accuracy. As shown in the first column of Table 4 the planets were listed in the order of their relative distance from the sun. The number 4 was written after each one. To the first was added 0; to the second 3; to the third, twice 3 or 6; and so on. Then by dividing through by 10 the numbers became the distances of the planets from the sun in terms of the distance of the earth as 1.0. (See Table 4.)

This curious series of numbers indicated a planet at a distance of 2.8 astronomical units between Mars and Jupiter. None was known in 1772 when Bode's Law was formulated. But in 1801 a minor planet or asteroid was found at that exact distance, and this led to the discovery of a large group of asteroids which once may have formed the body of a large planet. This may be the highest achievement of Bode's Law. As will be noted, the numbers give accurately the distances out to Saturn, the farthest known planet at that time. But for Uranus, Neptune, and Pluto, discovered in 1781, 1846, and 1930 respectively, Bode's Law does not hold.

In the last column of the table is shown the surprisingly same arithmetical series of numbers according to the metaphysical system of that enigmatic Russian mystic, Georges Ivanovitch Gurdjieff.[1] These numbers were not arbitrarily picked, as for Bode's Law. Gurdjieff held that cosmic emanations in the form of matter

238

or substance are transmitted by the planets, the solar system, the stars and suns in the Milky Way, and on out from the ultimate principle called the Absolute. The foundation of all matter is hydrogen, made up of carbon, oxygen, and nitrogen. The emanations of matter from the Absolute upon meeting those of the stars, the solar system, and the planets change in density according to an order which corresponds to the musical notes *do, si, la,* and on up the scale through different octaves. The order and relative densities is what is shown in Table 4:

TABLE 4

		Bode's Law		True Distance	Gurdjieff's Theory
Mercury	4 + 0	=	.4	.4	
Venus	4 + 3	=	.7	.7	H3
Earth	4 + 6	=	1.0	1.0	6
Mars	4 + 12	=	1.6	1.5	12
Asteroids	4 + 24	=	2.8	2.8	24
Jupiter	4 + 48	=	5.2	5.2	48
Saturn	4 + 96	=	10.0	9.5	96
Uranus	4 + 192	=	19.6	19.2	192
Neptune	4 + 384	=	33.8	30.1	384
Pluto	4 + 768	=	77.2	39.5	768
					1536
					3072
					6144
					H12288

Gurdjieff does not equate these categories of physical substance and psychical influence with the various planets as we have shown. He begins his progression with "Hydrogen" 6, Earth, but we can assume from his exposition that Venus' number was 3 and Mercury's 0. Also it is extended not only to Uranus, Neptune, and Pluto, but to four more possible planetary bodies or universal stages.

The coincidence of the numbering series in Bode's Law and in Gurdjieff's chemical-musical-metaphysical system is remarkable.

So too are their differences. Bode's Law breaks down at Saturn, the limit of the planets visible to the naked eye. The three outer planets are not only beyond human perception, but their respective cycles of 84, 164, and 248 years are also beyond the average span of man's life. Their physical existence was determined only by the formulation of an abstract concept subject to experimental verification. But what about their psychical influences, with which Gurdjieff was concerned?

As each of his categories of physical matter and psychical influence is connected with a definite plane in the universe, and every function of man is a result of their action, the relation between man's functions and the planes of the universe can be established. He posits in fact that all the so-called "hydrogens" up to 3072 are already found or play a part in the human organism. Does this mean that we are already experiencing to a slight degree the influences from two more universal planes or undiscovered planets beyond Pluto in another, higher octave? This metaphysical premise is based of course on the harmonic relationship of the planets as suggested by his vibratory or musical scale, and the corresponding relationship between the planets and man's functions.

Rodney Collin's theory develops this idea further. Beginning with the sun, the ultimate source of life in our solar system, in Table 5 he postulates the glands of the human body controlled by each of the planets according to their nearness to the sun, and the periods they were dominant during the evolution of man.[2]

The table is far too complicated to be developed here; we can summarize only a few salient facts. In the history of mankind, as in the lifetime of individual man, different functions are stimulated in the same progressive order as the relative distances of the planets from the sun. The origin of life cannot be measured, not even conceived. The periods of the pancreas and thyroid are prenatal, belonging to gestation. Hence the duration of time between periods becomes successively shorter, half as long; as in man, time speeds up, life grows fuller. This is reflected by the functions of the glands in the human body. The thymus, in the neighborhood of the heart, is the most primitive of all and tends to atrophy after adolescence. The pancreas is associated with the lymphatic system, controlling man's digestion of food. The thyroid gland, situated in the throat, controls the pulmonary system and respiration. The parathyroids, situated on the thyroid, control blood circulation, producing tissue and growth. The adrenal glands lie on the kidneys and control the cerebro-spinal system. Secreting hormones producing fear and rage, they are the "glands of passion," and people of this type are fierce and martial. The next two glands comprise the two lobes of the pituitary, a small organ behind the bridge of the nose. The posterior pituitary, associated with the sympathetic nervous system, controls physical sensations and reflexes. The anterior pituitary is connected with the cerebral cortex and skeletal system, controlling mind and reason. The gonads control not only physical sex functions but all processes of creation. The last gland, the pineal body, is located at the focal point of the brain and man's psychic system. Its little-known functions have yet to be realized.

On this grand time-scale Collin proceeds to locate various races, cultures, and civilizations of antiquity—Egypt, Babylonia, Assyria, and India—which held sway from 5,000 B.C. to 1,000 B.C. under the parathyroid influences of Venus, manifesting its characteristics of slow growth, poise, and solidity. This is generally confirmed by the rise of these civilizations during the Taurus Age beginning in 4152 B.C. Astrology, however, divides this Venus period of 4,000 years among the ages of Gemini, Taurus, and Aries.

TABLE 5

Date	Duration	Solar Body	Gland
60,000 years ago	32,000 years	Sun	Thymus
30,000 years ago	16,000 years	Moon	Pancreas
15,000 years ago	8,000 years	Mercury	Thyroid
5,000 B.C.	4,000 years	Venus	Parathyroid
1,000 B.C.	2,000 years	Mars	Adrenals
1,000 A.D.	1,000 years	Jupiter	Posterior Pituitary
Present		Saturn	Anterior Pituitary
Next		Uranus	Gonads
Future		Neptune	Pineal

In Collin's period 1000 B.C. to A.D. 1000 governed by the adrenal influences of Mars, the turbulent civilizations of Greece and Rome were dominant. But again astrology divides this period into the Aries and Pisces ages.

These differences show, of course, that Collin bases his theory on the effect of planetary bodies over a time-scale corresponding to their distances from the sun, whereas astrology measures its ages by the zodiacal signs or constellations far beyond the solar system. Can they be correlated by assuming that both the planets and the constellations exert influences on earth, the planets acting through the fields of cosmic force set up by the constellations?

Collin was not familiar with the cultures and civilization of pre-Columbian Mesoamerica, and does not mention them. So before developing further this difference, let us briefly inquire how these cultures fit into his time-scale.

One might assume from his theory that the rise of Mesoamerican cultures can be culturally equated with the rise of the Middle East civilizations, taking place in the Venus period 5,000-1,000 B.C. under its parathyroidal influences for growth. The major lifetime of the first—the mysterious Olmec culture—lies instead in the following Mars period, although the Olmecs seem not to have been martial. But if its origin is pushed back beyond 1,000 B.C. as it has been, Olmec culture did begin in the Venus period.

We might also suppose that the Nahuatl Toltecs developed the first great civilization whose metropolis was Teotihuacan, and the concept of Quetzalcoatl-Venus, in the same Venus period. This is far too early if we accept the founding of Teotihuacan slightly before the beginning of the Christian era as dated by archaeology. This places its rise and domination, and that of the classic Mayan civilization, in the Mars period governed by the adrenal glands of war and passion. Yet neither the Toltecs of Teotihuacan nor the classical Mayas were martial; they were predominantly religious.

But certainly, following Collin, the fierce and war-loving Aztecs presumably rose to supremacy under the impetus given by the adrenals during the Mars period 1,000 B.C. to A.D. 1000. Instead, the Aztecs rose to power during the first half of the following Jupiter period under the influence of the posterior pituitary controlling physical sensations and reflexes.

The succession of all these translations of psycho-physical drives into manifested civilizations is the same, but there is a time-lag of one period between them.

The ramifications and subtleties of Collin's profound theory warrant fuller study, for other cosmic influences as well as planets affect earth and man. So let us look now at Guenther Wachsmuth's pattern of changes as the equinoctial and solstitial points incline to different constellations.

It is based on the great 25,920-year cycle of the precession of the equinoxes, this "World Clock" being divided into twelve zodiacal sections or "hours." Wachsmuth stresses the fact that the Earth's axis keeps changing its direction, its north pole inclining toward one zodiacal sign after another during the clockwise cycle. When the four cardinal points are directed to Gemini, Sagittarius, Pisces, and Virgo, cosmic influences upon earth are especially strong and man is cosmically oriented. When the four points are directed to Taurus, Scorpio, Aquarius, and Leo, cosmic experience is no longer as direct but reflected in myths, and man is mythically oriented. In the third phase when the points are directed to Aries, Libra, Capricorn, and Cancer, earthly influences are dominant and man is oriented to the earth. Hence mankind during its evolution throughout the course of the World Clock goes through three different phases, resulting in three variations of man which Wachsmuth calls Prototypes 1, 2, and 3.

PROTOTYPE 1   PROTOTYPE 2   PROTOTYPE 3

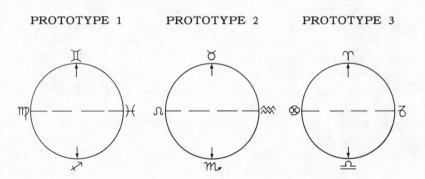

Each of the prototypes appears in four variations, once in each of the four quarters of the precessional year, as the axis of the earth keeps turning: ↑ , → , ↓ , → . The same four signs appear, but the equinoxes and solstices are differently placed among them. In each period mankind reflects in his consciousness and culture the varying influences upon it.

This terminology has a rough parallel in the current astrological naming of the signs to denote their type of energy: *cardinal* for soul energy, *fixed* to denote moral stability and stamina, and *mutable* for bodily energy and activity. These also appear successively in each of the four quarters, but do not correspond with Wachsmuth's schematic. The main difference is that modern astrology commonly ignores the progress of the vernal point, and is based on its position in the past Aries epoch.

What we observe in both cases, however, is a rhythm and measured periodicity which correspond to the Nahua-Maya succession of four eras or suns, each representing a different quarter, which dominate, vanish, and reappear, following the inexorable law of *movement*. Periodicity occurs in plant life, in human embryology, in the organic processes of the earth's evolution. Civilizations rise, fall, and reappear under similar conditions, but oriented differently. As shown in Table 6, astrology considers the time from approximately 6,000 to 4,000 B.C. to have been the Age of Gemini, ruled by Mercury. This roughly coincides with Wachsmuth's dating of the period from 6,500 to 4,500 B.C., a Gemini period during which Prototype 1 developed the ancient Persian civilization. Gemini is the sign of the twins, betokening a duality. So here were enunciated the dualities of light and darkness, of Ormuzd and Ahriman, later followed by Cain and Abel, and by the Greek twins Castor and Pollux whose names are still borne by two brilliant stars in the sign of Gemini. The period also fits into Collin's time-scale, corresponding to the last quarter of his 8,000-year period governed by the thyroid influences of Mercury.

The following Wachsmuth phase from 4,500 to 1,900 B.C. coincides with astrology's Age of Taurus from 4,000 to 2,000 B.C. In this Taurus phase, whose planetary ruler was Venus, Prototype 2 developed the civilizations of Sumeria, Babylon, and Egypt. Establishing social order on a cosmic model, their priest-kings devised the zodiac and calendar, and built pyramids whose four triangular sides inclined toward the four points of Taurus, Scorpio, Aquarius, and Leo. Collin, as shown, marks the four thousand years between 5,000 and 1,000 B.C. as the period ruled by the parathyroid influences of Venus, controlling growth. So this corresponds to the last part of his period.

TABLE 6

**Comparing dates and periods as given by
Collin, Astrology and Wachsmuth**

Collin

5,000 - 1,000 B.C.	Venus
1,000 B.C. - A.D. 1,000	Mars
A.D. 1,000 - 2,000	Jupiter
	Saturn

Astrology

6,000 - 4,000 B.C.	Gemini - Mercury
4,000 - 2,000 B.C.	Taurus - Venus
2,000 - 0 B.C.	Aries - Mars
0 B.C. - A.D. 2,000	Pisces - Jupiter
	Neptune

Wachsmuth

6,500 - 4,500 B.C.	Gemini - Mercury
4,000 - 1,900 B.C.	Taurus - Venus
1,900 - 100 B.C.	Aries - Mars
100 B.C. - Present	Pisces - Jupiter
	Neptune

The Taurus period was succeeded by the Aries period ruled by Mars—2,000 to 0 B.C. according to astrology, or 1,900 B.C. to 100 B.C. according to Wachsmuth. In this phase when man was oriented to earth, Prototype 3 established the Greco-Roman civilization, introducing mathematics, secular laws, Caesarism, and humanizing the gods in myths. It corresponds to the first half of Collin's Mars period from 1,000 B.C. to A.D. 1,000.

The Aries period in turn was superceded by the present Pisces period. Astrology sets its beginning at 0 B.C., Wachsmuth at 100 B.C. Both agree that its rulers are Jupiter and Neptune. Collin, on the contrary, dates the period from A.D. 1,000 to 2,000, asserting its planetary rulers are Jupiter and Saturn controlling the posterior and anterior pituitary glands. Prototype 3 under maximum cosmic influence now appears again.

This poses a number of questions. In the Old World, Christianity was introduced in the first half of the Pisces period, followed in the second half by the satanic climax of war, applied science, and materialism we are now experiencing. In the New World, the classical Nahuatl-Mayan religious empires rose, flourished, and died in the same first half of the period, and was replaced in the last half by the quarreling states dominated by the militaristic Tula-Toltecs and Aztecs. How could two such opposing manifestations derive from one cosmic source?

One answer already has been given. The symbol of Pisces is two fish; a *complexio oppositorium* as Jung calls it. The first thousand years of the Christian era is represented by Christ, the first fish; and the second thousand years by the second fish, the anti-Christ or Lucifer. If Quetzalcoatl may be equated with Christ, and Huitzilopochtli with the anti-Christ, the Mesoamerican application of this psychological interpretation seems valid.

There may be another explanation. The discovery of Uranus in 1781, Neptune in 1846, and Pluto as late as 1930 astrologically changed the traditional rulers of the signs. Uranus is now considered the ruler of Aquarius which, with Capricorn, was formerly ruled by Saturn. Pluto now rules Scorpio instead of Mars which was believed to co-rule both Scorpio and Aries. And more importantly, Pisces is now said to be ruled jointly by Jupiter and Neptune. As Jupiter's influences are harmonizing, and the cycle of Neptune is believed to be connected with the process of regeneration, this may astrologically confirm the division of the Pisces period. It may also shed some light on why the great Teotihuacan civilization, the first in Mesoamerica, took form early in the Pisces period under the harmonizing influences of Jupiter and Neptune, instead of in the far earlier Taurus period ruled by Venus.

The time-lag between the development of civilizations in the Old World and the New poses another question, assuming that the same celestial influences were received over the entire planet Earth. The civilizations of Asia take form first, followed by those in America, and finally that in western Europe. A lapse of centuries, of cycles and periods, of "hours" on the World Clock occur as civilization spreads around the globe. It is impossible to relate chronologically the building of the great pyramids in Egypt and the equally great pyramids of America built two thousand years later, but which so much resemble the Egyptian. Something else must be included in the patterns set forth by Collin, Wachsmuth, and astrology. A factor of geography, a westward movement of evolutionary centers around the globe from Asia to America to Europe, in phase with the precession of the equinoxes. And this, as we have seen, is similar to Nahuatl-Mayan chronology: a succession of world-eras equated with a succession of world directions or quarters, both forming a space-time sequence in accordance with the supreme law of *movement*.

How little we know of the history of mankind on this small planet and of the universal laws that govern it! And what little we know is constantly changing. Despite the differences between the interpretive systems of Collin and Wachsmuth, they are much alike. They approach the evolution of man with his successive cultures and civilizations from a cosmic viewpoint. They grapple with the problem of the effects upon the psychical-physical body of individual man and upon the social body of his civilization of influences from the celestial bodies with which he is organically related. They develop the ideas of movement, rhythm, and periodicity which govern plants, animals, men, the tides of the sea, the crust of the earth itself. If one interpretation postulates the effect of the planets in the solar system, the other the effect of the constellations during the precession, they but reflect the scope of man's ever-expanding consciousness. How can we doubt that its intuitive scope will expand still farther with the possible discovery of new planets, with more knowledge of distant galaxies beyond the Milky Way? Will another, a galactic zodiac be required, another expanded study of their effects?

Modern as these conjectures may seem, they are but projections of ancient beliefs found in Mesopotamia, Egypt, India, and Mesoamerica. They refute the current restricted belief that the evolution of man and his civilizations took place solely in response to physical and social stimuli. And they help us to understand a little better the Nahuas' concern with space and the Mayas' obsession with time, the two co-ordinates of Mesoamerican civilization.

5 THE LONG COUNT

The Mayas did not limit their time-reckoning system to the Calendar Round of fifty-two years as did the Aztecs. They vastly extended it in great cycles reaching millions of years into the past. To keep track of them the Mayas employed a unique numbering system.

Throughout the world several systems of numbering have been used. The quinary system is based on the five fingers of the hand, our decimal system on the ten fingers of both hands. The Mayas used the vigesimal system based on the twenty fingers and toes. Only three symbols were employed: a dot for the number 1, a bar for 5, and a stylized shell for 0.

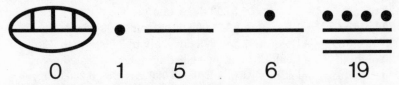

It seems probable that the Olmecs invented the dot and bar symbols, as they have been found inscribed on monuments at La Venta, but the concept of zero, or nought, appears to have been developed for the first time in world history by the Mayas. It was not known in India until a thousand years later, from there it was passed through the Arabs to Europe another thousand years later.

In addition, the Mayas worked out a system of place-value notation, placing their numerals in vertical sequence instead of horizontal as we do. Our decimal system increases horizontally by the power of ten: 1-10-100-1,000-10,000-100,000, etc.

The Mayas' vigesimal system increased vertically in terms of twenty:

1 Kabal	160,000
1 Pic	8,000
1 Bak	400
1 Kal	20
1 Hun	1

In reckoning time the names of these numerical values were changed and they were represented by glyphs of heads, each feature of which—a hand over the lower jaw, an earplug, filed teeth, and a squinting eye—designated a numeral. As yet only a third of the Maya glyphs have been deciphered; almost all of them are records of numbers and dates.

For the names of the time-periods, *kin*, meaning day or sun, was given to the primary number 1. This multiplied by twenty gave one *uninal* of twenty days, 18 *uninals* giving one *tun* of 360 days —and this, the only exception to the multiplication by twenty, was made to bring it in line with the 360-day calendar. This period of 360 days, the *tun*, was used as the unit for computation of the Long Count whose cycles are shown in Table 7.

TABLE 7

20 tuns	- 1 katun or 7,200 days, one year
20 katuns	- 1 baktun or 144,000 days, some 400 years
20 baktuns	- 1 pictun, 2,880,000 days, about 8,000 years
20 pictuns	- 1 calabtun, 57,600,000 days, about 158,000 years
20 calabtuns	- 1 kinchiltun, 1,520,000,000 days or 3,200,000 years
20 kinchiltuns	- 1 alautun, 23,040,000,000 days or some 64,000,000 years

... and on up to a hablatun of 460,800,000,000 days

Dates were inscribed from top to bottom in descending order of magnitude, expressing the number of days elapsed from the end of the last great cycle. These great cycles were periods of 13 *baktuns,* roughly 5,200 years.

Here, for example, is how the date 7.16.6.16.18 was recorded on the great Olmec Stele C at Tres Zapotes:

$$
\begin{aligned}
&= \ 7 \text{ baktuns} = 1{,}008{,}000 \text{ days} \\
&=16 \text{ katuns} \ = \ \ 115{,}200 \text{ days} \\
&= \ 6 \text{ tuns} \quad = \quad \ 2{,}160 \text{ days} \\
&=16 \text{ uninals} = \quad \ \ \ 320 \text{ days} \\
&=18 \text{ kins} \quad = \quad \quad \ \ 18 \text{ days}
\end{aligned}
$$

or 1,125,698 days since the end of the last great cycle.

This date, corresponding to the modern calendar date of 31 B.C., is only five years later than the oldest recorded date yet found in Mesoamerica. It is interesting to note that the stele was found by Matthew W. Stirling in 1939, but with the top numeral missing which he guessed would be the number 7. Fortunately in 1972 the missing fragment of the stele was found by a farmer, and it bore the number 7.

The date 13.0.0.0.0.4 Ahau 8 Cumku was the base from which this and all other dates were reckoned. Obviously it was not the starting point of the calendar, for 13 baktuns of 5,200 years each already had elapsed. Moreover Thompson reports the discovery of calculation of dates preceding it: the Tablet of the Cross at Palenque showing the date of 12.19.13.4.0 and Stele 10 at Tikál erected before 9.10.0.0.1. The origin of the Long Count is not known. Morley believed it was devised at the end of Baktun 7.[1] As the earliest recorded dates fall within Baktun 7, Thompson believes the Long Count was begun in that period.[2] So does Coe.[3]

In any case the date 13.0.0.0.0 4 Ahau 8 Cumku, was selected as the beginning of the time reckoning period. From it, backward projections of similar cycles were made far into the past. The two longest calculations into the past were made at Quirigua. According to Thompson's decipherment of their inscriptions, they date 90 million and 400 million years ago.[4]

And still time kept receding backward into a remoteness beyond comprehension. There could be no true starting point for the calendar, any calendar, for time itself. For time, like space, has no beginning, no end. Is this what the Mayas were beginning to discover as they kept probing ever farther and farther into the mystery of beginningless and endless time? That time receded ever

backward in a curve, describing a great cosmic circle and returning whence it came? The serpent swallowing its own tail, circum-
scribing the *pleroma,* the boundless and measureless infinitude of
all space and time and creation; "the complete circle" symbol of
the universe.

No other people on earth have been so obsessed with time. Our
imaginations balk at the astronomical figures of their mathematical calculations. Today with our limited knowledge of Maya
religious philosophy and our linear conception of time, we cannot
perceive fully the awesome and sublime mystery of time as the
Mayas conceived it. We can only stand reverently awed by their
genius in translating it so precisely into astronomical, mathematical, and philosophic terms.

The Mayan concept of limitless time is still a distinguishing feature of Indian mentality throughout America. In previous publi-
cations of my own the great difference between the Indian and our
own Euro-American concepts of time has been developed at some
length, using the Hopi view as an example.[5] To us time is a shal-
low horizontal stream flowing out from the past, through the present, into the future. We are increasingly obsessed with the sense
of its constantly accelerating pace. The clock ticks ever faster.
Every tick converts a segment of the future into the present, and
this present is swept so swiftly into the past that we have no present left to experience in its fullness.

The Hopis, on the contrary, have all the time there is. For to
them time is not a medium of linear measurement, a flowing
stream. Rather is it a deep, still pool of an element as livingly real
as the elements of earth, water, air, and fire. Whorf, in his analysis
of the Hopi language, found it has no three-tense system of past,
present, future like our own.[6] Man lives in an ever-living *now.*
The Hopi language thus avoids the artificiality of expressing time
in units of linear measurement. Our "length of time" is regarded
as a relationship between two events. A man plants his corn, and
in great ceremonials he plants his prayers. And in the great, still
pool of the element time both grow to fruition. Hence Hopi time is
not a motion. It is a duration, a storing up of power that holds over
into later events. A constant anticipation and preparation that becomes realization. A sense of ever becoming within a duration of

immovable time. This is the secret of the power of the nine great ceremonials in the annual cycle; for thought is power, the seed planted in durational time, the anticipation that grows into realization.

This time which has no beginning nor end, which is motionless and boundless, is also known as Duration, or *Parakála,* in the religious philosophy of India, Shakta Vedantism.[7] It has two aspects. It may be statically condensed into a point (now) which is the pivotal center of every event. And it may expand dynamically into a boundless continuum (always) which is Duration, involving past, present, and future.

Space, like time, has the same twofold aspect, shrinking to a center (here) and swelling in a boundless continuum (everywhere). The Hopis have the same concept of dimensional space. The distance between events is expressed not as a linear measurement, but as a relation between them. For the realm of objective events stretches away to the realm of mythical events which can only be known subjectively. Hence the immediacy and the emotional power of mythical happenings as enacted in Hopi ceremonialism, and the numinous power conveyed to us today by Nahuatl-Mayan myth.

This same synonymity of time and space is expressed by Einstein's theory of relativity—that the universe is a four-dimensional space-time continuum with three dimensions of space and one of time. Man, with his expanding perception, has perceived the spatial dimensions of length, breadth, and height. But he generally still sees time, the fourth dimension, as three-dimensional: past, present, future; birth, life, death. Yet gradually the fourth dimension of time spanning both past and future, is beginning to emerge from his unconscious in dreams, archetypal images, and the phenomena of telepathy and precognition. And all of these confirm the inner spaciousness and timelessness of "Indian Time."

This conception of time as duration, rather than linear, may suggest the reason why the great religious civilizations of the Toltecs of Teotihuacan and the classic Mayas were suddenly ended and their fabulous cities were mysteriously abandoned. Crop failures, revolt of the ignorant masses, economic, political, and other conjectural explanations are not the reason. They are but the effects, not the cause. The cause lies deeper, embodied in the cyclic relationship between man and the cosmic influences governing him.

An earlier chapter on "Life Spans and World Cycles" introduced the idea that there is an inherent duration, an *aion* or aeon, a measured period of existence for everything in the universe. Each has its own duration embodied within its genus—plant, animal, bird, man, his cultures and his civilizations. As Nicoll brings out, these aeonian lifetimes with their cycles of growth, maturity, and decay are all embodied within time.[8] Only the full fruition of the universe itself is beyond time; the one boundless, immeasurable, infinite aeon, which is equated with the *pleroma* of infinite space. The duration of the lifetime of a moth may be measured in seconds or minutes, those of animals and man in years, that of cultures and civilizations in centuries, those of the earth and planets in milliard periods beyond count.

The Mayas, with the extent and depth of their astronomical, mathematical, and astrological knowledge, were able to calculate the duration of such cycles extending from the hours of the day and night to the Great Cycle of 5,200 years. If, as suggested earlier, the governing priesthood astronomically picked the sites of their major ceremonial centers as focal points of astrological influence at the beginning of the great classic period, just as surely the priesthood knew when its cycle, the aeonian lifetime of their civilization, had ended. The World Clock was pointing to another hour with different celestial influences. The old invigorating impulse was gone. The priests felt within themselves a loss of power. And so they abandoned their religious rulership and their ceremonial centers to the ignorant multitude, leaving their learning and teaching embodied in their architectural monuments as seeds to flower anew in coming centuries. What they left behind are vast archaeological ruins embodying a living spirit that has the power to still communicate its presence.

Who has not felt it in many jungle ruins? Their great courts amid the lofty green rain forest, their majestic pyramidal platforms, their temples with their lacy roof combs, and quiet corridors lined with stucco relief panels or wall paintings, exert upon visitors from all continents and all walks of life a mysterious fascination. These visitors are not professionally concerned like archaeologists patiently excavating stone upon stone, deciphering the hieroglyphs engraved upon them. They do not appraise, like architects, the relationships of the structures to the ridges and valleys of the surrounding hills; or the sensual appeal of these dull stone walls once brilliantly colored to respond to the changing lights of the day and the seasons. Nor are they likely aware of the diverse interpretations of their symbolic art. Neither the motive of their terrestrial construction nor the celestial blueprint for them are known to us curious tourists who plod up the steps of steep pyramids, prowl through dusky passages. And yet all of us, ignorant as we are, are somehow subtly changed by this different aspect of a world beyond our comprehension, of values we have either lost and forgotten or have yet to learn. These ruins speak directly to our hearts, not through our minds. Just what they say we do not know. For their invisible and mysterious living spirit seems to be biding its time until its meanings finally come full circle. Not in our era perhaps. But to those souls in a later cycle who by a more highly developed faculty of intuition may translate their ancient Mayan meaning in a context of time different from our own.

Jung, who always affirmed the validity of astrology, observed, "Careful investigation of the unconscious shows that there is a peculiar coincidence with time, which is also the reason why the ancients were able to project the succession of unconsciously perceived inner contents into the outer astronomical determinants of time. This is the basis for the connection of psychic events with temporal determinants. So it is not a matter of an indirect connection, as you suppose, but of a direct one."[9]

This connection is precisely the Mayan problem which now confronts us here. By their phenomenal mathematical and astronomical knowledge the Mayas were able to project the beginning of their Great Cycle backward to 3113 B.C. and to project its end forward to A.D. 2011. But what psychic events perceived in the unconscious did they astrologically project upon these two astronomical determinates? What, in short, is the meaning of this Great Cycle?

6 THE GREAT CYCLE
ITS PROJECTED BEGINNING

Why the date 13.0.0.0.0 4 Ahau 8 Cumku was selected as the beginning of the last Great Cycle and the base from which all other dates were reckoned is not known. It seems most probable that it was conceived as marking the creation of the present world, the fifth.

As we recall, the first world was destroyed by jaguars representing the earth, the second by the element air, the third by fire, and the fourth by water, a great flood. Upon its creation, the present fifth world was predestined to be destroyed by a great cataclysm of earthquakes.

Just when, according to our reckoning, did its creation take place? The great difficulty has been in correlating the Maya date of 13.0.0.0.0 4 Ahau 8 Cumku with our present Christian calendar. Numerous scholars over the years have worked out various correlations: Willson setting the date at August 29, 3511 B.C., Spinden at October 14, 3373 B.C., Morley in 3340 B.C., Escalona-Ramos in 2853 B.C., and G. Zimmer in his *Geshichtle der Sterhunde* at August 29, 3512 B.C. J. T. Goodman in 1905 established another correlation setting the date in 3113 B.C. Juan Martinez Hernandez, a Yucatan archaeologist, corrected it by one day in 1918. And in 1927 it was further corrected by four days by J. Eric S. Thompson of the Carnegie Institute.[1] The combined Goodman-Martinez-Thompson correlation has now been accepted as the most accurate, and the projected start of the last Great Cycle is generally believed to be August 12, 3113 B.C.

Astrologically there are several critical points of change marked by the precession of the equinoxes. Every 2,160 years the equinoctial points move through thirty degrees of the zodiac, or one sign; and according to Wachsmuth another prototype of man appears, building a different civilization. This period, as we recall from previous discussions, seems to measure the lifetime of all major civilizations, including the overall civilization of Mesoamerica. The component cultures, each having its unique characteristics, have a measured lifetime ranging from 700 to 800 years, the primary cultures in Mesoamerica conforming to this. On a larger scale there are still more critical points of change. The end of the 6,480-year cycle, when the equinox has moved through three signs, is regarded as crucial, for the planets of the three signs form a ninety degree angle or square, an unfavorable aspect. The prognostic aspect of the half-point at 12,960 years when the planets of the six signs are in opposition at 180 degrees is considered dangerous, and that of the end of the precessional cycle even more catastrophic. If this is true, it would be interesting to know if the cataclysms accompanying glacial advances, the catastrophes which sank Atlantis, and the former catastrophes mentioned to Solon, fit into this cyclical pattern.

The Mayan cyclical pattern, based on multiples of fifty-two, also contains catastrophic implications. At the end of the Calendar Round cycle of 52 years, when the solar year and sacred year calendars coincided, the people extinguished all their fires, lamented and fasted, believing that the world would be destroyed. The end of two of these cycles every 104 years, when the cycles of the solar, sacred, and Venus calendars coincided, was also of a catastrophic significance. Of the end of the Great Cycle of 5,200 years there was no doubt; a catastrophe would completely destroy the world. Four previous worlds have been so destroyed, the present world being the fifth. The duration of these five worlds, granting each a life-span of 5,200 years, totals 26,000 years; and this closely approximates the great 25,920-year cycle of the precession of the equinoxes.

On the assumption that the Mayan Great Cycle, comprising 13

baktuns or 5,200 years and beginning on August 12, 3113 B.C., marked the end of the Fourth World and the beginning of the Fifth World, one would expect the great catastrophe attested by Nahuatl-Mayan myth. The end of the Great Cycle and the Fifth World, according to the same Goodman-Martinez-Thompson correlation, will occur on December 24, 2011 A.D., and it too will be destroyed by catastrophic earthquakes.

The Mayan priests with their phenomenal knowledge of astronomy may have been able to project the configurations of the planets to these two dates, and to interpret astrologically from them the predicted catastrophes. What were these portentous configurations? And how would modern astrologers interpret them?

Predictions of planetary positions can be made by treating the astronomical configurations as an abstract mathematical system, analyzing the astronomical data, and then modeling it as a system. One must start with a correlation of the Mayan Long Count with the Christian calendar: first with the Julian calendar of 45 B.C. whose beginning date of January 1, 4713 B.C. was selected as the beginning of world history; and then with our present Gregorian calendar which replaced it in A.D. 1582. The accepted correlation provides this, but it must be applied to individual planets. Knowing the regular synodic periods of the planets, and the Gregorian dates of the specified Mayan dates, one can convert these dates into Julian day numbers and find comparable dates when the positions of the planets with respect to the sun are known. One can observe the patterns these positions make, and reduce these positions to mathematical equations that can be used to predict the planetary positions for the specified Mayan dates.

For the present discussion Mrs. Roberta S. Sklower, a mathematician and a member of the Albuquerque Astronomers organization, has modeled this complex astronomical system and determined the positions of the planets at the beginning and end of the Mayan Great Cycle.[2] Her detailed study is included here as an appendix.

The premise of her study is pragmatic, based upon the observed astronomical phenomena of sidereal and synodic rhythms, and upon the current established view of the solar system as an harmonically organized system of planetary bodies whose positions at any time can be calculated. The well-known Neugebauer Tables of solar and planetary longitudes for some four thousand years were established on this premise, and Mrs. Sklower has utilized them in her calculations for 3113 B.C.[3]

Her predicted positions of the planets on August 12, 3113 B.C. are given in Table 8. This is followed by a rough sketch of the configuration showing their angles of elongation with the sun, (figure 2) and a zodiacal chart marking their positions in the signs (figure 3).

The configuration is so unusual that Sklower computes the probability of its occurrence as only once every 4,500 years. We observe that Mercury, only 6.2 degrees from the sun, Saturn 9 degrees, and Mars at −33 degrees, are all in Leo, squaring Jupiter in Scorpio, denoting a tremendous release of energy, a drive toward power. The most important aspect, the real power aspect, is the exact conjunction of the sun and Venus at 0 degrees in Cancer.

One would expect from Nahuatl and Mayan myth that the configuration, whatever it might be, augured a tremendous terrestrial catastrophe marking the end of the Fourth World and the beginning of the Fifth. And this configuration does confirm this tremendous burst of power.

The astrologer G. D' Onofrio reads the configuration from a different level. She interprets the sudden and tremendous outburst of energy as psychical, resulting in a swift change and creative growth in mankind, perhaps giving birth to a different mentality than that in the previous cycle. In explaining its effect upon man, she associates the sun with the thymus gland which "sets the spring of life uncoiling"—the regulator of that undifferentiated life impulse derived from the sun. Hence it seems to her that Venus, which controls the parathyroid gland, being in exact conjunction with the sun, distributed the energy that had the most effect upon mankind's sudden change and growth, alternating with Mercury, Saturn, and Mars squaring with Jupiter and producing stress energy during the cycle.

What actually happened of world importance about 3113 B.C.?

In Egypt the first dynasty began about 3200 B.C. when King Narmer united Upper and Lower Egypt. The Harakhte era, according to Fagan's calculations, began in 3130 B.C. The Chinese calendar

TABLE 8

August 12, 3113 B.C. Planetary Positions ☉λ = 115.6

All fixed stars and constellations adjusted by 73°

Planet		Angle of Elongation Degrees	Planetary Longitude	Zodiac Sign & Degree		Fixed Star	Main Constellation
Sun	☉	0	115.6	24° 4′	♋	Vindemiatrix	Virginnis
Mercury	☿	−6.2	121.8	1° 8′	♌	Algoric Segrinus	Corvus Bootis
Venus	♀	0	115.6	24° 4′	♋	Vindemiatrix	Virginnis
Mars	♂	−33	148.6	28° 6′	♌	Alphecca Acrux	Coronal Borealis Crucis
Jupiter	♃	−104	220	10°	♏	Aculeus Acumen Sinistra	Scorpi Ophliucci
Saturn	♄	−9	124.6	4° 6′	♌	Seginus Foramen	Bootis Argus

FIGURE 2

PLANETARY ANGLES OF ELONGATION
August 12, 3113 B. C.

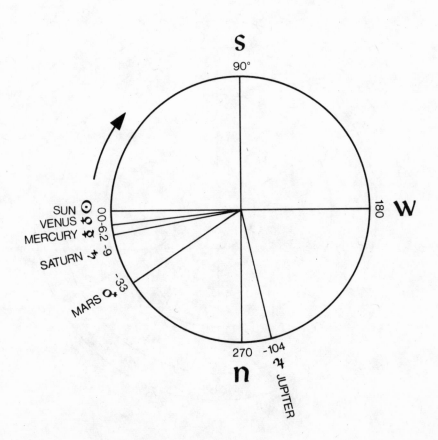

FIGURE 3

PLANETARY POSITIONS
August 12, 3113 B. C.

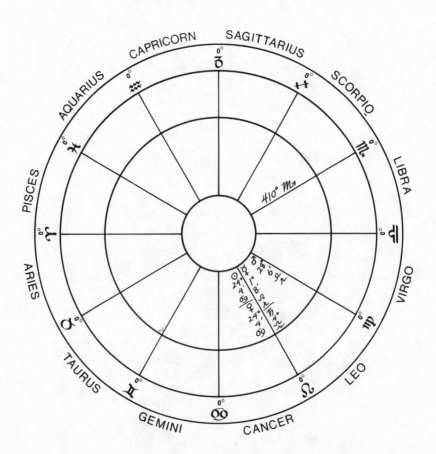

was inaugurated in 3082 B.C. The great Hindu cycle of Kali-Yuga began in 3101 B.C., according to the *Bhagavata Purana*. The Sumerian civilization began with the founding of Nineveh in 3100 B.C. Ixtlilxochtitl in the sixteenth century of the present era concluded from his study of Nahuatl sources that the creation of the Fifth Sun occurred in 3245 B.C. And the Jewish calendar began in 3761 B.C., marking their calculated date of creation.

All these closely associated dates conform to the timetables of Collin and Wachsmuth which show that these great civilizations of antiquity, with their invigorated mentality, solidity, and tranquil growth, rose during the cycle which began at this time.

But with this sudden and tremendous outburst of psychical and creative energy, was there no catastrophic manifestation of destructive physical energy as posited by Mayan myth and indicated by the planetary configuration?

We know too little of terrestrial catastrophes in the far past. That which comes most readily to mind is the one that sank Atlantis. This occurred in 9500 B.C. according to Plato and Zapffe's record of the date of the cataclysm which accompanied the last of the Wisconsin glacial ages, or in 1500 B.C. according to Velikovsky. Between these two dates, namely about 3113 B.C., there is no established historical record of a major catastrophe.

But when did the Deluge occur? It has never been precisely dated. Often it is assumed that it coincided with the catastrophic flood that sank Atlantis. But if it occurred in 9500 B.C., it is too early, or if in 1500 B.C., it is too late. Most probably the Deluge was another, separate catastrophe.

The great conjunction of Saturn and Jupiter in 3102 B.C. is believed to have introduced the great flood recorded in the ancient *Mahabharata* of India.[4] The Pyramid Texts of Egypt suggest that the unification of Egypt by the first human king, the first attempt to develop agriculture on a wide technological scale, and the erection of the great pyramids, occurred as a response to and immediately following the Deluge. The date suggested is about 3100 or 3200 B.C.[5] This same date also has been found to be the earliest date that can be obtained by calendrical means, thus setting the limit of recorded history.[6]

All these vastly significant dates in world history and the beginning of the Mayan Great Cycle coincide at about 3113 B.C. The unusual configuration of the planets betokens a sudden and tremendous outburst of physical and psychical energy resulting in the genesis of the great civilizations of antiquity. The significance of the date in both hemispheres is apparent, and so is the duality of the effects resulting from the occurrence.

7 THE GREAT CYCLE
ITS PROJECTED END

The configuration for the projected end of the Great Cycle on
A.D. December 24, 2011 is even more significant. The Sklower predictions of the angles of elongation of the planets on that date are:

Sun	☉	0 degrees
Mercury	☿	26.49
Saturn	♄	63.79
Mars	♂	98.44
Pluto	♇	− 3.08
Venus	♀	− 35.17
Neptune	♆	− 60.0
Uranus	⛢	− 90.66
Jupiter	♃	−118.84

The configuration is roughly sketched in Figure 4.

Dr. Dan Lairmore, associated with the Foundation of Akaschic
Research in London and now doing astrological work in New
Mexico, verified with his own calculations these planetary positions calculated by Mrs. Sklower. These in turn were verified by
a cross check with the observatory at Jodril Bunk, England. Mrs.
Sklower and Mr. Lairmore then prepared additional data. In the
following Table 9, Planetary Positions, they give the longitude of
each planet, its zodiacal sign and degree, fixed star, and main
constellation. In Table 10, Planetary Aspects, are given the as-

265

FIGURE 4

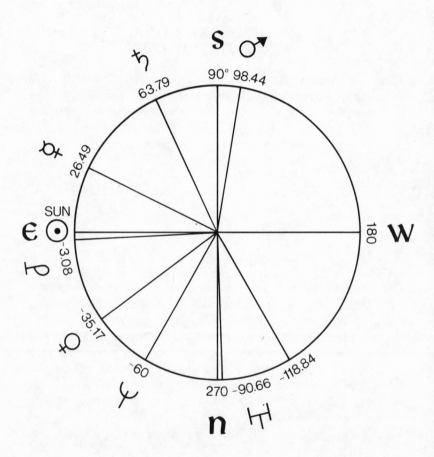

TABLE 9
Dec. 24, 2011 A.D. — Planetary Positions

Planet	Angle of Elongation	Planetary Longitude	Zodiac Sign & Degree	Fixed Star	Main Constellation
☉ Sun	—	272.82	3° ♐	Polis 2° 6' ♑	Sagittarii
☿ Mercury	26.49	245.33	15° ♐	Sabik	Ophiucci
♀ Venus	−35.17	307.0	7° ♒	Oculis 4° ♒ / Bos 5° ♒	Capricorni
♂ Mars	98.44	173.38	23.38° ♏	Denebola 20.5° ♏ / Copula 24° ♏	Leonis / 51 M Canum Vens
♃ Jupiter	−118.84	390.66	0° ♉	Mirach 29.2° ♈ / Shoruran 2° ♉	Andromeda / Arietes
♄ Saturn	63.79	209.03	29.03° ♎	Arcturus	Bootis
♅ Uranus	−90.66	362.48	2° ♈	Difda	Ceti
♆ Neptune	−60	331.82	2° ♓	Sadelmik	Aquarii
♇ Pluto	−3.08	275.9	6° ♐	Facic 7° ♑	22 M Sagittarii

TABLE 10

Planetary Aspects — Dec. 24, 2011 A.D.

	☉	☽	☿	♀	♂	♃	♄	♅	♆	♇
☉		CON +.5		SSX +2.3		TRI −2.3	SXT +4.8	SQR −1.9	SXT −3.9	CON +4.5
☽	CON +.5			SSX +1.9		TRI −2.7	SXT +5.3	SQR −2.4	SXT −4.4	CON +4.0
☿				SXT −6.0	SQR −7.2		SSQ −1.9	TRI −10.2		SSX −3.8
♀	SSX −2.3	SSX +1.9	SXT −6.0		SQQ +1.8	SQR −4.6	SQR +7.2	SXT +4.2		SSX −2.1
♂			SQR −7.2	SQQ +1.8		SQQ +2.8				TRI −11.1
♃	TRI −2.3	TRI −2.7		SQR −4.6	SQQ +2.8		OPP −2.6	SSX −.4	SXT +1.7	TRI −6.7
♄	SXT +4.8	SXT +5.3	SSQ −1.9	SQR +7.2		OPP −2.6		QCX +2.9	TRI +.9	QTL −6.7
♅	SQR −1.9	SQR −2.4	TRI −10.2	SXT +4.2		SSX −.4	QCX +2.9		SSX +2.0	SQR −6.4
♆	SXT −3.9	SXT −4.4				SXT +1.7	TRI +.9	SSX +2.0		
♇	CON +4.5	CON +4.0	SSX −3.8	SSX −2.1	TRI −11.1	TRI −6.7	QTL −6.7	SQR −6.4		
AC										
MC										

pects of each planet to the others. And on an astrological chart, Table 11, the positions of the planets in their respective signs.

Mrs. Sklower computes the probability of the planetary spacing in 3113 B.C. as once every 4,500 years, while that for A.D. 2011 is only once in 45,200 years. From this extraordinary pattern we might well expect an extraordinary effect.

From a quick look at the rough sketch of the planetary angles of elongation with respect to the sun, several aspects of the alignment seem at once apparent. One would normally expect the planets to be randomly scattered around the 360 degrees of elongation from the sun, but here they are spread with an ordered separation of approximately 30 degrees. Astrologers consider 60, 90, 120, and 180 degree separations as highly significant. All four of these are represented here. Oppositions of planets at 180 degrees and squares at 90 degrees are regarded as unfavorable or bad aspects. Squares occur here between sun and Mars, Saturn and Venus, Neptune and Mercury, Jupiter and Venus, Uranus and sun; and Mars and Uranus are in opposition to each other and squared with the sun. Offhand, the whole configuration seems decidedly negative and unfavorable at best.

Table 10, which meticulously details the aspects of each of the other planets, amply confirms this. And finally in Table 11 is given the interpretation planet by planet. In brief summary:

Mercury: polar shift, upheavals, violence, accidents

Venus: violence, auto accidents, love turns to hate, short-
sightedness

Mars: misfortunes from elements, blindness

Jupiter: destruction by fire and earthquake

Saturn: control of the seas

Uranus: self-destruction, people dying of sheer fright

Neptune: upheavals by volcanic action and earthquakes, psychic breaking up of homes

Pluto: accidents and violent deaths

Sun: fire

This current interpretation has been preceded by similar astrological predictions and prophecies for centuries. Nostradamus, the greatest European astrologer of his time, predicted in the sixteenth century that the world would undergo great upheavals due to

TABLE 11
Interpretation of Dec. 24, 2011 A.D.

Planet	Degree & Sign	Star	Degree	Nature of Star	Interpretation
Mercury	15° ♐	Saback	16° ♐	Same properties as Saturn and Venus	Lost energy—polar shift. Violence, accidents, conjunct North node of earth implying upheavals and extreme windstorms
Venus	7° ♒		4° ♒	?	Confrontation degree 11th House— Love turns to hate and violence
			5° ♒		Auto accidents, short sightedness. Makes people far-sighted
Mars	23.38° ♏ Virgo is an intercepted earth sign in chart	Denebola and Copula	20° ♏ 20° ♏	Venus & Saturn Moon	Tail of lion, judgements, the Lord to cometh. Swift judgement. Misfortune from elements of nature. Whirlpool nebula, its nature that of the moon causes blindness
Jupiter	0° ♉	Sheraton	2° ♉	Mars, Saturn	(one of names of devil) destruction by fire and earthquake
Saturn	29.03° ♎	Arcturus	23° ♎	Mars, Jupiter	control of the seas
Uranus	2° ♈	Difda	1° ♈	Saturn ?	Self destruction by brute force people dying out of sheer fright
Neptune	2° ♓	Fomalhout Sadelmelik	2° ♓	?	Earth upheaval, volcanic and earth-shaking degree, earth breaking apart. Psychic-breaking up of home
Pluto	6° ♑	Facie	7° ♑	Sun, Mars	Violent death and accident
Sun	2° ♑	Polis	2° ♑	Jupiter, Mars	Like Sagittarius—fire

the shift of its axis between 1999 and 2001. Famous Mother Shipton in England about the same time prophesied the world would come to an end in 1991. The late Edgar Cayce in his readings predicted that catastrophic changes in the world's physiography would begin during the last quarter of the twentieth century. Hundreds of similar predictions have been made during the last four centuries. There exists today a general belief among modern astrologers that about 2001 the axis of the earth will change, and the poles shift, causing cataclysmic upheavals.

Is there room for any hope in this pessimistic outlook? These predictions of world-wide physical catastrophes according to generally accepted astrology will be interpreted for us on a different, psychological level by G. D'Onofrio. But first let us get clear in our minds just what is the meaning of this archetypal catastrophe?

8 THE CATASTROPHE

The Catastrophe. The world-engulfing cataclysm. The memory of it, the dread of it, is still stamped on the collective unconscious of every Indian soul. Myth and legend tell of the last one, whenever it happened, followed by days of darkness and emptiness before the gods assembled to create a new sun. Predictions and prophecies tell of the one to come. Not only those of the Nahuas and Mayas, but that of the contemporary Hopis who believe the end of the world as we know it is not far off. The time will be marked when *Saquasohuh,* the Blue Star kachina, dances in the plaza. Far off and still invisible, the blue star will make its appearance soon.

According to Hopi prophecy, the previous worlds were destroyed when their inhabitants became corrupt. The present world is now also corrupt and will be destroyed; only those people who return to their original teachings will escape destruction. As the Day of Purification approaches, the True White Brother will come. He will bring with him sacred stone tablets to match those given the Hopis long ago. With him will come two helpers. One will carry the swastika, male symbol of purity, and a cross, female symbol of purity. The second helper will carry the symbol of the sun. These two will shake the earth. There will be a massive explosion, perhaps a volcanic eruption that will be felt throughout North and South America.

If these three fulfill their mission, finding a few Hopis who steadfastly adhere to their ancient teachings, they will lay out a new life plan. The earth will become new as it was in the beginning. The people saved will share everything in common, speak one tongue, and adopt the religion of the Great Spirit, Massau. But if the three sacred beings fail in their mission, and all people still remain corrupt, the Great Spirit will send "One" from the West. He will be many, many people and unmerciful. He will destroy the earth, only the ants being left to inhabit it.[1]

On Second Mesa near Mishongnovi an ancient petroglyph depicts a dome-shaped object resting on an arrow which represents travel through space, and the head of a Hopi maiden who represents pristine purity. As the Hopis believe the other planets are inhabited, this petroglyph represents a *patuwvota*, a "flying shield" similar to a "flying saucer" that came here in the Beginning. So now at the End the sacred ones will arrive from another planet, said to be Venus, by flying saucers. Many Hopi traditionalists recently have reported seeing flying saucers, all piloted by the beings they call *kachinas*.

On Friday, August 7, 1970 hundreds of Hopis and Anglos from miles around gathered at Prescott, Arizona to see the flying saucers or UFO's appear from Venus to confirm Hopi prophecy. That they were called by a white man, the "Flying Saucer Prophet" who had managed to gain the confidence of the Hopis, was doubtful. There was less doubt from many onlookers that something did appear. Reported the managing editor of the *Prescott Courier*: "It looked like a star—almost. It rose in the sky, stopped, hovered, wavered to one side and then continued across the sky repeating the maneuvers. It was a long ways away, but we thought it changed colors from a white to a reddish orange and then to a purplish blue and then a reddish white. And then it was gone. A flying saucer? Yes, if we could believe our eyes."

His Sunday edition headlined the story, with pages of photographs of six flying saucers, of the 100-year-old Hopi chiefs and the Flying Saucer Prophet; reports from many people in the area who had seen the saucers; feature stories from a dozen UFO research experts; and a full, detailed account of the Hopi prophecy.[2] Due to the wire service's policy not to publicize UFO sightings, no mention of this extraordinary story was made in any other newspaper. A second appearance of the flying saucers was to occur the following April, but due to a late spring snowstorm they either did not appear or could not be seen.

No comment is made here on the factual events as reported, nor on the claims of the Flying Saucer Prophet. What we do observe, however, is the remarkable similarity of the current Hopi prophecy to those of the ancient Nahuas and Mayas. Their contents contain the same principal elements: the catastrophic destruction of this world, as of the previous ones; the appearance of a star, followed by sacred beings from another planet; the symbolism of the sun and Venus, the swastika and the cross; and the necessity for reinstituting spiritual values in place of corrupt materialism, which accents their religious premise.

This current Hopi belief brings us back again to the Mesoamerican myth of the catastrophic destruction of previous worlds. Were they all caused by planetary aberrations, refuting our belief in an unalterably ordered solar system? Or were catastrophic disorders in both heaven and earth governed by laws of universal order?

Santillana asserts that the four corners of the quadrangular earth, as it was viewed by the Mayas, were determined by the four constellations rising heliacally at the two equinoxes and two solstices.[3] Since they existed only temporarily, the earth perished or drowned when the equinoctial constellations dipped beneath the equator, and a new earth emerged from the waters when four new constellations rose at the four points of the year. The progression of the vernal equinoctial points thus marked a succession of world-ages under different zodiacal signs.

Despite the violent changes that have continuously altered its surface, the Earth is the same organic entity, the "divine creature" as Plato called it. So has it been with mankind. Violent cataclysms have not obliterated it. Mankind has adapted itself to the changes. Races have vanished. One primitive culture, one civilization, arises and falls, to be replaced by another. But mankind remains. If terrestrial catastrophes have often altered the course of human history, all decisive changes in mankind's development have not been dependent upon them. Rather have they been determined by what seems to be the periodic synchronization of human and cosmic rhythms. Of this periodicity we know little, the scope of the periods is so large. We can only surmise that the physical changes in the surface of the earth and the psychological changes in mankind must be parallel phenomena determined by their coincidence in time. This is why myth, the oldest and most holy witness of the human spirit, is so relevant. It reveals the hidden world that has never faded from human consciousness and bridges the gap between physical and psychical realities.

The many quoted assertions throughout this text make us aware of the widespread belief that our religions have an astral origin, being but analogies for the movements of the stars. But also the belief is growing that the structure of man's psyche and the universe is the same, and that whatever happens in one happens in the other. This prompts the question whether the shape of man's universe and the images of his gods come to him from outside. Or whether the divine attributes which he has ascribed to celestial bodies and to his gods, which are natural and psychic forces, are but the projected inner contents of his own unconscious. If so, they existed in residual and primordial states before they were projected, and the creative cause of their archetypal imprints on the human psyche is beyond our comprehension. We only know that something rises in us to give shape to our groping for life's meaning, to the undying need of the spirit to be whole, on that uncharted plain of timeless time across which journeys into consciousness that which is unconscious.

For such a stamp of wholeness on the psyche, whose origin and nature is unknown, Jung first used the term primordial image or archetype. In later years he used the term "psychoid archetype" when he recognized it as a metaphysical entity both psychic and physical, which manifested its bipolar opposites as it rose into consciousness, imprinting both instinctive and organic life and the physical and inorganic world.[4]

The idea that the power of Creation, even the supreme Creator, embodied the principles of duality is not new. It stems back to the ancient belief in a primeval demiurge who existed before the beginning, standing behind good and evil, spirit and matter, all opposites; back to the Eastern teachings of one infinite power and consciousness finitizing itself in both matter and pragmatic consciousness. Through this great concept we finally reach the last

onion layers of the Mexico mystique with its fundamental theme
of cosmic duality.

For if the sacred twins of myth were such archetypes of the
dual forces manifested in man, so do the mythical cataclysms
which destroyed the previous worlds and gave rise to new ones
manifest the same bipolar forces in nature. The Catastrophe, then,
is also an archetype stamped on man's psyche and held in his undying memory. It too reflects the polarity of all Creation and embodies two meanings: it is a general symbol for change wrought
in a single process, as Cirlot says, but also a symbol for the beginnings of psychic transformation. They cannot be separated.
Hence myth attests both the horror of terrestrial destruction and
the constructive influence of its numinosity.

With this perspective we must now examine the Nahuatl and
Mayan prophecies that the present world-age will come to an
end with the cataclysmic upheavals indicated by the planetary
configuration on December 24, 2011.

Popular astrology affirms that a sextile of 60 degrees and a trine
of 120 degrees are good aspects, whereas a square of 90 degrees
and an opposition of 180 degrees are bad aspects. Goodness and
badness, however, have little to do with the nature of the aspect,
but with the nature of the planets involved. Any aspect between
two benefics is good, while any aspect between two malefics is
bad. The result of planetary influences cannot be determined
solely by their astrological aspects. Other considerations must be
taken into account.

D'Onofrio reads this configuration of A.D. 2011, as that of 3113
B.C., from the viewpoint of its possible psychological effects upon
man. Her interpretation parallels Collin's thesis that life energy
is diffused from the sun through the various planets to the corresponding glands in the human body which they control, but she
also takes into account the fields of force exerted from the areas
marked by the signs of the constellations.

The conjunction of the sun and Venus dominated the configuration marking the cycle beginning in 3113 B.C. This is why Venus
was so important throughout the cycle, and the great civilizations
of antiquity rose under its parathyroidal influence. Since then
three new planets have been discovered: Uranus in A.D. 1781, Nep-

tune in 1846, and Pluto as recently as 1930; and man is beginning to comprehend the roles he will play in the new cycle marked by the configuration of A.D. 2011.

The most significant aspect of this unusual pattern is the conjoining of the sun with Pluto, the last discovered and outermost of the planets, about which little is known. This conjunction of the sun and Pluto will dominate the coming new cycle, just as the conjunction of the sun and Venus dominated the previous cycle beginning in 3113 B.C.

Saturn at 29.03 degrees in Libra is ready to enter Scorpio, and therefore is in almost exact opposition to Jupiter at 0 degrees in Taurus. These two opposing planets influence the two lobes of the pituitary gland in the human body, one controlling physical sensations and reflexes and the other mind and reason. Their opposing forces present a conflict of polarities which we are well aware of today, and which must be reconciled if a balance is to be reached.

The next powerful angle is formed by Uranus squaring the conjunction of the sun and Pluto, directing at it the energy of stress for the purpose of change. Also Neptune at 2 degrees of Pisces makes a 60 degree angle to the Sun-Pluto conjunction, offering the opportunity of reconciling the opposing pituitary forces as partners by activating the pineal gland with its function of intuitive seeing or extrasensory perception. The difficulty of withstanding the Sun-Pluto conjunction squared by Uranus can be overcome only with the help of this Neptunian-pineal activation.

Since Venus at 7 degrees Aquarius makes a sextile to Uranus, it, like Neptune, helps mitigate the powerful stress energy arising from the square of Uranus to the Sun-Pluto conjunction. Venus, receiving the squares of Saturn and Jupiter from Taurus and Scorpio, also plays a part in harmonizing the two opposing forces of the pituitary.

Mercury in Sagittarius, making a sextile to Venus in Aquarius, will also produce harmonious energy particularly in the throat center, opening a way to the head. And since Mars and Mercury square each other, it seems that language will play a great part in the coming cycle; not the Gemini type of chatter now in use, but words used carefully and creatively with respect for their power.

FIGURE 5

PLANETARY POSITIONS
December 24, 2011
12:00 Midnight

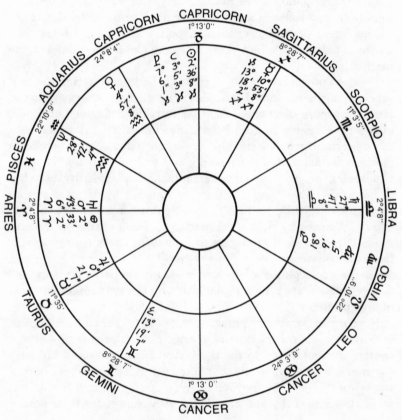

Even without reference to the astrological charts in Figure 5 D'Onofrio's conclusions are clear. The configuration reveals many harmonious aspects and opportunities for realizing them if we are receptive. She feels that we are already beginning to experience to a small degree what will culminate sometime about A.D. 2011—an intense bombardment of planetary forces of a new cosmic order, abetted or modified by those of outlying constellations.

The earth itself will of course receive the same influx of cosmic forces. That there may be areas and peoples unable to withstand the stress, will confirm the prediction of physical upheavals and human disturbances and casualties which always accompany world changes, some of which are already taking place. Yet the general prognosis is good. The world will not be destroyed by a great cataclysm despite all dire prophecies. Nor will mankind. Both will continue their evolution in a new phase. A phase significantly different from that we are now experiencing.

9 THE SIXTH WORLD
THE AGE OF AQUARIUS

The Egyptians, says Fagan, conceived the zodiac not only as the "Road of Life" but as the "Wheel of Life," for the movements of the sun and planets signified the movement of life itself,[1] as also expressed by the Nahuatl and Mayan law of *movement*. Comprising the rim of the wheel are the constellations of Cancer, Libra, Capricorn, and Aries, the ineffectual "busy bees." Its spokes are Gemini, Virgo, Sagittarius, and Pisces, caught in the conflict between the pairs of opposites. At its hub, moving the world, are Taurus, Leo, Scorpio, and Aquarius.

Mayan astrology seems to parallel this belief. Its Great Cycle began in the Age of Taurus; and it was predicted to end at the beginning of the Age of Aquarius, another constellation at the hub. How sure can we be of this?

If it is assumed that each astrological age lasts two thousand years, the three ages included in the Mayan Great Cycle began in the Taurean Age which started in 4,000 B.C., and will conclude with the end of the Piscean Age in A.D. 2,000. But Fagan, as previously discussed, establishes the opening of the Taurus Age in 4152 B.C. and its end in 1955 B.C. when Aldebaron, the "Bull's Eye," entered Aries. How long the succeeding Aries Age lasted is not known. The 2,000-year span, however, is only a rough approximation of an age of 2,160 years as measured by a precessional period. Hence if the Taurus Age covered 2,197 years, a closer

280

approximation, and the Aries Age extended for the same number of years, it would have ended in A.D. 221 coincident with the beginning of the Pisces Age. Here more confusion results. For as the Age of the Fish is synonymous with the Christian era, and it is not known when the birth of Christ and the advent of his era occurred, various dates have been set for the beginning of the Pisces age ranging from 144 B.C. to A.D. 496. Thus the end of the present Pisces age and the beginning of the following Aquarius age is also in wide dispute, with dates ranging up to A.D. 2381.

These variant dates are of less concern than the fact that Pisces, the twelfth and last age in the zodiacal cycle, signifies the final stage of dissolution which contains the beginning of a new cycle. Its sign portrays this dual aspect with two fishes parallel to each other but facing opposite directions. The fish on the left indicates the direction of involution, the one on the right pointing to the direction of evolution, the way out of the cycle. Jung goes a step farther in his interpretation.[2] One fish symbolizes the first thousand years of the age represented by the Christian principle, the other fish representing the Luciferian principle of materialism and destruction now under way.

The sign of the coming age is Aquarius, the Water Bearer. Water being a symbol of the unconscious, the sign betokens the emergence from the unconscious of those contents which unified with conscious elements will lead to a union of the opposite polarities.

The great significance of the Mayan date of A.D. 2011 is now apparent. There seems little doubt that this predicted end of the Mayan Great Cycle coincides with the end of the great precessional period concluding with the end of the present Age of Pisces. And if the past cycle constituted the Fifth World of the Nahuas and Mayas, the coming cycle will witness the emergence of the succeeding Sixth World with all that it implies.

Whether the turning point will be the exact date so fantastically calculated by the Mayas, it is already obvious we are now approaching another great verge in the history of mankind. We may ignore the predictions of cataclysmic upheavals in the Arctic and Antarctic regions, the sinking of Japan and the Atlantic and Pacific coasts of America, and the re-emergence of old land masses.

We are more uncomfortably aware of the statistical predictions that with the rate of our increasing population, our wasteful destruction of land resources, our pollution of rivers, lakes, and oceans, the very air itself, the world will become untenable between A.D. 2000 and 2020.[3] Are we on this ecologically doomed planet psychologically making efforts to leave it? Is this the unconscious prompting, akin to the instincts of migrating birds—or rats deserting a sinking ship!—behind our rationally engineered landings on the moon and preparations to extend our space travel to Mars?

We must also concede the psychical parallels accompanying these physical changes. Cataclysmic rumbles and ruptures in the human spirit are taking place everywhere. Revolutions have spread to every corner of the globe. Economic and social values are being discarded. Orthodox religious systems have lost their appeal; new beliefs, new sects, are springing up by the dozens. The engrossing interest in UFOs, or flying saucers, and the belief they may contain inhabitants from a distant body in outer space, is world-wide. Such phenomena are symptoms of psychic changes that always appear at the end of one precessional period and at the beginning of another—"changes in the constellation of psychic dominants, of the archetypes, or 'gods' as they used to be called, which bring about or accompany long-lasting transformations of the collective unconscious."[4] Transformations that occurred in the transition from the age of Taurus to that of Aries, then from Aries to Pisces, and now occuring when we are about to enter the age of Aquarius. Already we are psychically beginning our transition, or Emergence as the Pueblos call it, to the new Sixth World.

This may be the ultimate meaning we are able to derive from the Mesoamerican myth of the successive Worlds, Eras, or Suns, and from the Atlantis and other world myths of the successive Worlds or Continents—vast allegories for the psychological changes within man as he enters different stages along his evolutionary Road of Life.

During these stages our manner of perception changed with our expanding consciousness from the simple awareness of instinct and sensory perception to reason and our present excessive rationalization. And this is where we find ourselves today, alienated by the tyranny of mind from instinct, the earthy substratum of our essential being—a society whose psychic wholeness is split between opposite poles. Our intellectual development and fantastic scientific achievements have become too powerful to permit us to return. But the way out of this impasse is already indicated by increasing signs of a new faculty that will dominate both instinct and reason during the coming cycle. Through the awareness of intuition we may find that the material and the ethereal are aspects of the same essence; that sensory and extrasensory perception combine in one focus on the whole; and that all life itself is but a series of stages of cosmic evolution.

In the supreme law governing both external and internal realities, there seems to be a factor of cohesiveness that links in one great process the evolving life of every microscopic cell and giant star. Plants, animals, man, the Earth itself, may be but microcosmic reflections of that macrocosmic life which also informs all planets in our solar system and the farthest galaxies in a universe too great to be conceived by the human mind. All are embodied in the same cosmic process of the whole.

The religious philosophies of the East assure us there is no first creation. Worlds come and go eternally. Infinity, the irreducible real, periodically finitizes itself into the reducible real of the worlds of material form, of time, space, and causality. Then they are withdrawn again into the unmanifest alogical whole, only to be projected again; appearing and disappearing with the out-breathing and in-breathing power of all Creation, the pulse of life itself.

This process of involution and evolution, this perpetual movement, may be the deepest meaning of the ancient Mesoamerican hieroglyph for *movement,* for it takes place within the heart of man himself. Surely the validity of the Mexico Mystique must embody this universal truth, cloaked as it is in a mythical and symbolic medium of expression seemingly esoteric, strange, and barbaric to us. Uniquely American, it is a heritage that may serve to link us with a past people and with present peoples everywhere, as we approach a new verge in our common history.

Appendix

Predicting Planetary Positions

Roberta S. Sklower

All things are the same, familiar in experience
and ephemeral in time and worthless in matter.
Everything now is just as it was in the days of
those we have buried.

Marcus Aurelius Meditations

I. The Problem

Our present problem is to ascertain the planetary positions on two dates, one far in the past and one in the future—the conjectured beginning of the Mayan Great Cycle on August 12, 3113 B.C. and its predicted end on December 24, A.D. 2011. We wish to find out if there were unusual planetary arrangements for these extraordinary dates.

II. Methods of Planetary Predictions

Ancient astronomy had two basic approaches to the prediction of planetary positions. The Sumerians and Babylonians used an empirical approach. They observed the positions of the planets with surprising precision, discovered the patterns or cycles they formed over a period of time, and related these patterns to mathematical formulae which were then used to predict their future patterns. Modern astronomers call this method "curve fitting," but it is really an algebraic approach.

The Greeks used a geometrical approach. They set up models of elliptical orbits and solid bodies perambulating around these orbits, and defined precise equations of motion to describe them.

There is a crucial difference between these two methods. If we construct geometric figures we must precisely define what happens to the planets when they disappear below the horizon. We have to define gravitational and electromagnetic effects on these paths. We should be able to define long-range effects of these outside forces where these curves become discontinuous. And we really cannot define equations for all these outside effects.

But if we are seeking only algebraic formulae which will represent actually observed positions, we do not have to worry about the behavior of the planets when they disappear below the horizon, the effects of forces on the curves. And finally, we do not have to assume a continuity along a whole curve within the framework of a discontinuous nature.

For these reasons we shall use here the algebraic approach.

III. Definition of the Problem

Finding the planetary positions of August 12, 3113 B.C. is not quite the same problem as finding the positions of December 24, A.D. 2011. The general approach to both problems is the same. We use the underlying premise that the relative positions of the sun and the planets on any one specific date will be repeated on later dates and are themselves repeats of relative positions on earlier dates. If we can determine what these comparable dates are, we can determine where the planet is, in relation to the sun, on that specific date.

The information needed for the two problems is somewhat different. The short term problem (2011 A.D.) requires only the observations of the patterns of the last forty to fifty years in order to extrapolate from them a formula to predict the patterns of the next forty years. The long term problem (3113 B.C.) requires observations over the whole of man's recorded history. Dr. P. V. Neugebauer has taken the recorded observations, and using an algebraic technique to minimize the error, worked out a series of tables to approximate those patterns.

Since the Neugebauer tables minimize the error over a period from 2500 B.C. to almost A.D. 2000, the information contained in these tables is designed to minimize the error between calculated and observed positions over that extremely long period of time. While very applicable to the long term problem, these tables contain much more information than is needed to solve the short term problem—4,500 versus 40 years.

The 40 years of minimal error represent one per cent of 4,500 years of minimal error, so it is quite clear that we do not want the same information to solve both problems. And since the tables require a special method for their use, we shall be using a different method to solve the short term problem.

IV. Basic Concepts

Some basic concepts must be first defined. The ideas of meridian, right ascension, angle of elongation, synodic period, sidereal period, and Julian date are fundamental to the discussion.

A.   Meridian

Let a person stand facing due south. The highest point directly over his head is called his zenith. A semicircle can be drawn through this overhead point, starting at the point on his horizon which is due north of him, up through his zenith, and back down to his southern horizon at the point due south of him. This celestial semicircle is called his meridian. All heavenly bodies cross that meridian from east to west at some time during the twenty-four-hour day. The meridian we shall be concerned with is the Prime Meridian at Greenwich, England.

B.   Right Ascension

Right Ascension is the adjusted time, not the real time, that the sun or a planet crosses the meridian. It is adjusted in the sense that on April 21 every year the sun is assigned a Right Ascension of 0 hours. The other celestial bodies are assigned times corresponding to their time separation from the sun. A planet one hour ahead of the sun as these bodies cross the Meridian on April 21 will be assigned a Right Ascension of 23 hours, for zero hours can be considered as either zero hours or 24 hours. Similarly a planet one hour behind or to the east of the sun will have a Right Ascension of 1 hour.

This adjustment is necessary because the rotation of the Earth is not exactly twenty-four hours, but twenty-four hours and some four minutes. If the Right Ascension were taken as the absolute time, in August the sun would be overhead at Greenwich, England at 8:00 A.M. and on April 20 at midnight.

For purposes of this discussion, we need only to think of Right Ascension as some number which serves as a convenient reference point and which can be used to determine the separation of the planets and the sun by units of time which we can then convert to units of angular measure or degrees.

The earth rotates once a day, and the complete rotation describes a circle. Therefore, since there are 360 degrees in a circle, and it takes the earth 24 hours to complete 360 degrees, the earth must turn 360/24 degrees in one hour and it must take 60/15 or 4 minutes to turn 1 degree. Using these conversion factors, 4 minutes equal 1 degree and 60 minutes equal 15 degrees, we can then describe the difference between the Right Ascensions of the sun and any given planet, not only in units of time, but in degrees. We can then describe the relative positions of planet and sun as an angle.

C. Angle of Elongation

Looking at Figure 6, a planet, say Venus, as seen from the earth will form an angle with the sun. It is then said to be at a certain elongation from the sun. Another way of looking at this is that as an observer on earth looks at his meridian, Venus will cross his meridian separated from the sun by so many degrees at the rate of four minutes per degree. If the sun crosses his meridian

FIGURE 6

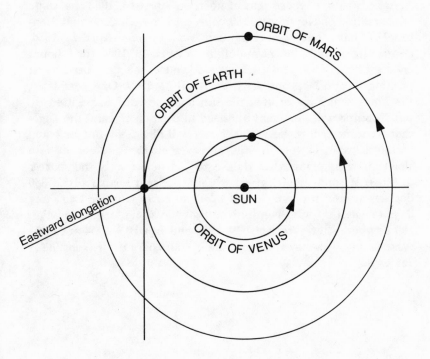

with a Right Ascension of 10 hours and 30 minutes, and Venus crosses his meridian with a Right Ascension of 12 hours and 30 minutes, Venus is two hours behind or east of the sun by two hours, which is equal to 30 degrees. Since Venus is behind the sun, the convention we use is that the angle is negative—it is a minus 30 degree angle. So we say that the angle of elongation of Venus is −30 degrees or 30 degrees east.

D. Synodic Period

The synodic period is the time required for a planet to move from a certain position with respect to the sun as seen from the Earth back to the same position or elongation. The second date is then comparable to the first date relative to the angle of elongation; in other words, we are defining a basic frame of reference as comparable angles made by the sun and a planet as seen from the earth.

To illustrate, suppose that at noon on April 14, 1953 the angle of elongation of Neptune is 180 degrees. The next time that Neptune will have that same elongation is not at noon, April 14, 1954, as one might think, but at midnight on April 16, 1954 (or 0 hours on the 17th). If we look at Figure 7 we can see that Earth is at position E_1 and Neptune at N_1 on April 14, 1953. One year later, the Earth will have orbited the sun and returned to position E_1, but Neptune will have moved ahead to position N_2, and the angle that Neptune will make with the sun will obviously not be equal to 180 degrees, as seen by the observer on Earth. Neptune is a slower moving planet than the Earth and moves only the shorter distance of some two degrees while the Earth has revolved 360 degrees around the sun. It will take the Earth another two some days to catch up with Neptune so that the angle formed is again 180 degrees. Therefore April 14, 1953 and April 16, 1954 are comparable days. We say then that the synodic period for Neptune is 367 days.

FIGURE 7

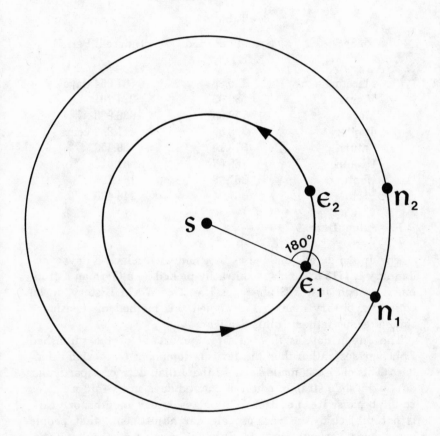

E. Sidereal Period

The sidereal period is the length of time it takes for a planet to orbit the sun and return to the same position as seen from the stars. Since the stars don't move, but are considered fixed on our celestial sphere, the sidereal period is simply the length of time it takes for a planet to orbit the sun.

The synodic and sidereal periods of the planets are given below:

Table 13

Planet	Synodic Period In Days	Sidereal Period
Mercury	115.88	87.964 days
Venus	583.93	224.701 "
Mars	779.95	686.980 "
Jupiter	398.89	11.862 years
Saturn	378.10	29.458 "
Uranus	369.67	84.013 "
Neptune	367.49	164.794 "
Pluto	367.74	248.430 "

F. Julian Date

The Julian date is defined as the number of elapsed days since January 1, 4713 B.C., a day arbitrarily picked by a German astronomer, Joseph Justus Scaliger, as Day 1 of World History. In an equally arbitrary manner, he named this method of measuring time after his father, Julius Scaliger.

The Julian date is the basis for almost all of the published Ephemerides, rather than the Jewish, Roman, or Gregorian calendars. This choice is made because the Julian date of a particular day is simply a straight count of elapsed days since 4713 B.C. This count, because it is not broken into days, weeks, months, or years, is not subject to the various calendar adjustments that people have made through history. Julius Caesar, nephew Augustus Caesar, the Roman Senate, and Pope Gregory all had to drop days or weeks in order to square accounts with the vernal equinox, which meandered all over the spring season.

The Julian day count does have one disadvantage, however. "December 24, 2011" is far easier to remember than 2455920.5 and "August 12, 3113 B.C." is far easier to locate in a textbook than Julian Day 584623.5.

V. Solving the Short Term A.D. 2011 Problem

As discussed briefly in an earlier section, the method we will use consists of finding the positions of the planets with reference to the sun on dates which are comparable in planetary elongations, observing the patterns that those elongations make, and reducing these patterns to some sort of mathematical formulae. We can then predict positions from those formulae.

The positions of the sun and planets for all dates and all years from 1896 on are recorded in the Astronomical and Nautical Ephemerides for each year. These Ephemerides then are the source of our observations from which we can determine the patterns.

The first step is to determine the comparable dates. We pick a reference date, any convenient date in a published Ephemeris, and for a given planet, determine the number of synodic periods between that date and December 24, 2011 A.D. We determine this by taking the number of days between them, and then dividing by the number of days in the synodic period of the planet in question. The answer will consist of an integer part and a remainder. If there is no remainder, then we have found a date which is comparable to 2011 A.D. Most likely there will be a remainder and this remainder is really the number of days over and above a whole synodic period, and should be eliminated.

For example, if we wish to determine a date for Venus comparable to December 24, 2011 A.D., we proceed in the following way:

1. We would like this comparable day to be some date for which the Ephemerides have been published so that we may compute the angle of elongation. Therefore we would choose December 24, 1971 as a convenient date. The Julian date is 2455920.

2.   We then take the number of days between the two dates,
14,611, and divide by the number of days in the synodic period
of Venus, 583.93 days.

The remainder is 1275. Since there are two decimal places in
the divisor, we can mark off two in the remainder and we get
12.75 days.

The answer is 25 $\underline{\frac{12.75}{583.93}}$ periods. To get an even number

of synodic periods we must zero out the remainder. Obviously
if we add some 12.75 days to 2441309, the result of 2455920
minus that number will be less than 14611, and this result
when divided by 583.93 should give us little or no remainder.

Therefore, adding 12.75 to 2441309, we get 2441321, the
Julian date of January 5, 1972. To ascertain that this is really
the comparable date, we must check the number of synodic
periods between 2441321.75 and 2455920.00, and the zero remainder assures us of a comparable date. The rest of the comparable dates are easier to find.

The second step is to find the relative position of the sun and
the planets on the comparable dates. These positions are to be
found in the American Ephemerides published yearly.

Still using Venus as the example, its Right Ascension as given
in the Ephemeris for January 5, 1972 is 21 hours, 14 minutes,
56.83 seconds, that of the sun 18 hours, 59 minutes, 41.13 seconds.
The time difference is found by subtracting the planetary Right
Ascension from that of the sun. In this case, Venus has the larger
Right Ascension, so the difference will be negative. Converting
this time difference into degrees, we find 33.82 degrees; and since
Venus is behind the sun, the angle is negative, i.e., the elongation
is −33.82 degrees.

The first comparable date back, as we saw earlier, was May 30,
1970, Julian day 2440737.07. The Right Ascension for Venus on
that date was 06^h 39^m 11.02^s. We have to consider, however, that
the Julian date that we computed included some time toward the
following day; this is what the 0.07 in the Julian date really
means. The Right Ascension for Venus on May 31, 1970 is given
in the Ephemeris as 06^h 44^m 27.04^s. There is a time difference of
some 316.02 seconds between the two days. If we take 0.07 of the

difference and add it to the Right Ascension for Venus on the 30th, we will have allowed for the 0.07 in the date. 0.07 of the difference is 21.12 seconds, which when added to the figure for the 30th gives a new corrected Right Ascension of 06^h 39^m 33.14^s. Following a similar procedure with the Right Ascensions for the sun on the two dates, we arrive at a corrected figure of 02^h 13^m 35.26^s. The angle difference then is −33.40°.

The next step is to study the pattern that emerges when the elongations for a number of synodic periods are calculated and plotted. If we compute the angles for the past twenty-five synodic periods of Venus and plot them, we can see that a definite pattern emerges: four complete cycles of five synodic periods per cycle. As it takes five synodic periods for the planet to go from one minimum value for the angle of elongation to the next, these five synodic periods or one cycle represent eight years. Looking at our chart we can see that Venus forms the smallest angle with the sun on the following dates: 3/28/35, 3/20/43, 3/23/51, 3/31/59, 3/19/67. If we pick any one of these dates, say 3/19/67, and find the number of synodic periods between it and December 24, 2011 A.D., we can then find which of the five points on the cycle that the target date corresponds to most closely.

The Julian date of March 19, 1967 is 2439568.21, that of December 24, 2011 A.D. is 2455920. There are 16351 days between the two dates or 28.0 synodic periods. Since there are five points to a cycle, 28 divided by 5 is 5 3/5. Counting 3 points past the start of the cycle, we find that the date corresponding to December 24, 2011 is January 5, 1972.

Other corresponding dates and values are:

Table 14

Date	Value
1/5/72	−33.9
1/6/64	−33.63
1/10/50	−33.41
1/11/48	−33.15
1/13/40	−32.89

The last step is to take the results of the pattern analysis, and develop some formula, either implicit or explicit. We discovered that there were five pertinent values, increasing as we go forward in time, starting with 32.89 in 1940 and ending with 33.90 in 1972. We can also see that the differences between the values are, 0.27, 0.22, 0.26, 0.26, starting with 1972 and going back to 1940. If we average out the differences, we find that the average difference between any two cycles is 0.255. In order then to predict a value in 2011 which is five cycles away from January 5, 1972, and which will be larger than the corresponding value in 1972, we take five times the average difference and add it to the value for January 5, 1972: $-33.90 + 5 \times 0.255$ or $-33.90 + 1.27 = -35.17$.

Applying the same method for the rest of the planets, we find the predicted positions relative to the sun for December 24, 2011 A.D. as shown in the text.

One further note. It can be shown that the corresponding points of cycles occur when the planet is in the same position relative to the sun and stars. We observe from this that each planet has a unique number of points in its complete cycle which depends upon the length of its synodic and sidereal period, so that the planet may return to the same relative position regarding sun and stars in a varying amount of time at the end of a cycle. Neugebauer used this principle of relative position as the basis for his method for planetary position calculation; this is the method we will use for solving the long term problem of August 12, 3113 B.C.

VI. Solving the Long Term 3113 B.C. Problem

Some scientific researchers like to play poker. Other scientists bet on the greyhounds. Another group of fatalists defines equations of geometric curves to make long term extrapolations to calculate planetary positions in antiquity. Factors that we cannot define completely such as long term effects in electromagnetic and gravitational fields, as well as some planetary masses (Pluto), add an element of suspense to the necessary equations.

Other complications in long term extrapolations are caused by the shifting of the Earth's axis. When we look up at the North Star, we look at a star called Polaris, the Pole Star, to which the

Earth's axis points. When the ancient Egyptians looked at the sky, the Pole Star was Draconis; 12,000 years from now it will be Vega.

This gradual change of direction in the Earth's axis is caused by the fact that the axis is not pointed straight up and down. There would be no change of Pole Star if it were. But in exchange for this convenience, we should have to give up our seasons, for they are a result of the Earth's axis being slanted some 23½° off the vertical. The Earth is spinning through space like a huge gyroscopic top, on a slant; and this slant causes the circular change in the direction that the North Pole points.

The change in direction of the pole is not apparent in our comparatively short lifetime, but over a period of five thousand years could play havoc with the calculated position of planets.

Neugebauer went back over an extremely long period of time—some forty-five hundred years—observing the cycles that the planets made as they orbited around the more or less same position relative to the sun and stars, and devised formulas to simulate their movements. These formulas are basically equations to minimize the errors between observed and calculated planetary positions over the whole of recorded history. Neugebauer, from these formulas, set up a group of twelve tables that describe planetary positions within synodic and sidereal periods. These remarkable tables describe the movements for thousand-year periods, two-hundred year periods, hundred-year periods, year, month, and day.

A full description of the Neugebauer method and reprints of the tables may be found in *Solar and Planetary Longitudes for Years −2500 to 2000* by William D. Stahlman and Owen Gingerich. Bryan Tuckerman of I.B.M. has also published an Ephemerides of Planetary Positions from 600 B.C. to 1 A.D. which are largely based on these tables.

In brief, Neugebauer's method involves the following steps:
1. The longitude and radius vector of the sun.
2. The planet's position or "age" within its sidereal and synodic period.
3. The position in relation to the sun after correcting for the varying motion of the planet in relation to its orbit, i.e., the directional change of the axis.

    4. The angle of elongation after setting the position in re-
       lation to sun and stars.
    5. The planetary longitude.

We might say generally that Neugebauer developed the correc-
tions needed for planetary orbit changes and Earth axis tilt, and
inserted them into his tables to make the tables workable. His
"anomalies" look at the patterns as a whole, and adjust for these
aberrations in a most remarkable manner. By these adjustments,
he avoided the pitfalls of trying to estimate long term field effects
and planetary mass determination which plagued so many later
attempts at planetary position calculation.

The planetary arrangement and plots of the angle of elongation
for the five visible planets on August 12, 3113 B.C. are shown in
the text.

VII. A Probability Theory

In the planetary alignment for December 24, 2011 A.D. we notice that the planets are spaced approximately 30° apart. Before
we decide that this is a highly unusual spacing mathematically
and astronomically, we must determine the probability, or the
odds that such a unique spacing would occur. We will not stipu-
late that a planet must lie on one of the thirty degree lines, but
only require that the planets be within a five degree band on
either side of the thirty-degree lines in their elongation from the
sun. Intuitively, we feel that such a spacing appears as highly
improbable, but we should back that up with statistical fact.

The question we are asking then, is: "What are the odds that a
planet will be elongated 90° approximately from the sun, a second
planet elongated approximately 60° from the sun, a third elongated approximately 30°, a fourth approximately even with the
sun, a fifth approximately 30° behind the sun, a sixth approximately 60° behind the sun, a seventh approximately 90° behind
the sun, and an eighth approximately 120° behind the sun."

Now when we wish to find the probability that one thing and
then another might occur, we multiply the probabilities of each
happening. If we throw a dice twice, and want to know the prob-

ability of a four on the first throw and a six on the second, we multiply the probability of throwing a four by the probability of throwing a six. Now, a dice has six faces, so the probability of throwing a four is 1/6; that of throwing a six is 1/6. The probability of throwing a four and a six is 1/6 x 1/6 or 1/36.

Now what is the probability that if we put the sun at 0°, the planets will be in the following arrangement: one in Band 1, one in Band 2, one in Band 3, one in Band 4, and one in Band 5 and so on to Band 8, as shown in Figure 8.

FIGURE 8

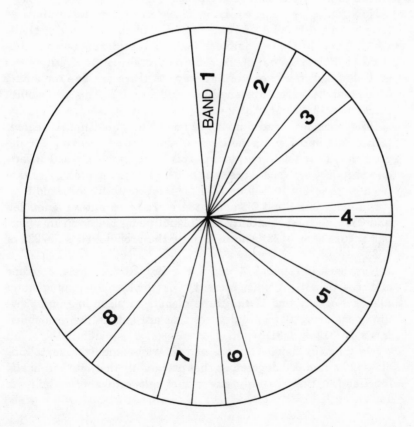

Mercury and Venus cannot be placed in other than Bands 3, 4, or 5; Mercury's maximum elongation from the sun is about 28° and Venus's maximum around 40°, because they move around the sun more rapidly than we do. This means that only the six outer planets, Mars, Jupiter, Saturn, Uranus, Neptune, and Pluto, are available for Bands 1, 2, 6, 7, and 8.

The probability of any one planet being placed in Band 1 is the probability that a planet is placed in one of the 10 specific degrees in Band 1, the five degrees on either side of 90° or from 95° to 85°. This band accounts for 10 degrees out of 360 degrees in the circle, or 1/36. Now we may choose any one of the six outer planets to fill that position in the band, so the probability of a planet being placed in Band 1 is 6 x 1/36 or 6/36.

Now when we consider Band 2, we must remember that we have used up Band 1 of 10 degrees out of the 360 in the circle, which leaves 350 to be eligible. So we are considering now another band of 10 degrees out of the 350 that are left, or 1/35. This band may be filled in any one of five ways as there are five remaining outer planets which are eligible to fill Band 2. This probability then is 5 x 10/350 or 5/35.

If we consider Band 6 next, we have eliminated the 20 degrees in Bands 1 and 2 from the circle of 360 degrees, leaving 340 degrees for a planet to be placed. This band may be filled in any one of four ways (there are four outer planets remaining) so that we now have 4 x 10/340 or 4/34 for the probability of Band 6.

Similarly, for Band 7 we find there are three outer planets left and 330°, so the probability of a planet being placed in this band is 3 x 10/330 or 3/33. And in Band 8 the probability is 20/320 or 2/32.

Now back to Bands 3, 4, and 5. For Band 3, we may choose one of three planets, Venus, Mercury, or the one remaining outer planet. For any one of the three planets to place in Band 3, we are considering 10 of 310 degrees that are left, so the probability is 3 x 10/310 or 3/31.

We may fill Band 4 in one of two ways, and we are talking about 10 out of 300 degrees, so that probability is 2/30. And finally for Band 5, there is only one planet left with a probability of 10/290 or 1/29.

Now the probability of a planet each in Bands 1 to 8 is the probability of the planet in Band 1 times the probability of the planet in Band 2, etc.

$$6/36 \times 5/35 \times 4/34 \times 3/33 \times 2/32 \times 3/31 \times 2/30 \times 1/29$$

or

$$\frac{6\text{-}5\text{-}4\text{-}3\text{-}2\text{-}3\text{-}2\text{-}1}{36\text{-}35\text{-}34\text{-}33\text{-}32\text{-}31\text{-}30\text{-}29} = \frac{1}{42\text{-}34\text{-}88\text{-}160\text{-}29}$$

or

$$1/584{,}006{,}960$$

But this is the probability that the planets will be spaced approximately 30 degrees apart from the position of the sun in one band of 10 degrees. There are 36 bands of 10 degrees that the sun might occupy in a circle. This whole business could happen then in one of 36 ways, so the odds are now up to 36/584,006,960. This is the same as 1/16,500,000, hardly a figure to make the friendly neighborhood bookie scream with delight. If anyone walked in and wished to bet against those odds, the bookie might figure that the pigeon knew something about the horse race.

There is one other way to look at these odds. As the Earth moves about one degree a day, the odds are that the event could happen only every 16,500,000 days or 45,200 years.

We might wonder, in the face of these odds, just exactly what the Mayas did know about December 24, 2011 A.D.

VIII. Mathematical Relationships Within the Solar System

To me, the most fascinating result of this inquiry is the mathematical ordering and relationships of the visible planets. It reveals that there is a unique number of points per cycle or synodic periods from minimum to minimum value of the angle of elongation for each planet (See Table 14).

Table 15

Planet	Points per Cycle	Difference
Sun	4	
Mercury	3	1
Venus	5	2
Mars	7-8	3
Jupiter	11	4
Saturn	14-15	4
Uranus	22	8

The number of these points or synodic periods is not accidental, but an integral part of the way the planet revolves around the sun; and the Right Ascensions of the sun show a pattern of four points per cycle. These all suggest that the planets lie in a well-ordered harmonious system which has many symbolic interpretations.

I have prepared graphs for all these planets, plotting the number of points per cycle for each. The graph for Venus is shown here as an example (Figure 9). Its five points confirm the significance of five given in the text to the five periods of Venus, to Quetzalcoatl, the Fifth World, the quincunx, the five regions of the world, and the five divisions of the Sacred Calendar.

I will not go into a fuller discussion of these points and the progressive differences between them, for this merges into metaphysical grounds beyond the scope of this mathematical inquiry. We can only wonder if astrology, symbology, and mythology could have been a shorthand to describe a galactic type of science of a different dimension than the conventional physics we use to describe earthly phenomena.

Mr. Waters in his text expresses the cautious reservation of many persons that conclusions such as reached here may be refuted by Velikovsky's theory of a disordering of the planets in the fifteenth and seventh centuries B.C. While I don't dispute the general theory, I do question whether Velikovsky's postulated catastrophes, whenever they occurred, materially disrupted the great ordering of the solar system as mathematically observed by my own study, and as partially confirmed by Bode's Law, by

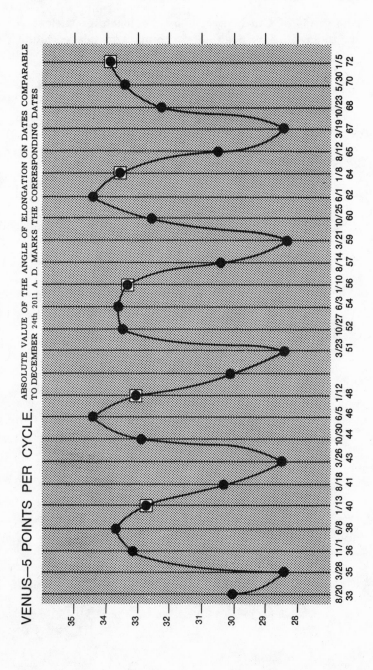

FIGURE 9

VENUS—5 POINTS PER CYCLE. ABSOLUTE VALUE OF THE ANGLE OF ELONGATION ON DATES COMPARABLE TO DECEMBER 24th 2011 A. D. MARKS THE CORRESPONDING DATES

the thesis of Gurdjieff, and by the tenets of ancient American mythology. I have dealt here with mathematical certainties, whatever interpretations may be given to them.

Notes

PART ONE

Section I

Chapter 1   Moctezuma and the Aztecs
1   Fray Bernardino de Sahagún, *Florentine Codex: General History of the Things of New Spain*. The translators refer to other commentators who state that these omens began to appear two years, not ten, before the Spaniards arrived.
2   Miguel Leon-Portilla, ed., *The Broken Spears: The Aztec Account of the Conquest of Mexico*.
3   Bernal Díaz del Castillo, *The Discovery and Conquest of Mexico*.
4   Sahagún, *Florentine Codex*.
5   Ibid. As all these locations mentioned are in the Land of the Dead, it is clear that Moctezuma was contemplating suicide.

Chapter 2   Cortes and the Spaniards
1   Russell C. Ewing, *Six Faces of Mexico*.
2   John Collier, *The Indians of the Americas*.
3   Bernal Díaz del Castillo, *The Discovery and Conquest of Mexico*.
4   Fray Bernardino de Sahagún, *Florentine Codex: General History of the Things of New Spain*.
5   As quoted in Pál Kelemen, *Medieval American Art*.
6   Sahagún, *Florentine Codex*.
7   Ibid.
8   Díaz, *Discovery and Conquest of Mexico*.
9   Miguel Leon-Portilla, ed., *The Broken Spears: The Aztec Account of the Conquest of Mexico*.
10   Ibid.

Chapter 3   Defeat of the Mayas
1   Russell C. Ewing, *Six Faces of Mexico.*

Chapter 4   A New Perspective
1   Gerald Sykes, *The Cool Millenium.*

Section II

Chapter 1   The Olmecs
1   Guenther Wachsmuth, *The Evolution of Mankind.*
2   Alexander von Wuthenau, *The Art of Terracotta Pottery in Pre-Columbian Central South America.*
3   See Miguel Covarrubias, *Indian Art of Mexico and Central America* and *The Eagle, the Jaguar, and the Serpent.*
4   Charles R. Wicke, *Olmec.*
5   Ignacio Bernal, *The Olmec World.*
6   William S. Webb and Raymond S. Baby, *The Adena People No. 2.* This supplements *The Adena People* by William S. Webb and Charles E. Snow.

Chapter 2   The Mayas
1   Jorge E. Hardoy, *Pre-Columbian Cities.*
2   American Institute of Man, *Special Publication No. 1.*
3   José Díaz Bolio, *Ruins óf Chichen Itza; Mayan Area.*
4   H. J. Spinden, *Ancient Civilizations of Mexico and Central America.*

Chapter 3   The Zapotecs and Mixtecs
1   Howard Leigh, "The Evolution of the Zapotec Glyph C," in John Paddock, ed., *Ancient Oaxaca.*
2   These parallels from Eduard Seler, "The Mexican Chronology, with Special Reference to the Zapotec Calendar," "The Wall Paintings of Mitla," and "The Bat God of the Maya Race," Smithsonian Institution *Bureau of American Ethnology Bulletin* No. 28.
3   Alfonso Caso, *Interpretación del Códice Selden.*
4   Ignacio Bernal, *The Olmec World.*

Chapter 4   The Toltecs of Teotihuacan
1   Inscription from the *Codice Matritense* on the wall of the Salas Preclassica y Teotihuacan in the Museo Nacional de Antropologia, Mexico City.
2   Fray Bernadino de Sahagún, *Florentine Codex,* Book 3.
3   Quoted in Laurette Séjourné, *Burning Water,* from an older translation in Spanish of the *Codex Florentine.* This is in variance with the English translation by Anderson and Dibble, who assume that Sahagún was referring to Tula, a far later city, instead of Teotihuacan, as the original Tollan. The academic squabble between these two schools of thought is aired in the following chapter.

Chapter 5   The Toltecs of Tula
1   J. de Acosta, *Natural and Moral Histories of the East and West Indies.*
2   Francesco Saverio Clavigero, *The History of Mexico.*
3   Fernando de Alva Ixtlilxochitl, *Obras Historicas.*

4 Primo Feliciano Velasquez, trans., *Codice Chimalpopoca, Anales de Cuauhtitlan.*
5 Charles Di Peso, "Casas Grandes and the Gran Chichimeca," *El Palacio, A Quarterly Journal of the Museum of New Mexico.*
6 H. J. Spinden, "New Light on Quetzalcoatl," International Congress of Americanists *Proceedings.*
7 Laurette Séjourné, *Burning Water.*
8 Robert Chadwick, "Native Pre-Aztec History of Central Mexico," in preparation for inclusion in *Handbook of American Indians*, Vol. 1 C. Galley proofs loaned me by Ross Parmenter of Oaxaca.

Chapter 6 The Aztecs
1 Francesco Saverio Clavigero, *The History of Mexico.*
2 Quoted in Miguel Leon-Portilla, *Aztec Thought and Culture.*
3 Ibid.

Chapter 7 In-Flowing Streams
1 Reported at the 1963 annual meeting of the U.S. Geological Society of America by Dr. Roald Fryxell, of Washington State University, and Dr. Harold E. Malde and Virginia Steen-McIntyre, both of the U.S.G.S.
2 This data from a letter by Lewis M. Greenberg, Department of History and Art History, Moore College of Art, Philadelphia, Pennsylvania, to *Pensée*, Winter 1973-74.
3 Harold Sterling Gladwin, *Men Out of Asia.*
4 Lee Eldridge Huddleston, *Origin of the American Indians.*
5 Henriette Mertz, *Pale Ink: Two Ancient Records of Chinese Explorations in America.* For further Chinese background, see Immanuel Velikovsky's *Worlds in Collision* in which he indicates that the voyage may have been made in the 15th century B.C.
6 Henriette Mertz, *The Wine Dark Sea.*
7 For a full account see Cyrus H. Gordon, *Before Columbus.*
8 Miguel Covarrubias, *The Eagle, the Jaguar, and the Serpent* and *Indian Art of Mexico and Central America.*
9 For a complete review, see the papers presented on this question at the national meeting of the Society for American Archaeology held in Santa Fe, New Mexico, in 1968, and published under the title *Man Across the Sea*, edited by Carroll L. Riley *et al.*

Chapter 8 Life Spans and World Cycles
1 J. Eric S. Thompson, *Maya Hieroglyphic Writing.*
2 Giorgio de Santillana, *Hamlet's Mill.*
3 Rodney Collin, *The Theory of Celestial Influence.*
4 Ibid.

PART TWO

Section I

Chapter 1 The Universe
1 Theodor Schwenk, *Sensitive Chaos.*

2   Miguel Leon-Portilla, *Aztec Thought and Culture.*
3   Frank Waters, *Masked Gods: Navajo and Pueblo Ceremonialism.*

Chapter 2   The First Four Suns
1   Frank Waters, *Book of the Hopi.*
2   W. Y. Evans-Wentz, *The Tibetan Book of the Dead.*

Chapter 3   The Myth of Atlantis
1   This Pythagorean tradition from American Institute of Man, *Special Publication No. 1.*
2   The outline here follows the pattern given in Guenther Wachsmuth, *The Evolution of Mankind.*
3   Edgar E. Cayce, *Edgar Cayce on Atlantis.*

Chapter 4   The Four Glacial Ages
1   Carl A. Zapffe, "A New Theory for the Great Ice Ages," *Physics Today.*

Chapter 5   The Fifth Sun
1   Included in Primo Feliciano Velasquez, trans., *Codice Chimalpopoca, Anales de Cuauhtitlan.*
2   Richard Wilhelm, trans., *The I Ching; or Book of Changes.*
3   Miguel Leon-Portilla, *Aztec Thought and Culture.*

Chapter 6   The Myth of Quetzalcoatl
1   Fray Bernardino de Sahagún, *Florentine Codex*, Book 3.
2   Included in Primo Feliciano Velasquez, trans., *Codice Chimalpopoca, Anales de Cuauhtitlan.*
3   Laurette Séjourné, *Burning Water.*
4   Sahagún, *Florentine Codex*, Book 1.
5   Alfonso Caso, *The Aztecs: People of the Sun.*
6   Lewis Spence, *The Magic and Mysteries of Mexico.*
7   Sahagún, *Florentine Codex*, Book 2.

Chapter 7   The Voyage of Venus Through Hell
1   Most of the present chapter is taken from Eduard Seler's Commentary on the Codex Borgia, especially his section "El Viaje de Venus por el Infierno."
2   Alfonso Caso, *The Aztecs: People of the Sun.*
3   Laurette Séjourné, *Burning Water.*
4   Fray Diego Duran, *Book of the Gods and Rites and the Ancient Calendar.*
5   W. Y. Evans-Wentz, *The Tibetan Book of the Dead.*
6   Hyemeyohsts Storm, *Seven Arrows.*

Chapter 8   Venus-Quetzalcoatl
1   Immanuel Velikovsky, *Worlds in Collision.*
2   Miguel Leon-Portilla, *Aztec Thought and Culture.*
3   Both included in Primo Feliciano Velasquez, trans., *Codice Chimalpopoca, Anales de Cuauhtitlan.*
4   Francesco Saverio Clavigero, *The History of Mexico.*

Chapter 9   Cosmic Catastrophism
1   Louis Pauwels and Jacques Bergier, *The Morning of the Magicians.*
2   H. S. Bellamy and P. Allen, *The Great Idol of Tiahuanaco.*
3   Arthur Posnansky, *Tihuanacu: The Cradle of American Man.*
4   Jorge E. Hardoy, *Pre-Columbian Cities.*

Section II

Chapter 1   The Mayan Twins
1   Delia Goetz and Sylvanus G. Morley, trans., *Popul Vuh.*
2   J. Eric S. Thompson, *Maya Hieroglyphic Writing.*
3   Frank Waters, *Book of the Hopi.*
4   Eduard Seler's Commentary on the Codex Borgia, especially his section "El Viaje de Venus por el Infierno."

Chapter 2   The Pyramid
1   William Mullen, "A Reading of the Pyramid Texts," *Pensée.*
2   Peter Tompkins, *Secrets of the Great Pyramid.*
3   Livio Catullo Stecchini, "Notes on the Relation of Ancient Measures to the Great Pyramid" in Peter Tompkins, *Secrets of the Great Pyramid.*

Chapter 3   The Seven Caves
1   Translated into English by Adrian Recinos and Delia Goetz under the title *The Annals of the Cakchiquels.*
2   Frank Waters, *Book of the Hopi.*
3   T. A. Willard, *Kukulcan, The Bearded Conqueror.*
4   J. Eric S. Thompson, *Maya History and Religion.*
5   Michael D. Coe, *The Maya.*
6   Quoted by Willard, *Kukulcan, The Bearded Conqueror.*
7   Thompson, *Maya History and Religion.*
8   Frank Waters, *Pumpkin Seed Point.*
9   Arthur Avalon [Sir John Woodroffe], *The Serpent Power.*

Chapter 4   People of the Sun
1   Alfonso Caso, *The Aztecs: People of the Sun.*
2   Fray Diego Duran, *Book of the Gods and Rites and the Ancient Calendar.*
3   Irene Nicholson, *Mexican and Central American Mythology.*
4   Laurette Séjourné, *Burning Water.*
5   Fray Bernardino de Sahagún, *Florentine Codex.*
6   Richard Wilhelm, trans., *Secret of the Golden Flower.*
7   Velikovsky has an interesting interpretation: that this "fire water" symbol represents the outpouring of naptha on earth.
8   Sahagún, *Florentine Codex.*
9   Ibid.

Chapter 5   Jaguar, Eagle, and Serpent
1   *Malinalco: Official Guide.*
2   Frank Waters, *Book of the Hopi.*

Chapter 6 The Gods
1 Fray Diego Duran, *Book of the Gods and Rites and the Ancient Calendar.*
2 Irene Nicholson, *Mexican and Central American Mythology.*
3 Laurette Séjourné, *Burning Water.*
4 A paper presented by Dr. Sullivan at the 40th International Congress of Americanists, Rome-Genoa, September 3-10, 1972.
5 Alfonso Caso, *The Aztecs: People of the Sun.*
6 Frank Waters, *Book of the Hopi.*
7 Nicholson, *Mexican and Central American Mythology.*

Chapter 7 The Sun
1 A full description of the races is given in my *Masked Gods, Navajo and Pueblo Ceremonialism;* the significance of ritual vis-a-vis the sun was related to C. G. Jung when he visited Taos Pueblo in New Mexico. It impressed him so much that he recorded it in his *Collected Works* and in his autobiography.
2 Rodney Collin, *The Theory of Celestial Influence.*
3 William T. Skilling and Robert S. Richardson, *A Brief Text in Astronomy.*
4 Collin, *The Theory of Celestial Influence.*
5 Kathleen Raine, *Blake and Tradition.*

Chapter 8 Mayan God-Pots and Crosses
1 Lilly de Jongh Osborne, *Indian Crafts of Guatemala and El Salvador.*
2 Evon Z. Vogt, *The Zinacantecos of Mexico.*
3 Christine Price, *Heirs of the Ancient Maya.*

Section III

Chapter 1 The Sacred Calendar
1 Vincent H. Malmstrom, "Origin of the Mesoamerican 260-Day Calendar," *Science.*
2 J. Eric S. Thompson, *Maya Hieroglyphic Writing.*
3 An interpretation of the Mayan procession of days as symbolizing man's cycle of birth, death, and resurrection is given in Irene Nicholson, *Mexican and Central American Mythology.*
4 Richard Wilhelm, trans., *The I Ching; or Book of Changes.*

Chapter 2 The Calendar Round
1 J. Eric S. Thompson, *Maya Hieroglyphic Writing.*
2 J. Eric S. Thompson, *The Rise and Fall of Maya Civilization.*

Chapter 3 The Zodiac—"The Road of Life"
1 Michel Gauquelin, *The Scientific Basis of Astrology.*
2 Eduard Seler, "The Venus Period in the Picture Writings of the Borgian Codex Group," Smithsonian Institution *Bureau of American Ethnology Bulletin* No. 28.
3 Lewis Spense, *The Magic and Mysteries of Mexico.*
4 Cyril Fagan, *Astrological Origins.*
5 Ibid.

Chapter 4   Space-Time Influence
1 George Ivanovitch Gurdjieff died in 1949. These paragraphs are derived from two sources: *In Search of the Miraculous* by P. D. Ouspensky, who carried on his work; and *Views From the Real World*, early talks of Gurdjieff throughout the world as recollected by his pupils.
2 Rodney Collin, *The Theory of Celestial Influence*.

Chapter 5   The Long Count
1 Sylvanus Griswold Morley, *The Ancient Maya*.
2 J. Eric S. Thompson, *Maya Hieroglyphic Writing*.
3 Michael D. Coe, *The Maya*.
4 Thompson, *Maya Hieroglyphic Writing*.
5 Frank Waters, *Pumpkin Seed Point*.
6 Benjamin Lee Whorf, *Language, Thought and Reality*.
7 Sir John Woodroffe, *The World as Power*.
8 Maurice Nicoll, *Living Time*.
9 C. J. Jung, *Letters*, Vol. 1.

Chapter 6   The Great Cycle—Its Beginning
1 This summary from Sylvanus Griswold Morley, *The Ancient Maya,* is confirmed by most scholars. For Robert W. Willson's interesting correlation and "Ahau Equation" see "Astronomical Notes on the Maya Codices," Peabody Museum of American Archaeology and Ethnology *Papers*.
2 Mrs. Sklower is a professional mathematician and a member of the Albuquerque (New Mexico) Astronomers Association.
3 This established premise is disrupted by Velikovsky's theory of cosmic catastrophism, already discussed, in which he posits a disordering and rearrangement of the planets in 1500 B.C. and 687 B.C. According to this theory, the configuration of the planets in 3113 B.C. was different than after 687 B.C.; and Venus, which Mrs. Sklower has included, was still a comet. Velikovsky's still-disputed theory may eventually be accepted, but the scientific establishment has not yet synchronized its gears to mesh with it. In any case, this present inquiry is into Mayan myth which has its own metaphysical validity.
4 Giorgio de Santillana, *Hamlet's Mill*.
5 William Mullen, "A Reading of the Pyramid Texts," *Pensée*.
6 Colin Renfrew, *Before Civilization: The Radiocarbon Revolution and Prehistoric Europe*.

Chapter 8   The Catastrophe
1 Personal communication given to me while doing research during 1960 and 1961 for the *Book of the Hopi* which contains this prophetic material. Ten years later, in 1970 and 1971, for reasons to be brought out, the full Hopi prophecy was given wide publicity by public releases from the Hopi Independent Nation, Hotevilla, Arizona, through Chief Dan Katchongva with the assistance of Ralph Tawangyawma and Carolyn Tawangyawma, interpreter, who also wrote letters to President Nixon, various senators, and dignitaries in Germany and Japan.
2 *Prescott Courier,* August 9, 1970.
3 Giorgio de Santillana, *Hamlet's Mill*.
4 C. G. Jung, *The Archetypes and the Collective Unconscious*. See also the excellent *The Myth of Meaning* by Aniela Jaffe.

Chapter 9   The Sixth World—The Age of Aquarius
1 Cyril Fagan, *Astrological Origins.*
2 C. G. Jung, *Collected Works,* Vol. II.
3 The Movement for Survival, formed by 33 scientists, predicts that the disruption of the life-support system on this planet will occur possibly by A.D. 2000. The Club of Rome, an organization of 70 international scientists and businessmen using a digital computer to predict increasing population and pollution and decreasing natural resources, sets the disaster date at A.D. 2020.
4 C. G. Jung, *Flying Saucers: A Modern Myth of Things Seen in the Skies.*

Bibliography

Books

Acosta, José de. *The Natural and Moral Histories of the East and West Indies*. 2d ed. Mexico City: Fondo de Cultura Económica, 1962.

Alcalá, Ermilo Solís, trans. *Códice Pérez*. Mérida: 1949.

Anton, Ferdinand. *Art of the Maya*. Translated by Mary Whittell. London: Thames & Hudson, 1970.

Avalon, Arthur. *See* Woodroffe.

Bellamy, H. S., and Allen, Peter. *The Great Idol of Tiahuanaco*. London: Faber & Faber, 1959.

Bernal, Ignacio. *Mexico before Cortez: Art, History, Legend*. Translated by Willis Barnstone. Garden City: Doubleday, 1963.

——————————. *The Olmec World*. Translated by Doris Heyden and Fernando Horcasitas. Berkeley: University of California Press, 1969.

——————————. *3000 Years of Art and Life in Mexico*. Translated by Carolyn B. Czitrom. New York: H. N. Abrams, 1968.

Bernal, Ignacio, et al. *The National Museum of Anthropology, Mexico*. Edited by Beatrice Trueblood. New York: H. N. Abrams, 1968.

Blom, Frans, and Duby, Gertrude. *The Lacandon*. Mexico City: Editorial Cultural, 1955-57.

Book of the Jaguar Priest. Commentary by Maud Worcester McKemson. New York: Henry Schuman, 1951.

Caso, Alfonso. *The Aztecs: People of the Sun*. Translated by Lowell Dunham. Norman: University of Oklahoma Press, 1958.

——————————. *Interpretación del Códice Selden 3135 (A.2)*. Mexico City: Sociedad Mexicana de Antropología, 1964.

——————————. *Interpretation of the Codex Bodley 2858 (A.75)*. Mexico City: Sociedad Mexicana de Antropología, 1960.

Cayce, Edgar E. *Edgar Cayce on Atlantis*. New York: Hawthorn, 1968.

Chadwick, Robert. *Handbook of American Indians*, Vol. 1: *Native Pre-Aztec History of Central Mexico*. (forthcoming).

Clavigero, Francesco Saverio. *The History of Mexico*. Translated by Charles Cullen. London: Thomas Dobson, 1817.

313

Codex Borgianus. Commentary by Eduard Seler. 3 vols. Mexico City: Fondo de Cultura Económica, 1963.
Codex Chimalpopocatl. See Velásquez.
Codex Dresdensis. See Willson.
Codex Florentino. See Sahagún.
Codex Peresianus. See Alcalá.
Codex Selden. See Caso.
Codex Telleriano. See Abrams.
Codex Xolotl. See Dibble.
Coe, Michael D. *The Maya.* Mexico City: Ediciones Lara, 1966.
Collier, John. *The Indians of the Americas.* New York: W. W. Norton, 1947.
Collin, Rodney. *The Theory of Celestial Influence.* London: Stuart & Watkins, 1968.
Covarrubias, Miguel. *The Eagle, the Jaguar, and the Serpent.* New York: Knopf, 1954.
——————. *Indian Art of Mexico and Central America.* New York: Knopf, 1957.
De Santillana, Giorgio. *Hamlet's Mill: An Essay on Myth and the Frame of Time.* Translated by Hertha von Dechend. Boston: Gambit, 1969.
Díaz Bolio, José. *Ruins of Chichen Itza: Mayan Area.* Mérida: 1969.
Díaz del Castillo, Bernal. *The Conquest of New Spain.* Translated by J. M. Cohen. Baltimore: Penguin Books, 1963.
——————. *The Discovery and Conquest of Mexico: 1517-1521.* New York: Farrar, Straus, & Cudahy, 1956.
Dibble, Charles E., ed. *Códice Xolotl.* Mexico City: Universidad Nacional, 1951.
Durán, Diego. *Book of the Gods and Rites and the Ancient Calendar.* Translated by Fernando Horcasitas and Doris Heyden. Norman: University of Oklahoma Press, 1971.
Edwards, Emily. *Painted Walls of Mexico: From Prehistoric Times until Today.* Austin: University of Texas Press, 1966.
Evans-Wentz, W. Y., ed. *The Tibetan Book of the Dead.* 3d ed. London: Oxford University Press, 1957.
——————. *Tibetan Yoga and Secret Doctrines.* London: Oxford University Press, 1935.
Ewing, Russell C. *Six Faces of Mexico.* Tucson: University of Arizona Press, 1966.
Fagan, Cyril. *Astrological Origins.* St. Paul: Llewellyn, 1971.
Gauquelin, Michel. *The Scientific Basis of Astrology.* Translated by James Hughes. New York: Stein & Day, 1970.
Gladwin, Harold Sterling. *Men Out of Asia.* New York: McGraw-Hill, 1947.
Goetz, Delia, and Morley, S. G., trans. *Popul Vuh: The Sacred Book of the Ancient Quiché Maya.* Norman: University of Oklahoma Press, 1950.
Goodavage, Joseph F. *Astrology: The Space-Age Science.* New York: New American Library, 1967.
Gordon, Cyrus H. *Before Columbus.* New York: Crown, 1971.
Greenman, Emerson F. *Serpent Mound.* Columbus: Ohio Historical Society, 1967.
Hardoy, Jorge E. *Pre-Columbian Cities.* New York: Walker, 1973.
Hoyle, Fred *Astronomy.* New York: Crescent Books, 1962.

Huddleston, Lee Eldridge. *Origin of the American Indians*. Austin: University of Texas Press, 1967.

Ixtlilxóchitl, Fernando de Alva. *Obras Historicas*. Edited by Alfredo Chavero. Mexico City: Editors Nacional, 1952.

Jaffé, Aniela. *The Myth of Meaning*. Translated by R. F. C. Hull. New York: G. P. Putnam, 1971.

Jung, C. G. *The Archetypes and the Collective Unconscious*. New York: Pantheon Books, 1959.

_____. *C. G. Jung: Letters, 1906-1950*, Vol. 1. Edited by Gerhard Adler and Aniela Jaffé. Princeton: Princeton University Press, 1973.

_____. *Flying Saucers: A Modern Myth of Things Seen in the Skies*. Translated by R. F. C. Hull. New York: Harcourt, Brace, 1959.

Keen, Benjamin. *The Aztec Image*. Brunswick: Rutgers University Press, 1971.

Kelemen, Pál. *Medieval American Art*. New York: Macmillan, 1943.

Leon-Portilla, Miguel, ed. *Aztec Thought and Culture*. Norman: University of Oklahoma Press, 1963.

_____. *The Broken Spears: The Aztec Account of the Conquest of Mexico*. Translated by Lysander Kemp. Boston: Beacon, 1962.

Le Poer Trensh, Brinsley. *Forgotten Heritage*. London: Spearman, 1964.

Mertz, Henriette. *Pale Ink: Two Ancient Records of Chinese Exploration in America*. Chicago: Swallow Press, 1973.

_____. *The Wine Dark Sea*. Chicago: 1964.

Morley, Sylvanus Griswold. *The Ancient Maya*. 3d ed. Revised by George W. Brainerd. Stanford: Stanford University Press, 1956.

Neugebauer, Otto E. *The Exact Sciences in Antiquity*. Philadelphia: University of Pennsylvania Press, 1941.

Neumann, Erich. *The Great Mother: An Analysis of the Archetype*. Translated by Ralph Manheim. New York: Pantheon, 1955.

Nicholson, Irene. *Mexican and Central American Mythology*. London: Paul Hamlyn, 1967.

_____. *A Study of Ancient Mexican Poetry and Symbolism*. London: Faber & Faber, 1959.

Nicoll, Maurice. *Living Time*. London: Stuart & Watkins, 1971.

Osborne, Lilly de Jongh. *Indian Crafts of Guatemala and El Salvador*. Norman: University of Oklahoma Press, 1965.

Ouspensky, P. D. *In Search of the Miraculous*. New York: Harcourt, Brace, & World, 1949.

Paddock, John, ed. *Ancient Oaxaca: Discoveries in Mexican Archeology and History*. Stanford: Stanford University Press, 1966.

Pauwels, Louis, and Bergier, Jacques. *The Morning of the Magicians*. New York: Stein & Day, 1964.

Plato. *The Dialogues of Plato*. Translated by B. Jowett. 2 vols. New York: Random House, 1937.

Posnansky, Arthur. *Tihuanacu: The Cradle of American Man*. 2 vols. New York: J. J. Augustin, 1945-58.

Price, Christine. *Heirs of the Ancient Maya: A Portrait of the Lacandon Indians*. New York: Scribner's, 1972.

_____. *Made in Ancient Egypt*. London: Bodley Head, 1971.

Raine, Kathleen. *Blake and Tradition*. 2 vols. Princeton: Princeton University Press, 1968.

Recinos, Adrian, and Goetz, Delia, trans. *Annals of the Cakchiquels.* Norman: University of Oklahoma Press, 1953.

Riley, Carroll L. *et al.*, ed., *Man Across the Sea: Problems of Pre-Columbian Contacts.* Austin: University of Texas Press, 1971.

Rivet, Paul. *Mayan Cities.* Translated by Miriam and Lionel Kochan. New York: Putnam's, 1960.

Roys, Ralph L. *The Indian Background of Colonial Yucatan.* Norman: University of Oklahoma Press, 1972.

Sahagún, Bernardino de. *Florentine Codex: General History of the Things of New Spain.* Translated by Arthur J. O. Anderson and Charles E. Dibble. 12 vols. Santa Fe: School of American Research, 1950-1963.

Scholes, Frances V., and Roys, Ralph L. *The Maya Chontal Indians of Acalan; Tixchel.* Washington, D.C.: Carnegie Institute, 1948.

Schwenk, Theodor. *Sensitive Chaos: The Creation of Flowing Forms in Water and Air.* London: R. Steiner, 1965.

Séjourné, Laurette. *Burning Water.* New York: Grove Press, 1960.

Silverberg, Robert. *Mound Builders of Ancient America.* Greenwich, Conn.: N. Y. Graphic, 1968.

Skilling, William T., and Richardson, Robert S. *A Brief Text in Astronomy.* Rev. ed. New York: Holt, Rinehart & Winston, 1959.

Soustelle, Jacques. *Arts of Ancient Mexico.* Translated by Elizabeth Carmichael. New York: Viking, 1967.

Spence, Lewis. *The Magic and Mysteries of Mexico.* London: Rider & Co., 1930.

Spinden, Herbert J. *Ancient Civilizations of Mexico and Central America.* New York: American Museum of Natural History, 1951.

Steiner, Rudolf. *Cosmic Memory.* Englewood, N. J.: R. Steiner, 1959.

Stevenson, Tilly E. *The Religious Life of a Zuni Child.* Smithsonian Institution, Bureau of American Ethnology, Annual Report. Washington, D.C.: Government Printing Office, 1887.

Storm, Hyemeyohsts. *Seven Arrows.* New York: Harper & Row, 1972.

Sykes, Gerald. *The Cool Millenium.* Englewood Cliffs: Prentice-Hall, 1967.

Thompson, J. Eric S. *Maya Hieroglyphic Writing.* 3d ed. Norman: University of Oklahoma Press, 1971.

──────────. *Maya History and Religion.* Norman: University of Oklahoma Press, 1970.

──────────. *The Rise and Fall of Maya Civilization.* 2d ed. Norman: University of Oklahoma Press, 1966.

Tompkins, Peter. *Secrets of the Great Pyramid.* New York: Harper & Row, 1971.

Toynbee, Arnold J. *Civilization on Trial.* New York: Oxford University Press, 1947.

──────────. *A Study of History.* Abridged ed. London: Oxford University Press, 1972.

Vaillant, George C. *Aztecs of Mexico.* Rev. ed. New York: Doubleday, 1962.

Velásquez, Primo Feliciano, trans. *Códice Chimalpópoca: Anales de Cuauhtitlan y Leyenda de los Soles.* Mexico City: Imprenta Universitaria, 1945.

Velikovsky, Immanuel. *Worlds in Collision.* New York: Macmillan, 1950.

Vogt, Evon Z. *The Zinacantecos of Mexico.* New York: Holt, Rinehart, & Winston, 1970.

Von Hagen, Victor W. *World of the Maya.* New York: New American Library, 1960.
Wachsmuth, Guenther. *The Evolution of Mankind.* Translated by Norman Macbeth. Dornach, Switzerland: Philosophic-Anthroposophic Press, 1961.
Waters, Frank. *Book of the Hopi.* New York: Viking, 1963.
——————————. *Masked Gods: Navajo and Pueblo Ceremonialism.* Chicago: Swallow Press, 1950.
——————————. *Pumpkin Seed Point.* Chicago: Swallow Press, 1969.
Webb, William S., and Baby, Raymond S. *The Adena People No. 2.* Columbus: Ohio Historical Society, 1966.
Wicke, Charles R. *Olmec.* Tucson: University of Arizona Press, 1971.
Wilhelm, Richard, trans. *Secret of the Golden Flower: A Chinese Book of Life.* London: Paul, Trench, Trubner, 1945.
Willard, T. A. *Kukulcan: The Bearded Conqueror.* Hollywood: Murray T. Gee, 1941.
Woodroffe, Sir John. *Mahámáyá.* Madras: Ganesh, 1954.
——————————. [Arthur Avalon]. *The Serpent Power.* Madras: Ganesh, 1924.
——————————. *The World As Power.* 3d ed. Madras: Ganash, n.d.
Wuthenau, Alexander von. *The Art of Terracotta Pottery in Pre-Columbian Central and South America.* New York: Crown, 1965.

THESIS, ARTICLES

Abrams, H. Leon, Jr. "Codex Telleriano, Remensis: Commentary on Colonial Section." Master's thesis, Mexico City College, 1950.
Acosta, Jorge R. "Archaeological Explorations in Teotihuacan." *Artes de Mexico,* No. 134, 1970, Mexico City.
Di Peso, Charles C. "Casas Grandes and the Gran Chichimeca." *El Palacio: A Quarterly Journal of the Museum of New Mexico,* Winter, 1968.
Heine-Geldern, Robert, and Ekholm, Gordon F. "Significant Parallels in the Symbolic Arts of Southern Asia and Middle America," in *The Civilizations of Ancient America.* Vol. II. Edited by Sol Tax. International Congress of Americanists *Proceedings.* Chicago: University of Chicago Press, 1951.
Malmstrom, Vincent H. "Origin of the Mesoamerican 260-day Calendar." *Science,* Sept. 7, 1973.
Marquina, Ignacio. "The Architecture of Teotihuacan: Art in Mexico." *Artes de Mexico,* No. 134, 1970, Mexico City.
——————————. "The Paintings of Teotihuacan." *Artes de Mexico,* No. 134, 1970.
Mullen, William. "The Center Holds." *Pensée,* May, 1972.
——————————. "A Reading of the Pyramid Texts (Immanuel Velikovsky Reconsidered)." *Pensée,* Winter, 1973.
Muller, Florencia. "Ceramics." *Artes de Mexico,* No. 134, 1970, Mexico City.
Ornstein, Robert E. "Right and Left Thinking." *Psychology Today,* May, 1973.
Rose, Lynn E. "Babylonian Observations of Venus." *Pensée,* Winter, 1973.
Seler, Eduard. First nine articles in *Mexican and Central American Antiquities, Calendar Systems, and History.* Edited by Charles P. Bowditch.

Smithsonian Institution, *Bureau of American Ethnology, Bulletin No. 28.* Washington, D.C.: Government Printing Office, 1904.

Special Publication No. 1 ("To the Members of the 1950 International Congress of Mathematicians"). Chicago: American Institute of Man, August, 1950.

Spinden, Herbert J. "New Light on Quetzalcoatl." International Congress of Americanists *Proceedings,* 1942.

Sullivan, Thelma D. "The Arms and Insignia of the Mexican." *Estudios de Cultura Náhuatl,* X, 1972.

——————————. "Tlaloc: A New Etymological Interpretation of the God's Name and What It Reveals of His Essence and Nature." International Congress of Americanists *Proceedings,* 1973.

Velikovsky, Immanuel. "The Orientation of the Pyramids." *Pensée,* Winter, 1973.

Willson, Robert W. "Astronomical Notes on the Maya Codices." Peabody Museum of American Archaeology and Ethnology *Papers,* Vol. VI, no. 3, 1924.

Zapffe, Carl A. "A New Theory for the Great Ice Age." *Physics Today,* October, 1954.

GUIDES

The following government guide books are all published by the Instituto Nacional de Antropología e Historia, Mexico City:

Chichen Itza: Guia Oficial. 1962.
Ciudades Maya: Guia Oficial. 1957.
Malinalco: Guia Oficial. 1958.
Monte Alban, Mitla: Guia Oficial. 1968.
El Tajín: Guia Oficial. 1966.
Templo Mayor de México: Guia Oficial. 1968.
Teotihuacan: Guia Oficial. 1966.
Tula: Guia Oficial. 1962.
Uxmal: Guia Oficial. 1966.

Index